P9-BJO-263

HOW TO SLICE
AN ONION

ALSO BY BUNNY CRUMPACKER

Perfect Figures

The Sex Life of Food

The Old-Time Brand-Name Cookbook

Old-Time Brand-Name Desserts

FOR CHILDREN

Alexander's Pretending Day

COWRITTEN WITH CHICK CRUMPACKER

Jazz Legends

HOW TO SLICE AN ONION

Cooking Basics and Beyond

Hundreds of Tips, Techniques, Recipes,

Food Facts, and Folklore

BUNNY CRUMPACKER

Illustrations by Sally Mara Sturman

Thomas Dunne Books

St. Martin's Press ⚘ New York

Send questions and comments to "Kitchen Conversations," on the author's
Web site at: www.bunnycrumpacker.com

THOMAS DUNNE BOOKS
An imprint of St. Martin's Press.

HOW TO SLICE AN ONION. Copyright © 2009 by Bunny Crumpacker. Illustrations
copyright © 2009 by Sally Mara Sturman. All rights reserved. Printed in the
United States of America. For information, address St. Martin's Press, 175 Fifth
Avenue, New York, N.Y. 10010.

www.thomasdunnebooks.com
www.stmartins.com

Book design by Maggie Goodman

Library of Congress Cataloging-in-Publication Data

Crumpacker, Bunny.
    How to slice an onion : cooking basics and beyond—hundreds of tips,
techniques, recipes, food facts, and folklore / Bunny Crumpacker.—1st ed.
        p. cm.
    Includes bibliographical references and index.
    ISBN 978-0-312-53718-0 (alk. paper)
    1. Cookery.   I. Title.
    TX714.C793 2009
    641.5—dc22

                                                          2009016741

First Edition: September 2009

10 9 8 7 6 5 4 3 2 1

To

CAROLINE

CASEY

CATHY

and

JIL

CONTENTS

Acknowledgments   xiii

INTRODUCTION
Cooking Is Easier Than They Tell You It Is
1

1. THE KITCHEN BATTERIE
Equipping Your Kitchen
7

2. THE ONION LEGACY
The Beginning: How to Slice an Onion
21

3. LIQUIDITY
The Magic That Is Water
39

4. HEAVENLY SOUP
Comfort and Joy in a Pot
60

5. THE BIRD

Getting to Know a Chicken

80

6. AND THEN THE EGG

If Chickens Came First

104

7. PASTA NOW AND FOREVER

A Basketful of Macaroni

123

8. THE BIG DISH

The Traditional Center

142

9. SIDES TO THE CENTER

Supporting Cast

163

10. THE DAIRY

From Milk to Cheese, with Stops Between

190

11. DESSERT IOI

At Last, the Sweetness

207

12. THE ANT AND THE GRASSHOPPER

For Now and for Later

242

13. AND . . .
Final Thoughts on Things It Helps to Know
264

Further Reading—Some Favorite Books 277

A Brief Glossary of Cooking Terms 281

Basic Measurements 283

Recipe List 285

Index 293

ACKNOWLEDGMENTS

I'm grateful to five good cooks: Joan Schermerhorn, with whom I've been exchanging recipes for years; Jil Picariello, whose excellent food is leavened with laughter and love; my dear sister June Alexander, who is the only other person in the world who remembers my mother's cheesecake (the best I've ever tasted); Cathy Wolz, once again, not for numbers this time, but for her lovely Apple Chili Sauce; and David Calicchio, who will probably never write a cookbook, alas. My thanks are also heartfelt to my editor, Peter Joseph, who works hard and does so well, and to my good agent, Kate McKean, who is always generous with her time and good cheer, Sally Sturman for her charming drawings, and to Sally's capable and helpful agent, Melissa Turk and The Artist Network. Not finally, but always, I'm grateful to Chick, first taster for all these years.

HOW TO SLICE
AN ONION

INTRODUCTION

Cooking Is Easier Than They Tell You It Is

I wish we hadn't turned cooking into such a rare art. Restaurants and food magazines present food in towers on our plates, and surround each by bits and smears of sauce dotted like a secret code; over all are sprigs of herbs waving their semaphored messages—Look! Herbs were used here! This is fancy! Show me your charge card!

Those beautiful towers are all very well, if you have a staff in the kitchen and a butler and a few maids in the dining room. But if you haven't, and you're hungry, you need to know what to do and how to proceed. This book is about cooking at home—for yourself, your family, and your friends—and it's meant to have the virtues of a good home: simplicity, ease, pleasure, and a flow of good conversation.

This is the first thing to say, then, by way of introduction: If you can slice an onion, you will never go hungry. If you understand how to make soup, you'll never lack for comfort—or company. There are things it helps to know, from what kind of knife to use to how to make ice cream—but nothing complicated, nothing secret, no cooking mythology. After all, if you know how to take basic ingredients—an onion, a carrot, a clove of garlic, a chicken, some pasta—you can prepare meals that are not only sustaining but also richly indulgent and intensely satisfying.

Put together, this is a book for beginners and also for practiced cooks. It's for people who want to learn how to cook, who want to find recipes that they can build on and that will take them farther along the road to good cooking. But it's also for people who already know what to do in the kitchen but who like to read about food, because they find at least as much pleasure in reading cookbooks as they do in pulling out the pots and pans and transforming the words of a recipe into a memorable meal, and who like to find some new recipes in the process. This is a book about the things you need to know in order to survive and then to flourish in your own kitchen.

How to Plan a Dinner for Those You Love— Including Yourself

Planning a dinner—whether it's for one or two, four, six, or eight—is really one of life's simpler and more pleasant activities, one that, again, sounds much harder than it is.

First, it gives you a chance to choose your own menu: What do *you* want to eat? If you don't want to eat it, chances are you won't enjoy cooking it (and your guests, if you've invited a few, won't enjoy eating it). If you're not eating alone, it gives you a way to know your friends in a way you might not have thought about before. What do they like and dislike? If you've eaten with them, you already have a few clues. If you haven't, you might have fun guessing. And you can always ask—promising to honor requests. Allergies matter. So do dislikes.

The next thought is about the season. Stew is too heavy and hot to eat in July; cold soup isn't appealing in January. To every thing there is a season, "a time to plant and a time to pluck up that which is planted," wise words that go back to Ecclesiastes. The time to cook—and to eat—is the time when that which is planted is ready to be plucked up. It's lovely that each thing feels right—and tastes right—in its season. Fresh blueberries in February are a novelty, but not a fraction as wonderful as the first blueberries of the summer. Each one of those February berries carries with it the knowledge that it grew in a distant place and so it also carries the cost of going from there to here. Corn and tomatoes at the supermarket in the middle of winter, no matter how beautifully they're displayed, never taste as good as they do from the local farmers' market, when they're dead ripe in the dog days of August. And with September come the first apples, crisp and rosy, and sweet pears. They're not the same, shipped in hard and cold from countries whose name we can barely spell, months after they were in their prime right here. The vegetables of winter—golden butternut squash, deep green Savoy cabbage—are as wonderful as the fruits of summer; they deserve their moment of glory. Spring brings rhubarb and asparagus, early onions, and then green peas, and strawberries, and then, in their long moment in the sun, blueberries. The wait is precious and filled with its own goodness. What a lesson to learn! Another of those the kitchen can teach us. There is indeed a moral force to cooking what's in season and what's locally grown, but it's our good fortune that morality tastes as good in the kitchen as it feels in the soul. (Do I need to say that I'm not talking about a morality of primness and prurience, but rather what feels right, is right, for the mind, the heart, and the body? After all, eating a ripe peach in August, with the juices running down your chin, is a sensuous act—full of the gratification of our senses—that just happens to be sensual as well.)

Having come this far—knowing what you want to eat, and what you believe suits your guests, if any, and what comes with the season and might be growing locally—you begin to have an idea of what you want to fill the plates on your table. Play with the possibilities—the tastes, shapes, and colors. Let ideas form in your head, as you leaf through the pages of your cookbooks, and, if you have them, the recipes you've clipped from magazines and newspapers. The recipes you read should fit the tastes in your mind, and so you can begin to form a menu: something to begin, something to focus on, something to add, and something to finish. The pieces begin to fit together, like a puzzle—an indentation here and a point there: They match.

Keep a record, when you cook for guests, of what you've made. Otherwise, you may find that it's not exactly that you're famous for your rice salad; it's just that you always serve it.

How to Manage Cooking

Begin backwards. It's that simple. If something can be done ahead, well, I blush to say, prepare it ahead. By the same token, when you're cooking, begin with the things that take the longest to cook; that's how you get everything ready to eat at the same time. Narrow it down from there, so that you're left at the end with only those things that need to be done just before they're served.

There are some basic things—aside from how to slice an onion—that it helps to know. One has to do with heat. Pans should be hot before food goes into them. Oil and butter go into a hot pan; food goes into hot oil or butter. When you're sautéing more than one thing in the same pan, push the first thing to the side before you add the next—right into the heat, to maximize its flavor. Then stir. The only exception to adding food to a hot pan comes when you're working with nonstick pans; their chemistry means they shouldn't be too hot without having something in them. In that case, start with butter or oil, and then heat the pan up. In general, though, don't be afraid of heat. It works for you.

Clean up as you go. Is that too motherly? The thing is that even though you may not feel like washing pots and spoons and whisks as you go along, you'll feel even less like doing them at the end. The sight of a sink filled with dirty dishes is a turnoff, just as much for you, the cook, as for anybody else. It's easier to clean up in stages than to be overwhelmed with the gloppy clutter at the end.

Make the best of what you have. If you have a small budget—or a small kitchen—figure out what you can do, and do it with good cheer. Don't worry too much. You're not on trial; somebody else is running the test kitchen. Whatever works works. And if it doesn't, figure out why, and don't do it that way again. The kitchen is a fine reflection of life. It's an excellent place to learn patience, to learn what you like and don't like, to discover what you can do and what you can't, and to enlarge every horizon, to challenge every truism, along the way. It's *your* kitchen—keep the seasons, keep the joy.

How to Use This Book

Traditionally, recipes have four sections: headnotes, about the recipe itself or the food that's in it; a list of ingredients; instructions; and endnotes—anything special that it might be helpful to know. In this book, the first part of every chapter is like recipe headnotes. It's meant to be fun—but it's also meant to be useful. In this section are notes about food—the history and mythology of what we eat. Sometimes, in this first section, there are recipes that have been written out in prose, as if they were a letter from me to you, instead of as formal instructions—how to roast a chicken, how to fry eggs, how to make rice pudding—and there are explanations of techniques it helps to know.

Recipes follow this headnote section in every chapter—and are organized in terms of difficulty, with the easiest recipes first. Most often, instead of using endnotes with each recipe, those special instructions (how to peel a tomato, for instance) are included in the body of the recipe itself.

The first chapter ("The Kitchen Batterie") is about equipping your kitchen, and the final chapter (chapter 13, "And . . .") includes some thoughts and notes about fruits and vegetables—buying them, storing them, preparing them. A few recipes are tucked in here as well, and some enthusiastic thoughts about leftovers. After chapter 13 are a glossary of cooking terms, a list of basic measurements, and a list of recipes included in this book.

Finally, these thoughts:

Home cooking is *your* cooking; it is personal and subjective. My pumpkin pie isn't the same as my mother's, and hers wasn't the same as your mother's. Recipes are not engraved in granite, like tombstones. They're living things; they evolve. They travel. They have variations. Recipes offer directions, but they also give inspiration. They are, writes

John Thorne, author of *Mouth Wide Open* and the food newsletter *Simple Cooking*, conversations between cooks. You don't need permission to adapt a recipe. You need both knowledge and a sense of adventure. Take the straight path first—try the recipe—and then feel free to wander and to enjoy the trip.

Good cooking is a gift. Good cooking is an act of love. Good cooking is a source of pleasure. It isn't arcane and secret; it's simple and full of joy. It means feeling the texture and weight of your ingredients. It means savoring scents and tastes, putting them together in your mind before you mix them in the pan. Good cooking is like your handwriting—it's personal, and it looks like you. After all, your knife begins in your fingers; your mixing spoon in your hand. All of this, I devoutly believe, is as true of cooking for oneself or one's family as it is of cooking for guests. It is one and the same thing—the best kind of cooking and certainly the best kind of eating. Food is love, we all agree about that—and one's own dinner speaks as much about love as does a feast for our closest friends.

In all of these ways, and in several others, I wish you a good kitchen as well as good cooking and happy eating.

THE KITCHEN BATTERIE

Equipping Your Kitchen

Pancakes and fritters,
Say the bells of St. Peter's.
Two sticks and an apple,
Say the bells of Whitechapel.
Kettles and pans,
Say the bells of St. Anne's.
—*"The Bells of London," anonymous*

The only equipment you need in your kitchen: a pot, a pan, a knife, a fork, and a spoon. That's what it all comes down to. (And in a pinch, you could give up the fork.)

But everything comes in small, medium, and large . . . and there are dozens of varieties of each . . . and there are so many other things it would help to have . . .

Just know that you can spend a fortune equipping your kitchen—but you really don't need to. Shiny pans do not a good cook make. Most good cooks use battered pots and pans they've had for years, and they love them and wouldn't part with or replace any of them. *Bon Appétit* magazine, some years back, asked a variety of well-known cooks and chefs about their favorite kitchen equipment. Julia Child chose an old nonstick frying pan, one she used with butter and oil—that is, not as nonstick—because it was just the right size for what she needed most often and the sides sloped the way she liked; the handle was metal, so she could put it in the oven. Other cooks chose such unexpected things as a compost bucket, a French coffee press, a glass teapot, and a whisk. Yes, somebody chose a copper pot—always nice, but so expensive— and somebody else, a heavy-duty mixer. But a surprising number of choices were for the simple and mundane. A teapot and a whisk.

Knives

There are a lot of myths about kitchen equipment. Most, it seems to me, have to do with knives. Yes, you need to know how to handle a knife. And, yes, your knives should be sharp. (Sharp knives cause fewer accidents to your fingers, because they need less pressure to cut. Jacques Pépin adds that if you do cut yourself with a sharp knife, at least it's a clean cut. Cold comfort when you're bleeding? Probably.) But knives needn't be wildly expensive. And above all, they needn't be—shouldn't be, for my money—stainless steel or carbon steel. High-carbon knives are a little harder to find than stainless steel knives, but they hold their edge much longer, and are much easier to resharpen. They're on the expensive side—but you'll keep them longer and find them easier to work with. Amazingly enough, you can find good ones on eBay, which can save a great deal of money. Last time I looked, the first two listings were for the Sabatier knife company's high-carbon chef knives at just over fifteen dollars each. (Sabatier guarantees their high-carbon knives for a lifetime.) New, they cost in the neighborhood of a hundred dollars and up. High-carbon knives are never shiny, ex- cept maybe on the day you buy them. They're quickly discolored by the acids in food; they tend to rust; they don't glow the way stainless steel knives do. But they're so much better to work with.

Care and Sharpening of Knives

Knife sharpening is part real, part myth. Real: You need a steel—the long, cylindrical blade that works like a file; it can be metal or ceramic. You run the entire length of the knife blade up and down the steel, holding the knife at about a twenty-degree angle, and doing both sides of the knife. That realigns the blade's edges. Official advice is to use the steel every time you use your knife. After I do that, I run my knife blade across the bottom of a stone mug—the unglazed bottom is rough, and helps keep knives sharp.

Every so often, no matter how diligent you are about using the steel, your knives will need more work. The best thing to do is find a knife sharpener—a person, I mean, who sharpens knives. You may have to mail your knives; if you're lucky, the knife-sharpening man will be local, and you can just bring your knives over. The Yellow Pages will help.

If you can't do that, use an electric sharpener or a sharpening stone. With a stone, use the rough side first, with a light coating of mineral oil, and run the entire length of the blade across the stone, heel to point, holding the knife at about a twenty-degree angle again. After you've done that on both sides several times (several means twenty or so, until it feels almost sharp), turn the stone over, repeat the mineral oil coating, and again run the length of the blade up and down the stone—both sides of the knife.

It helps to take good care of your knives. Keep them clean and dry. Don't put them in the dishwasher. (Use the steel, use the knife, wash it, dry it, put it away.) Don't use knives on hard surfaces like plates—they'll dull very quickly if you do that. Cut and slice on cutting boards made of wood or plastic; if you don't have a cutting board, add several to your list of what you need to find. (It helps to have at least three separate cutting boards—one for onions and garlic, one for chicken and meats, and one for everything else.) Knives shouldn't bang into each other, but you don't need a knife holder (one of those slanted boxes with slots on the top for knife blades).

Know, too, how to hold a knife. That's not kitchen equipment, but it is good kitchen practice. Don't extend your index finger to the top of the blade; that may feel right at first, but it doesn't work as well; it doesn't give you as much control or power as holding the knife with all your fingers curled around the handle. The fingers on your other hand—holding the food you're cutting—should be slightly curled under, so the knife works against your knuckles and doesn't cut into your fingers.

What size knife do you need? The standard answer begins with a chef's knife. A chef's knife is a large utility knife with a triangular blade; it can mince, chop, and slice, and is probably best known for "rocking" over a mound of herbs, onions, or garlic, chopping them quickly. The important thing is a knife you feel comfortable with—a knife that feels right in your hand. That's why I'm not going to say an eight-inch knife, or a twelve-inch knife—or even just a chef's knife. Hold various knives in your hand; whatever feels right works. That is not always the most expensive knife. Plastic-handled knives are fine. Some paring knives are so cheap (under five dollars) that you don't need to worry about resharpening them on a stone—when they get dull, buy a new one. I use very few knives: a five-inch paring knife is my favorite—I use it for almost everything. (Paring knives look like smaller versions of chef's knives.) I have another, slightly longer knife with a serrated edge; it's handy for things like slicing lemons, tomatoes, and—surprise!—sandwiches, because it doesn't press down on them as it slices. I also have a chef's knife, which I use much less often, a boning knife, a large bread knife, and a santoku knife (mine is not Japanese, and has hollowed-out scallops on either side of the blade). The only knife I couldn't work without is the paring knife. That's what feels best to me, and that's what matters. Whatever works works.

Pots and Pans

What, then, are the other kitchen essentials? And what would it just be nice to have? Pots and pans are essential, like knives, but they, too, needn't be top-of-the-line. I have several copper pots that I never use anymore—despite their excellent heat-conducting abilities, I don't want to spend time polishing them and I feel guilty if I don't; even worse, when they've been used enough, they need to be retinned, which means time, energy (taking them somewhere or packing them up and mailing them), and money. The pots I use most often are a set of four stainless steel saucepans in varying sizes, the kind with layered bottoms (aluminum, copper, and stainless steel); they were gifts an amazingly long time ago. If I had to, I could give up one of them, leaving me with small, medium, and large. One of the pots came with a double-boiler insert, which is very handy; it sits inside the two largest pots. (I also use the insert when I'm making ice cream without a machine, to put directly in the freezer.) But my favorite pot is bigger—it's an old Cuisinart pot, wide and deep, with a steamer rack insert. I use it to boil water for pasta, to steam vegetables and dumplings, and to make stock, soup, stew, braises, relishes, and jams, and it can go in the oven when I want it to. It, too, is stainless steel. It's a very happy pot.

Those are the saucepan essentials—one big pot and two or three smaller saucepans. Sauté pans also matter. Again, it's best to have two different sizes—a small (nonstick, if you like) pan that can be used to fry two eggs or make scrambled eggs or an omelet (it should have sloping sides) and a larger frying pan with straight sides. Metal handles are helpful, because they make it possible to put the pan in the oven. My favorite frying pan is ten inches across and has straight sides; it's very sturdy—but its handle broke off some years back. It was plastic, and I'm glad it's gone, though I didn't do anything to hasten its departure. The pan can now be used to brown and sear on the top of the stove, and then it can move along to the oven to finish cooking.

Short of my old stockpot, my favorite pot for stews and soups is a Le Creuset (heavy iron, coated with enamel) that can go on the top of the stove or in the oven and look lovely on the table. (My pot doesn't look lovely on the table, except to me.) They're available online, through catalogs, and in stores. Le Creuset pots and pans are heavy, sturdy, and handsome, and they're also expensive. (But they last a lifetime.) Iron pots (without enamel) are another possibility—they're considerably less expensive, last several lifetimes, become nonstick through good use and care, and almost always work well, assuming you have a lid, should you need one. Iron pots and pans can be found in hardware stores and at flea markets and garage sales. Unless you buy a factory-seasoned new iron pot, you'll need to season it, and used iron pots probably always need to be reseasoned.

That's what you need for the top of the stove, then: saucepans of varying sizes, a large stockpot, and at least two different size sauté pans. All can be made of stainless steel, plain or combined with other metals, or enameled cast iron, or just plain iron.

Seasoning Iron Pans

To season or reseason an iron pan, coat it with vegetable oil, solid shortening, or bacon grease (you'll have to cook some bacon first, but that's not too much of a hardship). Heat the oven to 250 or 300 degrees, and put the pan in the oven. Leave it for fifteen minutes, remove it, and pour out any excess grease. Put it back in the oven and bake it for two hours. Let it cool and wipe it dry. To keep it in good condition, use it at first with foods that are high in fat. Clean it while it's still warm by rinsing it with hot water and scraping away anything that has stuck to it—don't use a scouring pad, soap, or a detergent. Make sure it's thoroughly dry. Store it without a lid on top.

Mixing Bowls, Measurers, Tongs, Spatulas, and Whisks

Next up, in my own personal order of importance, are the things you need before you need the pots and pans: measuring cups and spoons, tongs, spatulas, whisks, and the bowls you mix things in. Mixing bowls don't have to be matched sets of three—though that's always nice. A mixing bowl, after all, is just something you mix in. If you're mixing a lot of things, you need a larger bowl. And if you're mixing small amounts of things—well, I don't need to tell you, do I?

I do my mixing, for the most part, in a large clear plastic bowl that looks like a giant measuring cup or a laboratory instrument. I use a small Portuguese bowl for smaller things—it's very pretty, but it's not part of a set. I have nothing against matching mixing bowls; I just happen not to have them, and I believe they aren't necessary. Matching, that is. Mixing bowls—whatever they may be—are definitely necessary.

You also definitely need measuring cups and spoons. Measure liquid in a standing cup—the glass or plastic kind that holds one or two cups. Measure dry things (like flour and sugar) in freestanding smaller metal or plastic cups, the kind that come in sets of four: one each for a quarter cup, third cup, half cup, and whole cup. (This is the kind you sweep the back of your knife across, when it's full, to level the measurement of flour, for instance—to be sure you have exactly what you think you have.) Measuring spoons come in bunches, too. I like metal ones—they're sturdier and a little easier to wash; they also feel good in the hand.

Tongs, spatulas, and whisks are all marvelous inventions. The best tongs are the long kind that you can lock into position when they're not being used. They're amazingly handy, like an extension of your fingers, and, among other virtues, they make it possible to move food around without piercing its surface. Spatulas are essential for folding

whipped cream or beaten egg whites into a batter, and they work for many other things as well; if they're heat-proof silicone, they're handier. Whisks are wonderful. Purely wonderful. They bring together all sorts of things, eliminating lumps, smoothing surfaces, expertly blending mixtures . . . I recommend two sizes: the normal, everyday size and a small one, handy for mixing things like salad dressings. Balloon whisks are considerably larger, and are essential if you're whipping cream or egg whites by hand.

Sheet Pans, Loaf Pans, Roasting Pans, and Racks

There are specialized pans that make various cooking projects easier and better: sheet pans for cookies, for instance. They should be heavy and sturdy—cookies on lightweight pans burn easily. Silpat baking pads on top of the pans make cookie making much easier when it's time to remove the cookies. Silpat is the brand name for silicone and fiberglass mats that come in various sizes and eliminate the need for pregreased baking sheet pans. Loaf pans work for bread, meatloaf, and paté, though all can be made on plain baking pans. Eight-by-eight-inch square pans are especially versatile and very handy to have. Supermarkets usually sell glass square pans in their pot section, no matter how small it may be. Big roasting pans work well for turkeys and roast beef—much better than the heavy-duty foil pans you can buy at the store. Those aren't heavy enough to be really sturdy, but I'm not nuts about cooking in foil, in any case; whether or not it's bad for you, it simply doesn't feel healthy to me. You don't use roasting pans terribly often, but when you need one, you need one—they're kind of hard to improvise. They need to be heavy and sturdy, with good handles, and if they come with their own rack, so much the better. Racks are a good idea, in

general—under a chicken (if you choose not to use sliced onions, the way I do—as on page 89), or for cooling cake or cookies, rather than keeping them in their pans, where they continue to cook, or piling them on a plate, where they steam as they cool and begin to look like something out of a Dalí painting. Also helpful is a smaller roasting pan (about nine by thirteen inches), to be used for all sorts of things, from lasagna to a batch of brownies.

Double Boilers

A double boiler is a tower based on water. It's a short tower, just two pots high—but two, it cannot be argued, is more than one. The bottom pot has to be larger than the other; it holds water, kept just below the boil. It's a fine way of making some sauces, melting chocolate, and— should you have the time and the patience (I rarely do)—scrambling eggs. It can be improvised, with two pots of different sizes, one sitting atop the other, but it's a great luxury to have one of your own. Double boiling in the oven means a large pan holding a smaller one, or several little heat-proof dishes; the larger pan holds hot water, to act as a blanket, steadying temperatures, for the inner pan—especially fine for making things like cheesecake and custard; the even heat works to their advantage and it's much safer than simply braving the oven, no matter what they say about how if you can't stand the heat, get out of the kitchen. No; if you can't stand the heat, use a double boiler. There are always choices.

Colanders, Strainers, Peelers, Skimmers, Graters, Mashers, and More

Kitchen toys are wonderful. You just have to restrict them to those that are moderately essential—not only because of money, but also because of space. There are limits to what can be squeezed into the kitchen junk drawer. Mine holds things I've had for years and have never used (three ice cream scoops, two ice picks [why?], and a variety of other gadgets)—but I'm not ready to part with them. Yet it also has stuff like a cherry pitter and a milk frother, perfect when I need them, even though I don't really need them often. I have learned not to buy too many new gadgets. I look at them, admire them, am tempted by them, and say to myself, "But where would I put it?" and my resistance is thus fortified.

There are things, though, that are enormously useful. Nothing works as well as a colander for draining pasta or salting eggplant, cucumbers, or cabbage. Strainers work for a variety of things—potatoes after they've been boiled, vegetables that have been blanched, custard sauce after it has thickened, stock after the bones and vegetables have given their all, and a host of other necessities. Strainers can also be used to sift flour. And, if necessary, they can double as colanders.

A swivel-bladed peeler is a simple thing, but blessed. Yes, you can—and perhaps should—scrape carrots with a knife rather than peel them (so many healthy goodies just under the skin), but nothing works as quickly or as well on a potato or a bell pepper. There are two kinds of peelers: straight edged and serrated. The former is for carrots and potatoes and other things of that ilk; the latter works nicely for peaches and tomatoes, which otherwise have to be dipped in boiling water and peeled by hand—perfectly doable, but not quite as fast.

A four-sided box grater works well for many things, especially thin-slicing things like cucumbers, but even nicer for grating are a microplane grater (for lemon zest, for instance, or hard cheese) and a zester (different from a grater, a zester is a small instrument that peels tiny strips off a lemon or an orange that can be used as they are, or stacked and sliced into even smaller pieces. 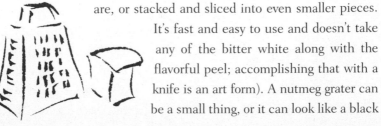 It's fast and easy to use and doesn't take any of the bitter white along with the flavorful peel; accomplishing that with a knife is an art form). A nutmeg grater can be a small thing, or it can look like a black pepper grinder (another essential!)—but when you want freshly grated nutmeg, nothing else works quite as well. Citrus reamers—for juicing oranges and lemons—help most if they double as strainers; otherwise, hold a lemon in one hand and squeeze into the other, letting the juice flow through your (clean) fingers, which catch the seeds. Such is the hope, at least.

There are a variety of potato mashers available—my favorite is the old-fashioned kind, which has curved thick wires on the end of a handle. It makes chunky mashed potatoes—and does nicely for crushing tomatoes or beans. If you like silky smooth mashed potatoes, a masher with a compartment for holding the potatoes and the need for a certain amount of arm strength is what you want. Don't use a mixer or a processor—they gum up the works.

Food mills serve a wonderful purpose when you need them—to sieve something you want to mash or purée at the same time. They're moderately expensive new, but you can find them at flea markets, and they usually work just as well when they're used.

Processors, Immersion
Stick Blenders, Spoons, and More

One of the most expensive things I'd recommend buying is a food processor—a good one. Yes, one can manage without a processor. But so many things are done more efficiently, faster, and better with a processor that I think they're well worth what they cost. Blenders are nice, but I don't have room on my counter for both a blender and a processor, and I don't like the idea of hauling either one out every time I want to use it. I choose the processor, and I leave it out all the time. Processors do things blenders can't—and in greater quantities. You can mix batters in a processor, make cold soup, blend frozen drinks, whip cream, grate or slice carrots or cabbage, chop nuts—make almost anything but mashed potatoes. They're fast and efficient for a wide range of tasks. I use mine not quite daily, but almost, and I love it for its speed and power. In it, I make everything from gazpacho to cheese-cake, from coleslaw to muffins. I whip cream, make egg salad, blend soup, mix guacamole or biscuits or pie crust, prepare smoothies . . . It is my favorite kitchen appliance—I use it more often than any other, except for the stovetop and the oven. I have a standing mixer, and I treasure it—but if I had to, I could manage without it, as long as I still had the processor.

Immersion stick blenders are lovely for puréeing soup right in the pot. They're easier to use with hot soup than a processor (and easier to wash), but they're a luxury—the standing processor does the same thing; you just have to be careful about splashes and spills. Ice cream machines are nice, too—the electric kind that don't need salt and ice. They're fun to use, and they make it possible to have frozen cream in twenty minutes. (But it's also possible to freeze ice cream mixtures in ice cube trays or freezer containers, as long as you remember to mix them in the middle of the freezing, and again before they're served. See page 230 for a recipe for ice cube tray ice cream.)

I haven't said anything yet about can openers. There isn't much to say. If you use cans, my dear, you need a can opener. And a beer-bottle opener, the church-key kind, because if you stick its point under a jar lid and pry it up just a little, you can open the jar without further ado. Yes, you can also open beer bottles with it. And you need corkscrews to open wine bottles. Then there are the big spoons—a giant table-spoon for serving up, a slotted spoon, and a ladle. Sometimes they come in sets on fancy racks you can hang on the wall, but I think they're handier in a kitchen drawer—or a big jar—near the stove. Wooden spoons are essential for stirring. It helps to keep a gathering of wooden spoons (and other long-handled gizmos) in a big muglike holder next to the stove. Also stuck in mine is a wooden rolling pin (the tapered kind), but I don't use it very often.

An instant-read thermometer is a great help when you're roasting a chicken or meat—it tells you exactly what you need to know, and all you have to do is remember to use it. An oven thermometer is good if you aren't sure whether your oven is accurate—if it heats to what you've set the dial for; and a thermometer for your refrigerator and freezer are helpful in the same sort of way. Clip-on-the-pan candy thermometers are nice when you're making jam, candy, or custard, but the only essential is an instant-read thermometer; without it, you're operating on guesswork, unless your fingers and your eyes and ears are truly experienced and trustworthy. Until they get to that point, it's best to use a thermometer.

Did you ask about salad spinners? They're nice. But they're big and bulky and take up a lot of room, wherever you keep them. An alternative is to fill a bowl with lettuce leaves and water, swoosh them around, lift out the lettuce (don't drain the bowl, which would get the grit back into the lettuce), shake it, and spread it on a terry-cloth towel, which can be wrapped and refrigerated—making for lovely dry, crisp lettuce whenever you need it.

A few years ago, Mark Bittman (who writes The Minimalist column for the *New York Times*) wrote that you could buy something very like this list of kitchen equipment—what the French call the batterie de cuisine—at restaurant supply houses in any city for under three hundred dollars for everything. Prices have undoubtedly gone up since then (as has the cost of the food this is all about), but the idea is still a good one, and close to true. Other possibilities: garage sales, flea markets, and eBay, the online auction Web site.

I've left out many things that are nice to have, because they aren't essential. In this category are microwaves, for instance, juicers, slow cookers, and rice cookers. I don't like the idea of microwaves, though I wouldn't mind making popcorn—or melting chocolate—in one. Slow cookers have advantages, but what they do can be duplicated on your stove, even if without the buttons. Rice cookers seem silly to me; all you have to do is use twice as much water as rice, bring it to a boil, turn the heat down, cover it, and cook for fifteen minutes. Did you add salt and olive oil or butter? Please do. Brown rice takes longer, but it's almost as easy. I do have a mandoline—not the big (beautiful but expensive) French kind, but a handy little plastic one, with just a handle, a frame, and the essential slicing blade. Mandolines make perfect thin slices, and they do it quickly. The expensive ones sit on your counter and are very sturdy; for less money, you get to hold one in your hand or rest it on your bowl. They're nice to have—but a box grater with a slicer on one side or a carefully wielded knife does almost as well. I also have a cherry pitter. I only use it once a year, when cherries are in season, but it's good to have when I need it.

There's more—there's always more. Some seem obvious: a pepper grinder; a saltbox to keep on the wall near where you work; cake and pie pans; pot holders and hand towels; a coffee pot; a kettle . . . And some aren't essential, but you might like to have them: an electric spice grinder; a toaster oven . . . It's nice to have a holder of pens and pencils nearby, so that you can make notes on a printed recipe for remembering next time ("too sweet—use less sugar!")—or for jotting notes on a shopping list. That means you need a pad of paper, too.

In the end, it comes back to the beginning: all you REALLY need is a pot, a pan, a knife, and a spoon. You can make miracles with just that little.

2

THE ONION LEGACY

The Beginning: How to Slice an Onion

Life is like an onion: you peel it off one layer at a time,
and sometimes you weep.   —*Carl Sandburg*

The place to start is with an onion. Not with an egg, as you might expect. Eggs may be more symbolic, but eggs are really kind of simplistic. Somebody's chicken is making an obvious statement. True, eggs may come first—unless chickens do—and, yes, eggs are lovely and delicious and nature's perfect package and all that, but they won't do for you what an onion will. And onions are not too shabby in the symbolism department, either, what with all those consecutive layers, each a degree smaller and more interior than the one before, and, at the center, a growing heart that holds the future—the next onion. Which doesn't even begin to speak of tears. Or taste.

Consider it a legacy from me to you: how to slice an onion—because if you can slice an onion, you can cook almost anything. Of course you wouldn't want onions in apple pie, but aside from dessert, onions can go pretty much anywhere. I count them as a desert island necessity (along with olives and lemons), and I recommend most highly learning to slice them quickly and neatly. It saves wear and tear on your fingers, your knives, and your morale. It's very simple. Once you have mastered it—a matter of minutes—you will have learned a basic cooking art.

Choosing Among Onions

Before you slice an onion, you have to decide what kind of onion to buy and to cook with. There are many onions out there, but basically, they can be divided by color: yellow, white, and red. And there are the onion relatives: scallions, chives, leeks, shallots, and garlic.

My favorites for most purposes are Spanish onions—the biggest yellow ones. They're sweet without having lost their oniony sharpness. Each Spanish onion goes a long way, so you don't have to peel as many. And they're easier to peel in the first place. (A quarter of a really large Spanish onion is about the equal of a medium-sized yellow onion, the kind often called Bermudas.)

Little white onions are marvelous for making glazed onions—a Thanksgiving perennial—and for a lovely sweet-and-sour onion relish (recipe on page 34). Red onions are a little milder and sweeter than other onions, but their greatest virtue is that they're red when you need them to be—when you want a bit of color in a salad, for instance, as well as flavor and crunch. Scallions are sort of what onions were when they were babies—they're sometimes called spring onions. They have white bulbs at their bottoms, out of which flat green leaves grow, turning dark green toward the tops. The green parts can be handles, or ribbons, if you blanch them (dip them into boiling water) briefly, or they can be a mild, crunchy garnish when they're used raw and sliced across. The white part is a mild alternative to onions in flavor as well as in texture—same note, but softer.

Chives are dark green, long and thin. They bring a crisp, gentle onion flavor to things like omelets, and they are a lovely garnish for a great many things. You can sometimes find garlic chives in a farmer's market in the springtime—they're the garlic version of onion chives, gentler and subtler than garlic, but still there. Both kinds of chives have small purple flowers, and if they haven't seen pesticides, it's lovely to use them, too—they're pretty, and they taste good.

Shallots are small but impressive onion cousins. They seem expensive, but a little of their wonderful flavor goes a long way. They're mellow—even a bit nutty—and sweet, and especially good minced in a vinaigrette. (More about vinaigrettes when we come to salads.)

Preparing Leeks for Cooking

Leeks are big and beautiful, like great big scallions, in soups and as a braised vegetable, hot or cold, with a vinaigrette dressing. They tend to be sandy . . . but who's perfect? Slice leeks in half, the long way, and hold them under running water, gently pulling the layers apart to see if there's any grit lurking in the shadows. Then you can slice them across in little half moons. Recipes usually say to throw away the dark green tops, but that seems awfully wasteful. I save them and use them to flavor soup (tied in a bundle, so they can be discarded at the end); if I were fancier, I'd use them to wrap things in or I'd slice them the long way and tie things up with them. But since I'm not, I keep them together in a plastic bag, and when I make soup—there they are, ready and waiting to give their all.

Garlic is inimitable and wonderful and I probably would take some to the desert island, too, in the shopping bag with the onions and lemon and olives. (I assume I'd be able to catch fish.) Garlic keeps fleas away when the cat eats it. Someone once told me that if your friends are offended by the smell of garlic, you ought to find new friends. The cat doesn't need to find new fleas.

Peeling and Crushing Garlic

The remarkably easy way to peel garlic is to slice a sliver off the stem end (flat and darker than the rest) of the clove. Then place it on your cutting board (the one you save for onions and garlic), and put your knife blade over it, flat (that is, resting on the garlic, *not* as if you're going to cut into it). Make a fist and give the knife a good whack. Pick up the garlic, and shake or pull off the peel—it'll come off easily. If there are any brown spots on the garlic, just slice them away. The rest of the clove is fine. If you're a hard puncher, you'll have begun to crush the garlic. All to the good, usually. If you want many cloves at once, use your fist to punch the top of the head, the funnel-shaped end. The cloves will separate easily.

The easiest way to crush garlic (without a garlic press) is to chop it fairly finely on your cutting board, sprinkle it with a little salt, and run the flat side of your paring knife back and forth over it, at a very slight angle, using a bit of pressure, until a paste forms. Use less salt in whatever you're cooking in order to compensate for that which you used in the crushing process.

Peeling Onions

The easiest way to peel an onion is to take a small slice off the growing end (the papery, funnel-shaped end) and, without letting go during the slice, pull back toward the root end (the hard, flat part) and, still holding on, slice the root end off, but just thinly, with that first peel. Another way to peel is to take a good slice off both ends, and then strip away the peel on the rest of the onion. Many professional cooks peel this way, because it's fast—but they work for other people, and other people pay for their onions, which means the cooks don't mind so much losing those first two moderately large slices. I'd rather keep the onion intact.

One of the wonderful things about big Spanish onions is that you can cut them in quarters without peeling them, and then peel each quarter as you need it. This is what I do when I need an onion: I take a big yellow Spanish onion, slice it in half—unpeeled—through the root end and then again in quarters. I peel one quarter, usually the required amount, and then slice it in whatever way I need. I put the other three sections, unpeeled, in a plastic bag and refrigerate them. To peel the quarter-onion (without any tears at all), I slice across the papery tip of the onion and, without letting go, pull back to the root end. That usually takes the papery layers off in one swipe. I leave the root itself unsliced—or very thinly sliced away, if it's hairy—so that I can cube the onion or slice it or chop it in whatever way I wish without its falling apart. Leaving the root intact also helps to minimize tears—the offending chemicals bunch up in the root. If things get drastic and tears flow, you can turn on the cold water and rinse the onion; that helps. A tiny bit of flavor may be lost; you may consider that a small sacrifice, but sometimes I think, having peeled and sliced, I'd rather cry.

Cubing, Dicing, Mincing, and Slicing

So far, we've been dealing with preliminaries. But now you've chosen your onion. It's peeled. You're hungry, or you will be soon. And you're ready to cook.

What you probably need to do is cube, dice, or mince your onion. To do any of those—and they are a matter of size (cube is the largest; mince is the smallest)—you need a checkerboard or grid effect across the onion, and this is how you get it:

1. Your working surface should be a flat wooden board or specially made plastic or, in desperate situations, a flat plate. If you use a wood cutting board, reserve one side of it for onions and garlic, or use a separate small board just for them, so that you can be sure when you're slicing bananas or pineapples that the flavors

of the bulbs don't inadvertently make their way into your fruit compote.

2. Slice a whole onion in half horizontally through the root end. The root end, you remember, is the flat end—one of the poles, North or South, of the onion, while the fat, round, and smooth middle is the equator. The other end, the other pole, is the end out of which green sprouts grow if you've had the onion too long. It's papery and funnel-shaped. So slicing in half through the root end means that your knife cuts through that funnel and through the root. The two halves, on the inside, are filled with whorls, like a fingerprint, and you can see the onion within the onion—the onion that might have been as well as the onion that is.

3. Place one of the onion halves (or quarters) cut-side-down on your cutting surface. Hold your knife (which is a good, sharp knife) over the onion so that its point is in front of and perpendicular to the root end. Begin at one side of the onion, and make up-and-down slices AL-MOST all the way through to the root. The onion has to hold together, and the root will perform that function, so be sure not to slice through the root end. Your slices will be at a right angle to the root end. The size of the final cubes is determined by how close or far apart the slices of your grid are, so make your slices close together if you want diced or minced onions, and farther apart if you're aiming for cubes or chunks. After you've done this once or twice, you won't need to worry about how to space your cuts; you'll know.

4. You can skip this next step without any great disaster: Leave the onion right where it is and make new slices that are horizontal to the cutting board—that is, the flat side of your knife blade is flat above the cutting board. Again, don't go all the way to the root.

5. Now slice the last way, with the blade of the knife at a right angle to the slices you've just made. Simply slice down across the onion, moving from the funnel end to the root end. What happens is magic: hundreds of cubes fall from your knife onto the cutting board.

Slicing and Julienning

That's how to slice an onion. Actually, that's how to cut an onion into cubes. If all you want is slices, life is simpler: just slice across. Using a quarter- or a half-onion, you can slice from pole to pole, the long way, making crescents, or across the body of the onion, making semicircles. If you slice across the whole onion, rather than a quarter or a half, you'll have onion rings.

Now that you know how to slice an onion, you can slice anything, making each slice at a right angle to the one before if you want to dice rather than slice. For julienne slices (which look like matchsticks, wide or narrow), make two sets of slices. The first set—as for a carrot—makes a kind of long panel; the second set slices little matchsticks from the stacked panels by slicing down through them. Onions aren't usually julienned—though in a pinch, the crescent slices (from pole to pole) could be considered julienned.

Storing Onions and Garlic

Keep unpeeled onions either in the refrigerator or at room temperature in an airy basket. I use an old French lettuce drier, the kind—before plastic spinners—you whizzed in great circles around your head after you'd washed the lettuce. You can still find those every so often; sometimes they come as three connected baskets of diminishing—or growing, depending on your point of view—size. I hang mine from a hook. Garlic should be kept the same way, out in the air. Why not, then, keep them together? I do.

Onions, it might be nice to know in a pinch, are antibacterial. During World War I, when surgeons needed to sterilize something and normal cleansers weren't available, they rubbed whatever it was with a piece of freshly sliced onion. Sorry, this does not mean you don't have to wash the cutting board.

The Great Pyramids at Giza were built by stonemasons and stone pushers who did all that work on a diet that consisted mostly of chickpeas, garlic, and onions. So you can be sure that onions and garlic are good for you. I'm sure the stone pushers would have liked other things to eat too, but in their world, where chocolate didn't exist (it was waiting to be discovered, across an uncrossable, unknowable sea), and mushrooms were reserved for the pharaoh, a diet of chickpeas, garlic, and onions was not half-bad. Put together with a little olive oil and vinegar, they make a lovely salad.

Using the Peel of Onions to Dye Eggs

Should you wish to dye eggs in the springtime (when, we are told, at the spring equinox, you can stand an egg on its end and leave it thusly for hours in the sunshine—though you can do that with an onion on any day of the year), one way to do it is by bringing together those two perfect symbols, the egg and the onion. Gently wash the eggs, and use a needle or a thumbtack or a hat pin to make a hole in the egg's broad end. (The purpose of this pointful endeavor, as you'll see in chapter 6, is to allow air to escape when the eggs cook, so that the bit of air inside the egg won't crack the shell as it's heated and expands.) Put the eggs in a saucepan with as many onion skins as you can conveniently gather—more skins mean a deeper color. Yellow onion skins will make for eggs with an earthy brown color; red onion skins will give you earthy reddish eggs. If you want a beautiful mottled effect, instead of just putting the skins and the eggs together in the saucepan, wrap the eggs snugly in the skins, using soft twine or cord to hold them together, or pack them tightly in the saucepan. Cover the eggs with water, bring to a boil, reduce heat, and simmer for ten minutes.

Simmering and Boiling

We haven't said anything yet about simmering, as opposed to boiling. Most often, a liquid is brought to the boil, and then the heat is reduced and cooking proceeds at a simmer. Simmering is kinder to most food than boiling, which can toughen them or break them into shreds. You need boiling water to make tea; but soup and stew and a wide variety of other foods need to be kept at a simmer. Boiling is vigorous, energetic, bubbly, and big. Simmering is just below the boil, and it means cooking with great gentleness. Simmering is soft, relaxed, and small. Big bubbles are for boiling; a gentle quiver is for simmering. Boiling is hearty and athletic; simmering is Victorian and delicate. Boiling is a belly laugh; simmering is a coy little smile. The *Mona Lisa* simmers. Use high heat for bringing a pot to a boil, and medium-low heat for a gentle simmer.

The eggs, then, have simmered for ten minutes. Let them cool in their hot water bath. Remove the eggs, and throw away the onion skins. You can polish the eggs with a bit of oil—olive or corn or canola, it doesn't matter at all. You'll have lovely, marbled, magical symbols of the earth (the onion) and the future (the egg). Ecologically sound, too.

Using the Peel in Soup

Another note about what onions are wrapped in, and another moment of glory for the skin of an onion: When you're making soup, especially broth or stock (stock is the basis for other things; broth is very similar, but is its own purpose, an end in itself), add some onion skin to the basic ingredients. It gives a lovely golden color to the soup. Just be sure to take it out at the end.

Baked Onions

. . . .

Think of baked potatoes, and how good—how comforting—they are. Why not baked onions?

For Each Serving:

1 medium-sized yellow (Bermuda) onion (*do not peel*)

Optional: chicken broth (homemade or low-sodium canned or packaged)

Either: one or two teaspoons unsalted butter

Or: ½ tablespoon balsamic vinegar and one tablespoon extra virgin olive oil

Salt and freshly ground black pepper

Optional: ¼ teaspoon thyme, fresh or dried

1. Preheat the oven to 400 degrees.
2. Place the unpeeled onion in a baking dish lined with foil. It should be a fairly snug fit. (If you're baking more than one onion, keep about an inch between the onions and the sides of the pan.) You can bake the onion as is, or you can add chicken broth to a depth of about ½ inch.
3. Bake for 1 hour, or until the onion feels soft when you press it.
4. Cut a cross in the top of the onion, as you would for a baked potato, and pull the peel down about an inch. Tuck a pat of butter inside the cross, some salt and pepper, and, if you like, a sprinkle of thyme, or sprinkle it with vinegar, olive oil, salt, and pepper and eat hot or cool as a portable salad. Either way, eat from the top down, with a fork or spoon.

SERVES 1

Variation: Use red onions. Boil them briefly—for no more than 5 minutes—and then peel them and place in a baking dish that has a tablespoon or two of olive oil in it. Stir, so that all sides of the onions are covered with oil, and bake at 375 degrees for about 45 minutes to an hour, or until the outer layer is crisp and the insides are soft. Finish as above, with butter, thyme, salt, and pepper, or with balsamic vinegar, oil, salt, and pepper.

Roast Onions with Thyme and Honey

Exact quantities don't matter for this recipe; the list below is merely a guide. If you like, add unpeeled cloves of garlic. At the table, one end of each clove can be sliced off and the soft roasted garlic pushed out and spread on good bread. It's also lovely to add peeled shallots. That makes three in the onion family: onions, shallots, and garlic. They go together beautifully; they're fond cousins at a family reunion.

    2 tablespoons olive oil
    4 onions—two each red and yellow, roughly the same size, peeled
        and quartered
    2 cloves of garlic peeled and chunked into small pieces
    Optional: cloves of garlic, unpeeled, and peeled shallots
    ½ teaspoon thyme
    Salt and freshly ground black pepper
    1 tablespoon honey
    ½ cup orange juice
    1 tablespoon balsamic vinegar

1. Preheat the oven to 350 degrees.
2. Cover the bottom of a baking dish large enough to hold the onions with olive oil. Add the onions and garlic (and the optional garlic and shallots, if you're using them) and stir to coat with the olive oil. Sprinkle with thyme, salt, and pepper, and dot the onions with honey. Pour the orange juice over all.
3. Bake for 45 minutes to an hour, until the onions are soft and lightly browned. Sprinkle with the balsamic vinegar.

6 TO 8 SERVINGS

Variation: A very simple thing to do with onions—not quite a relish—is to cook them slowly and gently in butter or olive oil: Slice the onions thinly; sauté them in butter or oil (with, if you like, thinly sliced garlic, a bay leaf, a sprig of thyme, and salt and freshly ground black pepper—or instead, if you'd rather, a little brown sugar and a dash of wine vinegar). Stir; then cover the pan and cook over very low heat, stirring from time to time, for 30 minutes to an hour, until the onions are very soft and golden. Good on bruschetta, as an accompaniment to beef, pork, or chicken, or to top mashed potatoes.

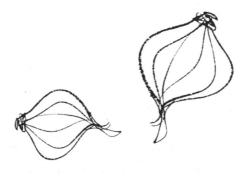

Mediterranean Onion Relish

I think there must be a gene that predisposes one to love sweet and sour food. There's a gene for everything else, so why not this? I have the gene, and I love this recipe, despite having to fuss with the peeling of the small onions; it's worth the effort. I first learned how to make this from Julia Child's Mastering the Art of French Cooking, Volume Two, *from which this recipe is adapted; I've seen variations since then. After all, the recipe's heritage is the northern shore of the Mediterranean, and they know what to do with an onion there. The relish is lovely with hot or cold meats, poultry, or fish.*

3 cups small white onions
½ cup chicken broth
½ cup water
1 teaspoon dry mustard mixed with 1½ tablespoons wine vinegar
2 tablespoons olive oil
1½ tablespoons brown sugar
½ cup tomato, fresh or canned, peeled and chopped
⅓ cup dried currants
2 large cloves garlic, minced
½ teaspoon thyme
1 bay leaf
Salt and freshly ground black pepper
Optional: freshly squeezed lemon juice and extra sugar (see Note
    about adding a few extra cloves of garlic)

1. Peel the onions by covering them with water in a saucepan. Bring the water to a boil; then turn off the heat, drain, and, when the onions are cool enough to handle, pull back the peel and take a very thin slice off the root end. As you finish each onion, cut a shallow X

into the root end. It'll hold the layers together as the onion continues to cook.

2. Combine all the ingredients in a saucepan. Bring to a boil, lower
the heat, and simmer, covered, over low heat until the onions are
tender and the sauce is syrupy, about an hour.

3. If the sauce is too thin, remove the onions to a bowl, and continue
to cook the sauce, uncovered, over high heat until it becomes somewhat syrupy. Taste to adjust the seasoning and the sweet and sour
balance, adding a bit of lemon juice or sugar to make it right. Pour
over the onions. Serve hot or at room temperature.

YIELD: ABOUT 3 CUPS.

Goes beautifully with hot or cold meats or poultry.

Note: If you like garlic, add whole peeled cloves of garlic with the
other ingredients—not too many; you don't want to overpower the
other flavors; just enough to make you that much happier at the table.

Shallot Butter · Garlic Butter

Shallots are sweeter and milder than onions, with a mellow flavor of their own. They're excellent roasted along with vegetables, meat, or poultry, and they make a lovely butter. Melted, it can be a sauce; chilled, it's a fine spread for good bread. Why not put some on top of a baked potato (page 169)? Or, for that matter, a baked onion (page 31)?

¼ pound (one stick) unsalted butter, at room temperature
2 shallots, peeled and finely chopped
1 tablespoon parsley, finely chopped
1 teaspoon lemon juice
1 teaspoon Worcestershire sauce

1. Mash the butter with a wooden spoon until it's light and creamy.
2. Stir in the remaining ingredients.
3. Chill, wrapped in foil or plastic. To use as a sauce for hot food, either place a pat of shallot butter on the top, or heat the butter until it's melted and spoon over. Use cold as a spread for bruschetta.

Variation: Garlic Butter—either substitute a teaspoon of minced garlic for the shallots, or simply add minced garlic to the above recipe.

To Make Garlic or Shallot Bread: Slice a baguette horizontally; place it on a foil sheet and cover both halves of the bread with garlic butter. Re-form the bread; wrap in the foil; bake 10 minutes at 350 degrees; unwrap and bake 5 to 10 minutes longer, or until crisped. You can also place the two halves (on a sheet of foil, but unwrapped) on a baking sheet and put it under the broiler until the bread is lightly browned.

Simpler: Toast slices of good Italian bread (or diagonally cut baguette slices); while the bread is hot, rub each slice with halved raw garlic cloves. Dribble extra virgin olive oil over each slice. In the summer, it's lovely to also rub half a ripe tomato over the toasted bread before adding the olive oil.

Turkish Leeks

Leeks, left in the garden to go to seed, make beautiful flowers. They also make beautiful food after they've left the garden. They're the not-so-secret ingredients in vichyssoise (cold potato soup strained, and mixed with cream—see page 74); they're lovely braised and served with vinaigrette dressing; and they're excellent in this classic Turkish way of preparing vegetables. (It's also very good made with celeriac—a knobby round root, cousin to celery—if you can find it.)

    4 leeks, trimmed
    ¼ cup extra virgin olive oil
    2 carrots, halved the long way and sliced into half-moons
    2 tablespoons raw rice
    1 cup water or low sodium chicken broth
    2 teaspoons sugar
    ½ lemon, juiced
    Salt and freshly ground pepper to taste.
    Garnish: fresh dill, chopped

1. Wash the leeks well (see page 23). Then halve and slice them in ½-inch-thick half-moons.
2. Warm the olive oil in a saucepan; add the leeks, carrots, rice, and water and mix. Cover and cook over low heat for 30 minutes, checking from time to time to stir and to be sure the mixture isn't dry. (If it is, add more water.)

3. Add the sugar, lemon juice, salt, and pepper, cover again, and continue cooking for another 15 minutes, again checking to see if more water is needed. The mixture should be moist, but not soupy. Cool to room temperature. Taste to adjust sweet and sour balance. Serve sprinkled with chopped dill.

SERVES 4

3

LIQUIDITY

The Magic That Is Water

> Thank God for tea! What would the world do without tea?—How did it exist? I am glad I was not born before tea.   —*Sydney Smith*

You can live for about three weeks without food, but you'll last not much longer than three days without water. It's remarkably easy to forget how much we need water. Our bodies are roughly 60 percent water, and we need water in order to exist. We can get it in the form of soup, juice, and food (coffee, tea, and soda are diuretics—which means they increase the body's rate of pee, not a good idea if you're trying to add water to your diet), but we also need to drink plain water as we go along. Water aids the digestive process, and it doesn't need large amounts of physical energy for its own digestion; what it does, aside from many other things, is replenish what we've used. The ideal goal used to be eight to ten eight-ounce servings of water a day, though scientists are now challenging those numbers as being too high. There aren't any recipes here for water. (Ingredients: hydrogen and oxygen, in carefully measured amounts.) I won't even get into a discussion of tap water versus bottled water. Everything depends on where you live, how good your water is, how much you're willing to spend on plain old water, how much you trust the bottler (you could be buying some-body else's tap water, after all), and how you feel about all those bottles, both plastic and glass, and their packaging and transportation.

Let's assume, instead, that you have a source of good drinkable wa-ter (and that you're aware of your good fortune). Think of all the things you can do with it! I don't mean boiling eggs or making soup, though they definitely count; I mean making fluids out of solid substances—turning a stalk of rhubarb, for instance, into a glass of spring tonic, a sturdy banana into a sweet foam, or a solid mass of chocolate powder into a silky smooth cup of sweet cocoa.

Boiling Water

I suppose there are rocket scientists—or brain surgeons—who don't know how to boil water. But there really isn't anything to it—you need heat, a pot, and water. The water goes in the pot; the pot goes over the heat; and the heat gets turned up high until the water is in obvious mo-tion and bubbles are breaking on its surface. That takes care of how to boil water.

There are things to know about boiling water, for all of that. Keep-ing water at a boil for a few minutes kills any stray bacteria (or other contaminants) that may be in it. Boiling water at high altitudes takes longer because boiling is related to atmospheric pressure, but if you live on top of a mountain, you probably already know that.

More esoterically, the word boil is derived from the Latin *ebullire*, to boil up, in turn from *bulla*, bubble. Someone who is ebullient is bubbling with enthusiasm or excitement—a pot of water is excited too, when it comes to the boil and is full of bubbles.

Cooking with Water

Boiling, steaming, poaching, double boiling—these are ways of cook-ing in which heat is transferred from its source to the food being

cooked through the medium of water. Dropping something into a
pot of water and bringing it to a boil is the simplest—think of hard-
cooked eggs.

There's a certain amount of controversy—not exactly what you'd
call heated, but still—about whether food should be added before water comes to the boil or after. The simplest way to think about it is that
if you want the food (meat in soup, for example) for its own sake, add
it *after* the water has begun to boil. If you want the liquid itself (broth,
for example) for what it has to offer, start food and water at the same
time. In the first way, juices stay relatively intact; in the second, more
seeps into the liquid and adds its flavor to it.

Steaming and Poaching

Steaming means that there is something between the water and the
food—a bamboo shelf, for instance, in a Chinese steamer, or a metal
rack, or, most simply, a bowl that holds the food above the water,
thus allowing the steam, rather than the water itself, to cook the
food. Water is kept just below the boil, at a constant level of heat,
and a lid keeps the steam inside the pot. It's a good idea to keep a
second pot of water at the boil, should it be necessary to add more
water to the steamer. Properly steamed food is juicy and flavorful, and
it's especially healthy—fewer vitamins and other nutrients seep into
the water; everything tends to stay where you want it: in the food
itself.

Poaching is another delicate way of cooking, and, like steaming, it
usually means especially moist and juicy food. To poach, food is kept
in water just under the boiling point, barely simmering. (See chapter 2
for more about simmering.) Ideally, poached eggs aren't hard-boiled—
the yolk, should you dare it, is still runny, while the white is softly set.
(See page 110 for directions on how to poach eggs.) Poached salmon
(which cooks in what's called a court bouillon—water flavored with
lemon, wine, herbs, carrots, and onions), is silky smooth; poached
chicken is sweet and uncomplicated.

Braising

Braising is another way to cook with liquid—sometimes water, sometimes wine or broth or even juice or cider, and sometimes a mixture. It's sort of like a very short—that is, height-challenged—soup; the goal is not broth, but a rich sauce surrounding meltingly tender meat, chicken, or vegetables. It's best for cuts of meat that need slow cooking, like chuck roast. What it does is twofold: It breaks down tough fibers and connective tissues and makes the meat tender, and it adds body and flavor to the liquid to make a rich, flavorful sauce. To make a braise (from the French *braiser*), begin with vegetables cut into small cubes and "sweated"—cooked over low heat in butter or oil until they're slightly softened. So many kinds of food begin with that step— the vegetables (usually onions, garlic, carrots, and celery) are called a mirepoix in France, a soffritto in Italy and Spain (where it is spelled sofrito). Different vegetables are cooked this way in different cultures— Indonesian cooks include shrimp paste, for instance; Thai cooks use curry pastes; in India, hot chilies and chopped ginger may join onion and garlic—but the process is almost always the same. The result is that the vegetables have a more intense flavor because the water they contain has evaporated, and their flavor becomes part of the larger sauce.

In the traditional meat braise, after the vegetables have been sweated and the meat browned, a liquid—stock, wine, tomatoes, even beer, sometimes juice or cider or just plain water—is poured into the pot. The liquid doesn't cover the meat, as it would if soup were the goal; it reaches partway up, and the meat, be it beef, lamb, pork, or chicken, emerges proudly several inches above the water level; look, Ma, I'm swimming!

The pot is covered, and the heat is lowered. The food cooks at a gentle simmer (perhaps it's investigated from time to time to make sure sufficient liquid remains or to see if the meat needs to be turned) for quite a while until the whole becomes more than the sum of its parts.

Reducing a Sauce

Sometimes, the meat and the vegetables are removed when they're done and the liquid is brought to the boil and cooked until it has reduced and it has become a thick and irresistible sauce. Reducing a sauce concentrates its flavor, because what boils away is water; it also means a sauce that is naturally thickened, without using flour or cornstarch or any other thickening agents. All you need to do is turn up the heat to bring the liquid to a boil; then turn the heat down slightly and continue to boil until it's the consistency and flavor you want. That obviously means tasting it—cooks have so much good fortune! It also means watching the pot (it has already come to a boil, so you needn't worry about old proverbs) just to be sure that it doesn't boil over—not good fortune at all when that happens.

About Juices

There are at least two ways of making juice: squeezing (by hand or with a juicer), or cooking, with added water and sugar or salt. Commercially made juice involves pressing (squeezing) as well as heating, and often concentrating the result—taking out the water—and then later reconstituting the result with different water. Sometimes it's fun to skip all of that, and go right to the source. I don't have a juicer, but I do have a good right arm when it's needed, and the pleasure of turning a solid into juice all by myself—well, with a little heat from the stove—is enormous; I taste it in every glass. The easiest way to make fresh orange juice is to squeeze oranges, a half at a time; nothing else is needed. Apple juice involves high pressure; I don't think I could do that by hand, but I can cook apples with a little sugar and water and strain the result. I think I'd rather buy apple juice—or even better, cider—so juicing involves both a sense of adventure and the other sense, known as common.

Smoothies are just one step removed from juice—they're usually made with more than one kind of fruit, and they're sometimes thickened with yogurt. Possible combinations of fruit are almost endless—melons and apple juice, bananas and peaches, blueberries and anything . . . on and on, through the refrigerator and the fruit basket. Even frozen fruit works—sometimes it works better, because it turns everything deliciously cold. Peaches, blueberries, strawberries, raspberries—I'll stop myself; the list is nearly endless. The recipe for Banana Anna on page 55 demonstrates a very simple smoothie. Get fancier from there, as your fancy leads you.

About Coffee

According to coffee legend, it all started with a herd of goats in Ethiopia. One day, as the goats grazed on the red berries of coffee bushes, the goatherd noticed their unusually high spirits, and decided to try a few himself. He was soon gamboling with the kids and, in his turn, was noticed by a monk, who took his own turn by picking some berries for the brothers back home. That night, they too felt strangely uplifted—not by sudden spiritual illumination, necessarily, but by the energy and clarity of thought which was the gift of the coffee berries. Word spread, and so did coffee bushes.

Beans were roasted for the first time in Arabia in about 1000 A.D.; by the thirteenth century, Arabians were drinking coffee regularly. They kept the bushes secret, boiling and parching the seeds—the coffee beans—so they wouldn't reproduce. According to another coffee legend, an Indian pilgrim smuggled a collection of fertile coffee seeds out of Mecca by taping them to his belly. The beans were planted, eventually bore fruit, and coffee spread around the world, reaching Europe in the seventeenth century, going first from Turkey to

Italy. In 1696, the Dutch founded the first European-owned coffee plantation in colonial Java, now Indonesia. That's why we call it a cup of java.

There have been plenty of rumors about the unhealthiness of coffee; it has been reputed to cause everything from stunted growth to cancer. Not to mention the heebie-jeebies. The news isn't all bad, though—there are many reports of the good things that coffee is supposed to do (aside from keeping us awake during boring meetings). On its Web site, the National Coffee Association tells us that coffee reduces the risk of type 2 diabetes, Parkinson's, colon and skin cancer, cirrhosis, gallstones, depression, "and more." Among the "more": The site says that a morning cup of coffee helps reduce "the pain experienced during moderate-intensity cycling exercise" in your morning workout. That, of course, assumes that you *have* a morning workout, and that it's painful. As for me, I'll have a cup of tea and think about it.

Making Coffee

First thing to think about when you set out to make a healthy cup of coffee is the beans, and then whether or not to grind them at home, how to keep them, how to brew them, and even how to serve the result—which could be anything from a mocha macchiato to a plain old cup of joe. (Among the theories explaining the origin of Joe's cup of coffee, one of the most believable is that the phrase originated after Admiral Josephus Daniels, secretary of the navy, abolished the officers' wine mess aboard U. S. Navy ships in 1914, leaving a cup of coffee as the strongest drink available on board. One imagines that naming a cup of coffee after him wasn't necessarily the worst thing said about the admiral.)

The only way to find the beans and roast you like best is to test various possibilities—not an onerous chore if you like coffee, just a bit time-consuming. Grinding the chosen beans at home as you need them (in a small, inexpensive electric grinder) maintains maximum freshness, but sometimes that isn't what you feel like doing first thing in the morning. The alternative, and there is no shame attached, is to purchase coffee that has already been ground. Purists will tell you that coffee beans lose flavor after they've been roasted, and lose more after they've been ground; they advise buying small amounts—about what you need for a week. That isn't always possible. However much you buy, the best way to store coffee—whole or ground—is in a lidded container or a jar; a fold-down bag doesn't work as well. Keep coffee in a dry, dark place—but not the refrigerator or the freezer.

There are ways and ways to brew coffee—percolators, filter machines, drip pots, French presses, small brass pots, espresso pots. . . . The sound of coffee perking is one of those kitchen legends—like bacon sizzling, or stew simmering. But good as it sounds—and smells—perked coffee isn't *good* coffee. The water is too hot for too long, and it drips down through the grounds too many times. There are those who think that percolators were responsible for the slow decline in coffee drinking in the middle of the twentieth century. Drip pots make much better coffee, whether they are coffee machines or—my favorite—a pot that you keep on the stove. Grounds go in the middle compartment and the hot water in the top drips (once) through them; the coffee is poured from the bottom compartment. A lot of people swear by French presses; they're attractive and inexpensive, and they make good coffee.

However you make your coffee, this is the secret: Measure carefully, following the directions for your pot or machine, and add a tiny pinch of salt. The overall rule is one heaping tablespoon of ground coffee for every eight ounces of coffee you're going to end up with—that is, at the finish, not the amount of water at the start. If hot water goes into your coffee pot, it should be just a bit less than boiling—bring it to a hard boil on the stove, remove the pan from the heat, let it stand while you count to five, and then pour it into the pot. It's essential, too, for your coffee pot to be scrupulously clean. Coffee oils tend to stick; they need to be scrubbed away each time you brew up a pot.

About the various ways to drink coffee: The basics are latte (pronounced lah-tay), which is espresso and steamed milk with milk foam on the top, and the quite similar cappuccino, which has more foam and a sprinkling of cinnamon. Café mocha is like a latte, but with chocolate added (mocha is always a combination of coffee and chocolate). Café au lait (my favorite) is coffee with a lot of milk—it should be half of each, and as long as I'm talking "should," the coffee and the hot milk should be poured simultaneously into the cup. That rarely happens.

For those who would rather not gambol with the goats, the customary way of decaffeinating coffee is to steam the raw coffee beans and then rinse them in a solvent—a process repeated and repeated until most of the caffeine in the beans is gone. Not terribly appetizing, that word "solvent," especially when you're told that benzene was once used as the most efficient solvent. Benzene comes from coal tar and petroleum and it's probably carcinogenic; yum. There are nicer ways of accomplishing decaf today, but none of them, not even water, is wildly appetizing. Hope for the future lies in a naturally caffeine-free coffee bean. Though it couldn't possibly be discovered by Ethiopian goats.

About Tea

There are tea legends, too. One tells about an Indian sage named Bodhidharma, who visited China to spread Buddhism; one night, he chewed leaves from a nearby bush to stay awake during meditation; it worked because the leaves he chose were tea leaves. A more poetic and much more grisly version of the story has it that Bodhidharma was so frustrated by his sleepiness that he tore off his eyelids and threw them to the ground; where they fell, the first tea bush sprouted and grew.

Another once upon a time: About five thousand years ago, the Chinese emperor Shen Nung, who was a good ruler and an investigative scientist, ruled that all drinking water was to be boiled in order to ensure that it was clean. One summer, during a visit to a corner of his realm, he and his court stopped to rest. According to his ruling, water was boiled for the court to drink. A breeze blew dried leaves from nearby bushes into the boiling water and turned it brown. The emperor—who collected herbs—tasted it and found it refreshing and good. An aha! moment in the story of tea, probably not too far from the facts.

And the facts are these: China is thought to be the birthplace of tea; there are written mentions of tea as far back as 1000 B.C. The English word *tea* comes from *te*, a Chinese dialect word. There are dozens—no, hundreds, maybe thousands—of different kinds of tea, and, just as with coffee, the best way to find the tea you like best is to sample different kinds. The basic division is between black tea—the kind that comes in a mug at the corner diner—and green tea, the kind you get in a Chinese or Japanese restaurant. Officially, there's also white tea and oolong tea. White tea is the least processed tea, and has a fresh, grassy sort of taste. Green, black, and oolong teas have each been processed in a different way, affecting their taste, with oolong sort of the middle, in taste, between green and black. Some teas, like Earl Grey, have been scented or flavored with oils or flower petals during processing; chai tea is black tea brewed with spices.

There are tea wars between tea bag and loose tea aficionados. Tea bags don't contain whole tea leaves, just what tea snobs would call tea dust—the pieces left after the whole leaves have been packaged. This means that some of the essential oils in the whole leaves are lost to the tea drinker. According to this theory, all the whole tea leaves are packed into tins to be sold; what's left is put into tea bags. I wonder, though: so much tea is sold in tea bags—how can there be so many bits and pieces lying around after the packaging of the whole leaves? For me, the true difference is in the way the tea is brewed. When loose tea leaves are measured into a pot or cup, the boiling water circulates freely all around them and the tea leaves can swell, expand, and unfurl, but when a tea bag is used, the tea just sort of sits there, surrounded by boiling water, but not dancing in it, not glowing in quite the same way. How enormous is the taste difference? As always, it's a matter of personal taste. And yes, there is a time and a place for a tea bag. (Either way—whole leaves or tea bags—tea should be kept in opaque containers, safe from light and air, and never in the refrigerator.)

There are only two tea things I feel really wildly strongly about. One is what happens in even the best restaurants when you order a cup of tea: The cup is filled with hot water, and the tea bag is in its package on the saucer. No! The tea has to be *in* the cup when the water—boiling hot—is poured in. The other thing I feel strongly about is reusing a once-used tea bag. It has to do, I believe, with attitudes about coffee and tea. Coffee is a symbol of hospitality in the United States; restaurants offer a bottomless cup—refills until you float away, if that's your choice. But if you ask for more tea, you are politely and sweetly offered another cup of hot water. Not a new tea bag. Not even a clean cup. How much does one tea bag cost? How much does a second cup of coffee cost? Why is one—the latter—free and the other, the tea bag, nonexistent? Tea has a sort of upscale quality to it, on a subliminal basis; it's for ladies—who drink it in thin china cups with their pinkies sticking out. Coffee is for men, and for folks. If you drink tea, you take your chances with the scornful multitudes who provide it. Console yourself by considering yourself elite.

Russians have an interesting way of dealing with multiple cups of tea. A samovar is essentially a container that boils water—traditionally by using coal or charcoal in a central, cylindrical pipe surrounded by a water chamber. (Modern samovars are electrically heated.) A teapot sits on the top of the pipe cylinder; it holds concentrated tea, made by steeping tea leaves in a small amount of water. The teapot is kept warm by the cylinder's heat. To make a cup of tea, a little concentrate is poured into a cup and diluted with hot water from the main container—there's a faucet at the bottom. The samovar works in small settings (there's a Russian expression that translates as "to have a sit by a samovar"—it means to sit and talk with friends and family while drinking tea from the samovar); it does equally well in large ones— long-distance cars on the Trans-Siberian Railway had samovars at the end of each car's corridor. Tea in England involves refills, too, by placing a pot of hot water on the table to dilute the concentrated tea left in the teapot. In the United States, we think of British high tea as an elegant gathering with strawberries and whipped cream, fine china and sterling silver. But in England, high tea is really just an early evening meal—combining afternoon tea and dinner. It's eaten at the "high"—main—table, instead of on a smaller tea tray. It usually consists of cold meats, eggs, or fish, cakes and sandwiches, and it is the very definition of informal. Afternoon tea, on the other hand, can be special; it's what we think of when we think of English tea. It can mean finger sandwiches (traditionally cucumber, egg, cress, fish paste, ham, smoked salmon), scones (with butter, clotted cream, and jam), and cakes and pastries. If the tea is served with a three-tiered stand, the sandwiches, scones, and cakes each have their own layer. At home, afternoon tea is somewhat less involved, perhaps just tea and a slice of cake. In hotels, cafés, and tea shops, afternoon tea is still a fine three-way treat, afternoon delight of its own kind. Afternoon tea began as the bridge between noontime lunch and a late dinner served at eight or nine o'clock. It's the sustainer—as *Jause*, the Austrian tea and coffee break time, gets Austrians from lunch to dinner (and sometimes from breakfast to lunch); it's just that in Austria, there's more whipped cream. It's the same thing in the United States: the coffee break, morning and afternoon. We haven't gotten to tea breaks yet.

Brewing Tea

Time to brew. The imperative: Start with fresh *cold* water. Good water. Bring the water to a rolling—that is, big—boil, but move quickly; it shouldn't stay at the boil because then the oxygen content of the water will be diminished. Along the way, when the water is hot but not yet boiling, preheat the teapot or teacup by pouring a little of the cooking water into it and letting it sit for a minute or two while the rest of the water comes to a boil. Spill out the warm-up water, and, if you're using loose tea, measure one teaspoon of leaves for each six to eight ounces of water. Bring the teapot or the cup to the water pot and as soon as the water comes to a boil, fill the teapot or cup with boiling water, and let it steep to the strength you like—at first, you may want to taste it every minute or so until it's as strong as you like. Don't let black tea steep for longer than five minutes; it will have too much tannic acid and taste acidic and bitter. Green tea, by the by, shouldn't be made with water that's at the boil, as black tea should; let the boiling water sit off the heat for a minute and then pour it over the green tea leaves, which should steep for a minute or two.

Black or green, the leaves need to be strained off—otherwise, they'll continue to steep. When I'm making just one cup, I use a small Japanese bamboo strainer to hold the tea leaves; it's about the shape of a cup or a mug, but smaller, to fit inside a cup so the leaves are still free; when the tea is ready, the bamboo strainer is lifted out. Metal tea strainers work, too, but mesh ball infusers of any shape, it seems to me, are just metal tea bags—not an improvement. With attention to brewing time, it's very possible to make a reasonably good cup of tea with a tea bag. It happens every day.

I make iced tea with tea bags. My favorite has sustained me through many a hot day: I use two bags of herbal lemon zinger and one of black currant black tea in a two-cup measure; cover with boiling water; and let steep until cool. Dilute to taste (usually by another cup or two) and serve over ice. It's refreshing and sweet without a drop of sugar. Standard iced tea means four to six tea bags steeped in two cups of hot (just off the boil) water for five minutes. Don't squeeze the tea bags; add sugar, if you like it sweet, while the mix is hot. Cool at room temperature to avoid cloudiness and dilute in a two-quart pitcher until it tastes the way you like it.

The story of tea bags, like so many other things, is the story of a single ingenious idea—simple, that is, after somebody else has thought of it. Coffee and tea merchant Thomas Sullivan wanted a way to give his customers small samples of the tea he had to offer; he used small hand-sewn silk muslin bags to ship the tea, and the people who received them understood immediately their potential. Aha! So simple! So easy! So clean! Please, Mr. Sullivan, could I have more of those tea bags?

Directions for making coffee, tea, and iced tea are on pages 45, 50, and 51.

Rhubarb Juice

....

Rhubarb juice is an absolute tonic after a long winter. Rhubarb is one of the first food plants of spring, and its taste feels head- and body-clearing, full of the sharpness of early spring. Did you know that rhubarb is hermaphroditic? Male and female together, that is. This information is surely unrelated to the fact that its leaves are poisonous. We eat only the stems.

Rhubarb, washed and chunked
Fresh cold water
Sugar
Pinch of salt
Lime juice

1. Place rhubarb in a non-aluminum saucepan and cover with water. For every stalk of rhubarb, add 1 tablespoon of sugar. Add a pinch of salt.
2. Bring to a boil, reduce heat, and simmer for 10 minutes, or until the rhubarb is soft. Strain.
3. Taste the juice and add more sugar if needed. Add a bit of lime juice—the amount depending on how much rhubarb juice you have, but begin with the juice of a quarter of a lime; taste, and add another quarter if you like.

Note: It's possible to use the strained rhubarb as a dessert (or to make a crisp); add more sugar, if you like; and a little cream—whipped or otherwise—would also be beneficial.

Tomato Juice

. . . .

Homemade tomato juice is a revelation, especially when made from ripe garden tomatoes. "Aha!" one's mouth says. "So this is what tomato juice is supposed to taste like!" And then it asks for more.

You can give your mouth more because homemade tomato juice is easy to make. And it is very, very, very good for you.

8 medium tomatoes, quartered, or, in the winter, 1 28-oz. can
    tomatoes (Muir Glen is highly recommended)
½ cup water
¼ medium onion
1 rib celery with leaves
3 sprigs parsley
¼ teaspoon paprika
½ teaspoon sugar
1 teaspoon salt
Freshly ground black pepper

1. Combine the tomatoes, water, onion, celery, and parsley in a saucepan. Bring to a boil, reduce the heat, and simmer for 30 minutes.
2. Pass through a food mill or strain, pushing hard on the solids with the back of a spoon.
3. Add the paprika, sugar, salt, and pepper to the juice and mix well. Taste and adjust seasonings—more salt may be needed. Chill before serving.

YIELD: ABOUT 2 CUPS

Banana Anna

Banana Anna was a smoothie before smoothies were invented. Or, to say the same thing differently, smoothies are descended from Banana Anna. Whence Banana Anna? I'm told it was sold, several generations back, in a San Antonio restaurant that also sold other similar fruit drinks and called them all Anna. Clever restaurant—this is a recipe that makes a great deal out of very little. It's delicious, refreshing, and very filling.

1 banana
½ cup milk (whole or low-fat)
3 ice cubes
1 to 2 teaspoons sugar
½ teaspoon vanilla
Garnish: freshly ground nutmeg or a sprinkle of cinnamon, or both

1. In either a blender or a food processor bowl, combine the banana, milk, ice cubes, sugar, and vanilla.
2. Process for 3 to 5 minutes, until the mixture is thick. Pour into glasses and garnish with a sprinkle of nutmeg or cinnamon. Serve immediately.

2 TO 3 SERVINGS

Variations: Use yogurt instead of milk. Add blueberries. Or strawberries. Or both. Or brandy. There are all sorts of possibilities, but Banana Anna tastes so good just the way it is, and it's so pure and simple . . .

Russian Coffee

. . . .

Russian Coffee as I learned to make it is half coffee and half cocoa—what we would call mocha (mocha is any combination of coffee and chocolate). Somehow I doubt that anybody in Moscow drinks coffee this way. On the other hand, I've never been to Moscow. But I love this Russian coffee, hot or cold.

Hot:
  2 cups freshly brewed coffee
  2 cups freshly made cocoa (see Note below about how to make cocoa)
  2 teaspoons sugar
  Tiny pinch salt
  Milk or cream
  Optional: Whipped cream

1. Mix the coffee, cocoa, sugar, and salt together. Serve hot and pass a pitcher of milk or cream. Why not serve with whipped cream?

SERVES 4

Cold:
Additional ingredients to those above:
  1 teaspoon sugar
  ½ cup milk
  Optional: Whipped cream and vanilla ice cream

1. Make Hot Russian coffee, adding an additional teaspoon of sugar. Cool. Taste to adjust sweetness, and add ½ cup more milk.
2. Pour into glasses over ice cubes. Pass, if you like, a bowl of whipped cream. And even better: a scoop of vanilla ice cream. Best: both.

SERVES 6 TO 8

Frozen:

    2 cups freshly brewed coffee
    ½ cup sugar
    2 cups freshly made cocoa (see Note below about how to make
       cocoa)
    Pinch of salt
    1½ cups heavy cream
    1 teaspoon pure vanilla extract
    Garnish: cinnamon
    Optional: additional whipped cream

1. Pour the hot coffee over the sugar in a heat-proof bowl or saucepan and stir until the sugar is dissolved. Add the cocoa and salt; stir. Cool.
2. Whip the cream and vanilla until stiff. Fold the cooled coffee mixture into the cream until well blended. Pour into a serving bowl and place in the freezer for at least 3 hours. If hard frozen, let stand at room temperature for 10 to 15 minutes before serving. Dust top lightly with cinnamon. Serve with additional whipped cream, if you like.

SERVES 8

Note: To make cocoa, mix a heaping tablespoon of cocoa and 2 level tablespoons of sugar in a heat-proof cup or a small saucepan. Stir in two teaspoons of milk or cream to make a thick paste, adding a bit more milk if necessary, and then stir in hot milk or water (or a mixture) to make 2 cups. Taste to see if additional sugar is needed.

Mango Lassi

....

Mango Lassi is a wonderful combination of mango, sugar, and yogurt. Drinks of yogurt and flavoring are offered throughout Asia and the Middle East. In Turkey, a drink known as aryan (yogurt, salt, and water— refreshing and much better than it sounds) is so popular that it's on the menu at McDonald's. There are variations of lassi and aryan drinks throughout Asia and the Middle East, but at Indian restaurants in the United States, the lassi on the menu is always mango.

> 1 cup plain whole milk or low-fat (*not* no-fat) yogurt
> ½ cup whole milk
> 2 fresh mangoes, peeled and pitted (see Note below about how to
>   peel and slice mangoes)
> 1 tablespoon sugar or more to taste

1. Combine all the ingredients in the bowl of a food processor and blend for 2 minutes. Add more sugar if you like. Either pour into glasses to serve or chill for several hours before serving.

4 SERVINGS

Note: To peel a mango, wash it and hold it upright (that is, with the stem end at the top). Use a serrated knife to slice the two larger sides (sometimes called "the cheeks") down from the top, avoiding the large central pit. Use the tip of a paring knife to make crisscross slices in each cheek without going through the skin. Push the skin up to invert, and use the knife or a spoon to scoop the flesh away from the skin. Cut the remaining sections away from the pit; peel them.

Variations: Use 2 cups of hulled strawberries instead of mango. In either case, add, if you like, ½ teaspoon of ground cardamom and a tiny pinch of salt.

Black and White Ice Cream Soda

Where does one go to buy a black and white ice cream soda? Back in the day, they were served at candy stores, drug-stores, and coffee shops. They had a clean, cold, sweet taste, and they came in tall V-shaped glasses, with real whipped cream spooned over a scoop of ice cream and everything spilling sweetly over the side. Oh, nostalgia! Oh, sugary, milky foam! Oh, chocolate and vanilla! You'll just have to make your own.

For each serving:
  2 tablespoons chocolate syrup
  2 tablespoons milk
  Unflavored seltzer
  1 scoop vanilla ice cream
  Whipped cream

1. Place the syrup in the bottom of a large glass. Add the milk and stir well to mix. Keep stirring as you add seltzer to within 2 inches of the top of the glass. Stir briskly.
2. Add the ice cream. Top with whipped cream.

Variations: Add 2 tablespoons strong coffee with the milk to make a mocha soda. Add a scoop of vanilla ice cream to a glass of root beer to make a Brown Cow; add vanilla ice cream to a glass of cola for a Black Cow. My mother's favorite was a chocolate soda with strawberry ice cream instead of vanilla.

4

HEAVENLY SOUP

Comfort and Joy in a Pot

Chowder breathes reassurance. It steams consolation.
—*Clementine Paddleford*

Onions are the first basic; soup is the second. The onion principle holds that if you know how to slice an onion, you can slice anything. Soup principle: If you know how to make soup, you'll always be able to have a good meal. Possibly even a heavenly one.

It isn't difficult to make heavenly soup. The process is described in a single paragraph in *The Street Where the Heart Lies*, by Ludwig Bemelmans (author and illustrator of the Madeline books for children):

"What is this heavenly soup made of?" he asked. . . .

"Oh, nothing at all. You take an onion, and a little clove of garlic, and cut them finely and brown them in hot oil. Then you put in small pieces of leftover meat and ham, then tomatoes, cut up, and a bouquet of herbs, a little thyme and basil, a laurel leaf. Then you throw in some rice or a handful of pasta, add a shot of red wine, and you serve it with grated cheese and bread, very simple. You let it cook slowly on a small fire before you throw in the rice and the pasta."

"May I have a little more?"

Heavenly soup, simply made, simply described. Bemelmans isn't supplying a recipe; he doesn't feel it's worth saying that the soup is made with broth or water or juice, or that the rice or pasta should be cooked before it's thrown into the soup—otherwise it has to be cooked after it's thrown into the soup—or that the wine will taste better if it, too, has a chance to simmer for ten minutes or so along with the other ingredients. And that the ham isn't an imperative—or that the ham you buy in France, the ham that was, the France that was, may not be quite like the ham you buy at the supermarket. And that the cheese will be positively divine, which is what you need for a heavenly soup, if it's Parmigiano Reggiano, freshly grated. Or that you will undoubtedly need a bit of salt and freshly ground black pepper. Doesn't matter; you can learn how to make soup from that paragraph.

Bemelmans's soup is fairly classic, but you can make soup out of just about anything, even as the old folktale tells us: A group of soldiers coming home from war stop at an old woman's house and tell her they can make a delicious soup out of nothing but water and a stone. Completely awed by the prospect of free soup, she agrees to let them use her fire and soup pot. Stone soup is good, they tell her, as they begin to cook, but if you add an onion, it is magnificent. And onions cost only pennies. So she gives them an onion. Ah! they say, what superb stone soup! Just think what it would be like if we added a carrot! So she gives them a carrot. And in turn, all the soup vegetables, and finally a soup bone, and some wonderful meat. Just think, she marvels, as she avidly spoons up the finished soup from her bowl. What marvelous soup you can make just from a simple stone!

There are dozens of different kinds of soup, aside from fabled soup. There's Chinese winter-melon soup cooked and served inside a carved melon, okra-thickened gumbo in the American south, and Greek avgolemono, a chicken soup thickened with lemon, egg, and rice. In Middle European countries, sweet fruit soups are cherished; in Slavic neighborhoods, sauerkraut soup is what hits the spot. There are recipes for chocolate soup out and about in the world. Why not? Chocolate sandwiches (sweet butter, dark bittersweet chocolate, good white bread) are absolutely wonderful, and chocolate soup—not a dessert soup, but something like Mexican mole poblano (a peppery sauce with chocolate in it)—might be, too.

There's a difference between soup and stock, by the way. Stock can be a basis for soup, but it doesn't work the other way around. Soup is consumed for its own sake; stock—a rich broth of meat or seafood with vegetables (or plain vegetables)—is made to be added to soup or stew or a sauce. There are specific families of soup: Bisque is thick and creamy, usually made with seafood; chowder can be made with seafood, corn or chicken, but it often begins with salt pork, has onions and potatoes in the middle, and ends with milk, unless it's Manhattan clam chowder, which replaces the milk with tomatoes. Consommé, bouillon, and broth are clear soups; some cream soups are thickened with egg, with butter and cream, and some with puréed vegetables. Whatever you call them, soups are a kind of magic: If you've got it, you can make soup out of it.

Basic Ingredients

To be soup-friendly you should always keep these stone soup basics in your refrigerator:

onions
garlic
carrots
celery
parsley

It's perfectly possible to make good soup out of just that much, if you get right down to it. French garlic soup isn't much more than garlic and water—with a bit of olive oil and a few herbs and, if you like, a bit of toast and good parmesan cheese. That sounds like the stone soup process, I admit. But just the garlic and water is truly a heavenly beginning.

Storing Carrots, Celery, and Parsley

Let's examine those basics. We've already discussed onions in chapter 2. Onward! Carrots and celery last a very long time if you need them to. Keep them wrapped; what they came in is fine, if what they came in is a sealed plastic bag. If they eventually start to look nervous, put them, cleaned and sliced into convenient sizes and wrapped well, in the freezer. The wrapping keeps them safe from the effects of extremely cold air—what's called freezer burn, which is about as unattractive as it sounds . . . things get whitish and smell inert and have an electric—not electrifying—flavor, and have to be thrown away, into the garbage, where they defrost and drip and generally make a mess, so it pays to wrap them well in the first place. And label. Otherwise you'll never remember, weeks later, what you've so carefully wrapped. I've done that with valuables—bacon without preservatives and pork pieces for pasta sauce and other things carefully saved for a rainy day, all gone up in freezer burn smoke.

Carrots and celery are generally great things to have in the refrigerator because they do so many things: They can be eaten raw, they can be used as vegetable side dishes, they are marvelous under a chicken as it roasts, and they can be added to all sorts of things to make them better, including soup. Frozen, you can still do a lot with them, except eat them raw.

Parsley next. Use the flat-leafed (Italian) kind rather than the curly kind; more flavor (and softer in your mouth). There are choices about how to store it; pick the one that you like best: You can put parsley in the refrigerator in its plastic bag, just the way you've brought it home from the store, and wash it as you use it. Or you can wash it when you first bring it home, shake off most of the water, wrap it well in paper towels, and keep it in a plastic bag. Or you can wash it well, carefully removing yellowed or spoiled leaves and stems, shake off excess water, pat it as dry as you can with paper towels, and then cram it into a big jar, cover the jar, and refrigerate it. Finally, you can stand the stems in a glass of water and cover the water and the parsley leaves with that same plastic bag and keep the glass in the front, where you won't knock it over by accident. I would, of course, so I don't do that.

You can also freeze parsley. After you've washed it, of course. However you keep it, you can slice stems as you need them; usually, you have to chop the leaves. (Don't ignore parsley stems before or after you have cut off the leaves; cut crosswise into tiny rounds, they add texture and flavor to anything you put them in—stew and chili and pasta sauce and salads as well as soup.)

Making Soup

At heart, soup is a simple thing. It starts, inevitably, with a few variables. They depend on your mood, your purse, your time, and the state of your refrigerator. But there are certain basic ingredients that are part of almost every soup, no matter what its name or its most prevalent substance may be. Think of them as variables, because essentially they are a series of choices. They are:

1. The Fat

Depending on what you have on hand, and the ultimate flavor you wish to achieve: olive oil, butter, bacon drippings, chicken fat, meat drippings, salt pork, canola oil. The fat should be compatible with everything else: butter and olive oil go with almost anything, but you wouldn't want to use beef drippings with fish, for instance. Bacon drippings are good with bean soups and split pea soup. Salt pork is classic for chowder. Chicken fat has a strong flavor, best in chicken soup. Canola oil is bland; it goes with almost everything.

2. The Bones and Meat

Bones and meat can be chicken, beef, ham, lamb, bacon, turkey, salt pork, fish. Of course you can make soup without meat and without bones. Then you have to find another way to give it richness. Beans, potatoes, or miso will do the trick. Roasting bones before proceeding with other ingredients gives broths and stocks a beautiful color and more intense flavor.

3. The Vegetables

The basics (onion, garlic, carrots, celery, parsley—called the "aromatics"), plus tomatoes, potatoes, mushrooms, beans, cabbage, broccoli, string beans, peas, peppers, etc. Not all at once. Some vegetables (broccoli, turnips, cabbage, even bell peppers) have an assertive taste—use them where you think they match, or for their own sakes, as in cream of broccoli soup. Others (peas, mushrooms, beans, potatoes) go with most other flavors—peas are especially nice for their bright color. Let the taste buds in your mind help you decide what goes where.

4. The Seasonings

Salt and pepper are necessities no matter what kind of soup you have in mind, but most recipes tell you whether you want any kind of herbs or spices. Perhaps the soup will need a pinch of sugar, lemon juice, or vinegar to underline its flavor.

5. The Liquid

By definition, soup is liquid. But what kind of liquid? That's your choice: water, wine, broth, tomato juice, etc. Again, it's a question of what goes with what as well as what you like. Recipes tell you and sometimes give you choices; if you're improvising, trust those mental taste buds again.

You don't always have to start from scratch. Canned broths can have many moments of glory. Buy low-sodium broth, organic if possible (in addition to being better for you, it tastes better). Look in the ingredients list on the label to see if carrots and celery are included; they tend to make a tastier canned broth. Keep a couple of cans or packs on a shelf for a soup emergency.

6. The Thickener

And sometimes your soup needs body, or thickening: flour, eggs, bread, potatoes, pasta, rice, or puréed vegetables are most often used—eggs in cream soups, not otherwise. Puréed vegetables add flavor and body to any kind of soup.

That's the idea of soup, in six steps. You usually start with a fat, because you need to sauté onion (and sometimes garlic) at the beginning. The meat or the bones give the soup richness; the vegetables add flavor and texture; the seasonings emphasize and underline; and the liquid carries the day. Thickening makes the soup feel good in your mouth—good for your soul as well as your body; it shouldn't feel like water with things floating in it.

You start soup by sautéing (from a French word that can be loosely translated as frying, with a stir from time to time) the basic vegetables in oil or butter until they're softened. Sautéing the aromatics is called "sweating" the vegetables—it means that the water they contain evaporates and their flavor is intensified. The meat and liquid are added to the soup next, and the main vegetables (as broccoli for cream of broccoli soup, for instance) after that. Dried herbs are added at the beginning; fresh herbs are added close to the end. Different thickeners have their own schedule—potatoes come relatively early; pasta relatively late. Recipes will tell you, and after only a little while, you'll know without looking.

Removing Surface Fat

Soup often tastes better the second day—and if you refrigerate it, the fat will rise to the surface, forming a solid sheet that keeps the rest of the soup fresh, and then can be lifted off and discarded before you reheat the soup. But if you're making soup to eat right away, skim off as much fat as you can. Use a large spoon, hold it just under the surface so that the fat floats into it, and keep doing that to spoon off as much fat as possible. There are those who say they remove surface fat by holding a paper towel lightly on the top of the soup and then throwing the paper towel away; I think that, at best, chemicals in the paper towel would leach into the soup, no matter how briefly the paper was there, and at worst, bits of paper towel would break off into the soup, even if I worked as quickly and deftly as a soup ballerina. It seems like an unpleasant idea; I stick to the spoon; so does most of the fat.

If it's appropriate, several minutes before the soup is done, add any quick-cooking vegetables you'd like (fresh or frozen peas, for instance), simmer another ten minutes, spoon off more surface fat if you can, sprinkle with parsley and any other fresh herbs you choose, and serve. Or purée the vegetables for a lovely, smooth soup with an appealing texture. Puréeing can be done in a food mill or in a food processor. Even a sieve and an arm muscle will do in a pinch. If you want to use the soup you've made as a basis for something else—you might just want to keep broth, for instance, in the refrigerator or freezer as a basis for great soup whenever you want it—then strain it before you put it away. You can't keep it indefinitely—which means longer than three days—unless you freeze it. If you keep it in the refrigerator, on the third day remove it, bring it to a boil, and boil it for twenty minutes. Get it back into the refrigerator as soon as you can—while it's still warm—to keep it fresh. Then there are people who pour their broth into ice cube trays, and, when it's frozen, pop the cubes into freezer bags. That's nice. Just don't add chicken broth to your iced tea.

Making Quick Soup

A simple, quick, and lovely vegetable soup can be made with just sautéed onions, a can of broth, and a single vegetable. After sautéing the onions (and garlic, if you like) in butter or olive oil, add the main vegetable (carrots, broccoli, peas, celery, beans, potatoes, tomatoes—whatever you like), and stir for a few minutes over medium heat. Add a can of low-sodium broth, cook for about ten minutes, and then purée in the food processor or food mill (with some pieces of the vegetable left whole for texture, if you like). Add a sprinkle of herbs or a dollop of sour cream or yogurt. Serve with good bread, and you have heavenly stone soup.

Garlic Soup—and a Variation: Onion Soup

Here we may have the world's simplest soup (not counting stone soup). This one is a Provençal recipe, but there are variations around the globe. It can be served as a clear broth or elaborated with thin pasta (vermicelli or angel hair), orzo, or poached eggs. (Egg poaching is described on page 110.)

The amount of garlic called for in various recipes ranges from as little as three or four cloves to as much as two heads. It depends on the cook as well as the territory. In for a penny, in for a pound, the English say, but the English didn't create garlic soup.

6 cloves of garlic, peeled and lightly crushed (see page 24)

2 tablespoons extra virgin olive oil

6 cups chicken broth or water (Use low sodium broth if canned; fresh broth can be made by simmering a few chicken parts—or bones—in water with onion, carrot, celery, parsley, salt and pepper for 20 to 30 minutes.)

1 bay leaf

½ teaspoon dried thyme or 1 teaspoon fresh

1 tablespoon chopped fresh Italian parsley

Salt and freshly ground black pepper

Optional garnish: 6 slices French bread and Parmigiano Reggiano or Gruyère cheese, grated

1. Sauté the garlic in the olive oil in a soup pot over low to medium heat for a few minutes, until it is softened. Don't let it brown, which would make it bitter. (If using bread garnish, see instructions below.)

2. Add the broth or water and the herbs. Bring to a boil; reduce the heat and simmer for 10 minutes. Add salt and pepper to taste.

3. Optional garnish: Remove the garlic from the pan after it has softened and, using the same oil, quickly sauté the sliced bread on both

sides until it's golden. (Add more oil if needed.) Remove and re-serve; return the garlic to the pot and continue cooking. When you're ready to serve, reheat if necessary, ladle into bowls; heap grated cheese on the top of the bread slices and float a slice in each bowl.

Note: Remove the bay leaf before serving.

SERVES 6

Variation: A lovely quick onion soup can be made similarly: Sauté two large onions, sliced, in extra virgin olive oil until they're softened and are just beginning to brown. Add 2 cloves of garlic, chopped, and either 1/2 teaspoon of dried thyme or 1 teaspoon of fresh; sauté a few minutes longer. Add 6 cups of broth or water and simmer for 10 minutes. Garnish again with good bread—which can be sautéed in the flavored oil after the onions or simply toasted—topped with grated cheese. If not using the bread garnish, top the soup with chopped chives or parsley. Serves 6. Classic onion soup is made with beef broth and a little brandy or wine; the onions are sautéed slowly in butter until they're golden brown, and it's always topped with bread and cheese, toasted until the cheese melts and is golden and bubbly. It's not radically different from this quicker variation.

Bean Soup

The quick soup I've already described on page 68 is like this recipe—sauté onions and garlic in olive oil, add beans and chicken broth, a bit of tomato paste, a sprinkling of thyme, simmer, and presto! Bean soup. Where can you go wrong?

½ medium onion, diced

2 tablespoons olive oil

1 clove garlic, minced

1 15-oz. can cannellini beans, rinsed, or ½ cup dried beans, soaked, cooked, and drained

4 cups chicken broth (if canned, use low-sodium)

3 tablespoons tomato paste

½ teaspoon dried thyme or 1 teaspoon fresh thyme

Salt and freshly ground black pepper

Garnish: Extra virgin cold pressed olive oil and minced flat-leaf Italian parsley

1. Sauté the onion in the olive oil in a soup pot over medium heat until the onions are soft and translucent. Add the garlic and cook 2 minutes longer.
2. Add the beans, chicken broth, tomato paste, and thyme and bring to a boil. Reduce the heat and simmer for 15 minutes.
3. With a fork, a potato masher, or the back of a spoon, mash some of the beans in order to thicken the soup. Add salt and pepper to taste. Serve in soup bowls, with, if you like, a bit of extra virgin cold pressed olive oil dribbled across the top, and a sprinkling of minced parsley over that.

4 SERVINGS

Variations: Any quick soup can be made this way—sauté onion and garlic, add a vegetable and broth, simmer briefly, and there you are.

Dried herbs can be added with the vegetable; fresh herbs do better at the end, a few minutes before finishing. If you like, some soups, like cream of broccoli, mushroom, or celery, do nicely with an addition of milk or cream.

Summer Borscht

This is a fast and easy recipe. And what's more, it's beautiful. You can start from scratch—with beets cooked in water or broth—but I'm not convinced that's sufficiently better than this fast and easy recipe using bottled borscht.

You can find bottled borscht in the ethnic food section of your super-market, usually on a bottom row. Ignore bottles that are labeled diet borscht. Borscht by its very nature is low-calorie; at least it is before you add the sugar and sour cream. Also ignore unsalted borscht. Borscht needs salt, just as everything else does. If you absolutely cannot have a speck of salt, I won't argue with you; but otherwise, don't buy unsalted borscht.

You may find the idea of clear borscht appealing—in that case, try it without adding the onions and cucumber called for in the recipe below, and strain out the beets. Clear borscht isn't transparent, because it has sour cream mixed into it. Served in a glass as if it were a beverage, beau-tiful and pink, it becomes a beverage.

Traditionally, borscht is very cold and the potatoes and eggs are very hot, and they're all served in the same bowl, with a small cloud of sour cream on the top. It's to die for, and I don't mean the calories or the cho-lesterol count. But beets are good for you, well worth what's added to them. Don't—do not—use no-fat sour cream. That's blasphemous. And what's worse, it doesn't taste good. Sour half-and-half (30 or 40 percent less fat) is perfectly good, and has considerably less fat than full-fat sour cream. On the other hand, my doctor tells me that everybody has to die from something.

1 bottle of borscht—salted, and with beet pieces

2 kirby cucumbers or half an English cucumber, washed, peeled, and
   diced

½ cup sliced scallions or diced red onion

1 lemon, juiced

2 to 3 tablespoons sugar, to taste

½ cup sour cream or sour half-and-half (*not* fat-free sour cream)

Freshly ground black pepper to taste

Optional: small, hot, freshly boiled potatoes, and hard-cooked eggs

1. Empty the borscht into a mixing bowl. Add the cucumbers, scallion,
   lemon juice, and sugar. Adjust the sweet-sour balance to your taste,
   adding more lemon juice or sugar if you feel that's needed.

2. Refrigerate until chilled (unless you've kept the borscht bottle in
   the refrigerator, which makes it cold to begin with). Stir in the sour
   cream. Add freshly ground black pepper and salt to taste. If you
   like, serve with hot boiled potatoes and hard-cooked eggs.

4 SERVINGS

Hot: Potato and Leek Soup
Cold: Vichyssoise

This is a soup that's so simple it almost seems like magic. But as simple as it is, it's also amazingly versatile, and that's part of its magic too. Hot, it is a classic French peasant soup, either chunky or smooth. Cold and puréed, it turns into vichyssoise, smooth and cool and, after all these years, still sophisticated. And there's more, as they say. Add carrots and it becomes hot carrot soup or cold carrot vichyssoise. Put julienned beets in the potato vichyssoise and it becomes a lovely blushingly pink summer soup. All that magic, from a few potatoes. You don't even need a wand.

4 large leeks, cleaned, trimmed, and sliced (see page 23)
3 large Yukon Gold potatoes, washed, peeled, and cubed
6 cups chicken broth (low sodium if canned) or water
Salt and freshly ground black pepper

1. Combine the leeks and potatoes in a soup pot, and add broth or water to cover. Bring to the boil, reduce heat, and simmer for half an hour, or until the potatoes are soft. Add salt and pepper to taste.

SERVES 6

That's all there is to it. You can do more: You can add a pat of butter in each bowl; you can sprinkle the soup with chives or parsley or dill— or all three; you can add a little milk, cream, or sour cream; you can leave it chunky or you can put it through a strainer or a food mill (not a processor or a blender, which would make the potatoes gummy). But basically, that's all there is to it.

Vichyssoise: Pass the soup through a food mill, chill it, and add ½ to 1 cup of cream. Taste it carefully for salt—cold soup needs more salt than hot does. Garnish with chopped chives.

Carrot Vichyssoise, Cold or Hot: Add 4 carrots, scraped and chunked, to the vegetables before you begin the simmering. Serve hot, or put through a food mill and serve chilled, garnished with chopped dill or parsley, or both.

Pink Vichyssoise: Add a heap of julienned beets (fresh—boiled or roasted—or canned) in the center of each bowl of cold vichyssoise, as a garnish, before serving.

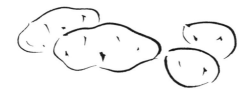

Corn Chowder

We eat a great many things that, if we follow them back far enough, are made from corn. Most obviously, corn is used as food for livestock, so a simple hamburger is, in that way, corn-based. Most soda is sweetened with high fructose corn syrup—more corn. There's cornstarch, corn oil, and corn chips, but corn is also present in cereal and ice cream—and a host of other food products as well. It's hard to find anything at the supermarket that isn't linked to corn. And we don't even have to eat it; corn is used to make wallpaper paste, toothpaste, ethanol, crayons, plaster board, and fillers for blankets and pillows. And a whole lot more.

Maybe one of the purest—and most comforting—uses of corn, short of a perfectly cooked ear of corn on the cob, is corn chowder. It's comfort food by the bowl, naturally sweet and reassuring.

3 tablespoons butter (or 4 ounces of salt pork, blanched—cooked briefly in boiling water—and diced, or a combination of salt pork and butter)

1 large onion, chopped

6 cups milk or chicken broth, or a mixture (use fresh or low-sodium canned broth)

2 large potatoes (Yukon Gold or red or white boiling potatoes), peeled and chopped

Salt and freshly ground black pepper

3 cups corn, cut from 3 or 4 ears of corn (or, use frozen or canned corn). See Note below about adding the cobs to the broth, and how to cut corn kernels from the cob.

Optional: ½ cup red bell pepper, chopped and sautéed briefly in butter

Garnish: chopped parsley or chives, or both

1. Melt butter in a large saucepan. Or, heat the salt pork in the saucepan until it is melted and beginning to brown; remove the crisp bits and save them to use as a garnish at the end. Add butter, if you're using both, after the pork fat has melted. Add onion and cook over moderate heat until the onion has softened and become translucent. Add the milk or broth, the potatoes, salt, pepper, and bay leaf, and cook for 20 minutes, until the potatoes are tender.

2. Stir in the corn and, if you're using it, the red bell pepper. Bring to the simmer and cook for a few minutes longer. Taste to adjust the seasoning, and garnish with the parsley or chives and, if you used salt pork, the crisp bits.

SERVES 6 TO 8

Note: If you're using fresh corn, strip the kernels into a bowl, and add the bare cobs to the milk or broth to be cooked with the potatoes. Remove the cobs before adding the cut corn. The best way to cut the kernels off the cob is to hold the cob vertically in a bowl or on a plate, and cut diagonally down from the top with a paring knife.

Yellow Pea Soup (Split or Whole)

Yellow split pea soup is more than a cousin to green split pea soup. It's a fraternal twin, separated at birth, but sharing the same heritage. Both are national dishes in Scandinavia, Holland, and Canada, where they vary not only from region to region but from household to household. That means it's flexible, and you can easily make it your own—with or without ham, sausage, or barley, for instance. For nonvegetarians (who will use ham in the basic recipe), sausage goes beautifully with split pea soup, as does salt pork. If you use salt pork, add it (sliced or cubed) to the pot with the vegetables in the beginning. Sausage can be fried separately, sliced, and added to the pot at the end. Kielbasa is good; so are hot dogs, breakfast sausages, and a variety of German sausages.

Marjoram is the secret ingredient in this recipe. If you can find whole yellow peas (Ikea stores often have a grocery section that includes bags of whole yellow peas, as do Scandinavian import stores), by all means use them. In any case, the soup can be made with either whole or split peas— and, truth to tell, yellow or green peas.

3 tablespoons unsalted butter

1 large onion, diced

2 carrots, diced

2 ribs celery, diced

½ pound yellow whole or split peas

Optional: ham bone, ham hock, or smoked pork chop

1 large baking potato, peeled and cubed

½ teaspoon dried marjoram

½ teaspoon dried thyme or 1 teaspoon fresh

6 to 8 cups fresh cold water

Salt and freshly ground black pepper

Garnish: chopped fresh Italian parsley or sliced sausage (as above),
    or croutons, made by cubing good bread and browning the cubes

in the oven, or—delectable—frying them in butter or oil until they're lightly browned on all sides. Be careful—they can easily burn if they're left too long; they start to cook slowly, and brown quickly.

1. Melt the butter in a large soup pot. Add the onion, carrots, and celery and sauté for five to ten minutes, until softened but not browned.

2. Pick over the peas to remove any small stones. Wash and drain the peas and add them to the pot with the potato, the ham or pork chop, if you're using meat, the herbs, and the water. Bring to a simmer over medium heat. Use a large spoon to skim off any scum that rises to the surface. Cover loosely and simmer for 1 hour, stirring occasionally, adding more water if it's needed. The peas should be soft, but not totally dissolved. Add salt and pepper to taste.

3. If you like your soup chunky, leave it as is. If you'd rather have it smooth, purée it in a processor (carefully! don't fill the processor all at once or it'll splash when you turn it on), or use an immersion stick blender. You can also purée just some of the soup to have a smooth soup with a little texture—thus can you have it all. Either way, remove the meat if you've used it, slice or shred it, and return it to the pot. Garnish with chopped parsley, sliced sausage, or croutons.

SERVES 6

Like most soup, split pea soup is better on the second day. To reheat, add a little water—the soup thickens as it stands—stir, and reheat over low heat, stirring occasionally. Garnish and serve.

5

THE BIRD

Getting to Know a Chicken

Poultry is for the cook what canvas is for the painter.
—Brillat-Savarin

I always give my bird a generous butter massage before I put it in the oven. Why? Because I think the chicken likes it—and, more important, I like to give it. —*Julia Child*

What you can't do with a chicken is have it for dessert. Otherwise, you can do anything. Like onions. And they go so well together, too!

It was Henry IV—back in the day in France, where he was king from 1589 to 1610—who wished that there "would not be a peasant in all my realm so poor that he could not have a chicken in his pot every Sunday."

Was Henry elevating the peasant by giving him a weekly chicken? Or was he lowering the chicken? Today, fried chicken is good honest soul food, working class and proud of it. Chicken à la king once had aspirations, but its name is pretentious, it tends to be gooey, and its place on the social ladder is low, the king notwithstanding. Chicken breast, in all its many menu variations, is now ubiquitous and thus very much of the middle. But roast chicken, oh my dear, is a kitchen aristocrat, full of grace and dignity, surely among the best of virtues. Along with humor, of course, which may not always appear with grace and dignity. But chicken has humor, too. Chickens are funny—from Chicken Little, poor little worried soul, to chicken ice cream, which (along with Yuk!) is the punch line of a very old joke about the dozens of flavors of ice cream.

Ignoring the chicken and disdaining the eagle, Benjamin Franklin said that the turkey ought to be our national bird. Two hundred years later, according to popular legend, Herbert Hoover campaigned on the idea of a chicken in every pot (see Henry IV, above). Since then, eagles have flirted with extinction, turkey is a holiday meal or a low-fat substitute for better things, and chicken has come out of the pot and into the salad bowl. So maybe the chicken ought to be our national bird. Not noble, not beautiful, not even very smart, but honest, loyal, and hardworking, scratching out a living just like most of us.

In the kitchen, chicken is virtuous on all counts, including taste and versatility. There is, therefore, much to say about chickens. The first thing is that it's important to get to know your chicken—in the process of buying it and after you bring it home.

Buying a Chicken

The chicken you get, when you buy a whole chicken, is more than a package; it's a lovely plump body of a thing—it has arms and legs and a liver and a heart. Hold it in your hand; admire it; notice its virtues and its flaws; make friends with your dinner.

I write this on the assumption that you have bought a whole chicken. Yes, it's much easier to buy parts than it is to buy a whole chicken and cut it up; I know that in the interest of health, with cholesterol at heart, one ought to have the breast and disdain the leg. (Where do all those chicken legs go? Do they walk to another universe?) But parts do cost considerably more, and besides, sometimes you just want a whole damn chicken. Even aside from that, dealing with a whole chicken even when you don't want to cook a whole one is part of the process of getting to know your bird. And a very economical, sensible, and precious bird it is, too.

So: My advice, at the beginning, is to buy a whole chicken. Buy a little one—3 to 4 pounds—if there are just a few of you, or you're eating alone. You'll need a bigger one (or two small ones) if you're feasting with friends and want to pick on the leftovers after they've gone. A roast chicken on a refrigerator shelf is a beautiful sight—it's a promise, an invitation, a reward, a secret, and a resource.

You can roast a small chicken; it's just that there isn't as much of it. There are varieties of chicken—broilers, fryers, roasters, capons, hens, stewing fowl. Fryers and roasters (little chickens and bigger ones) are what you're after. Capons are for true feasts—they're a luxury, and hard to find, in any case. (They're castrated roosters, sadly enough, and because they're not as active as roosters are, they're mellower in taste and juicier, because they're fatter.) Hens and stewing fowl are for long, slow cooking—they're tough birds, best for broth. Avoid them. Unless your goal is broth.

Buy the best chicken you can find and afford: if possible, free range, natural diet. After all, how good can anything taste that has spent its life crammed—with other chickens—into a tiny cage with only wires for a floor, lights left on day and night, and no sight of earth or sky? If God had wanted chickens to live like that, he would never have made bugs.

Brand-name, mass-market chickens may not be awful. It's just that free-range natural diet chickens are a whole lot better—and better for you as well.

Handling a Chicken

After you've found your chicken (whether whole or in parts) and brought it home, the next thing you need to know is that you have to be careful in your dealings with it. **This is important:** Handle it carefully, and wash up twice as carefully afterwards. What I do is put the package in the (empty) sink and unwrap it and cut it up right there, so I don't have to worry about residual bacteria on the counters or cutting boards. When I've finished, I put the chicken directly into its pan, and if anything is being frozen, it goes right into freezer bags that have been prepared ahead. Then I wash the knife with soap, rinse the sink thoroughly, and wash my hands well and dry them on paper towels, which are then thrown away. (When not dealing with chickens, I keep a hand towel on a hook under the counter—a clean one every day—and use that for hand wiping.) The reason for all this is that raw chicken—like raw meat of any kind but more so—harbors potent bacteria that can make you sick if they migrate onto your hands or your kitchen sponge or your cutting board and later inadvertently reach your mouth.

If your chicken is whole, when you unwrap it—now nestled at the bottom of the sink (you have already removed the dirty dishes)—you'll find it often comes with additional supplies that once were important to it, like the neck, heart, liver, and gizzard. Sometimes the neck is tucked into one of its cavities, and other bounties are in a bag where the stuffing ought to go; sometimes everything is together. Remove whatever you find. (Sometimes there's nothing there at all. Life is a mystery.) Rinse everything off—including the chicken itself—and prepare yourself to make choices.

You can freeze the innards together and use them later to make soup or broth; or you can freeze them in categories—chicken livers, necks, hearts, gizzards, separately—and use them later (fricassee the necks, for instance, when you have a collection; sauté the livers; and use the hearts and gizzards for soup or stew); you can tuck the innards around the chicken as it roasts and make them part of the feast; you can, as an industrious cook, make soup right away and put the innards in it; or you can wash them well and give them to the cat and forget this whole paragraph. Lucky cat!

I usually freeze the livers in one batch—in a plastic bag, adding new livers as they arrive and everything else in a lump separately, for soup. I use chicken livers for paté or classic chopped liver or spaghetti Caruso or just for themselves.

If the freezer is full, I give the current bunch of innards to the cats. The trouble with giving the goodies to the cats is that they come to expect it. They know when chicken is in the bag—keen little pink little noses—and they can barely contain themselves. And when they do manage to contain themselves, it's in the clear expectation of a reward. Otherwise why bother with self-containment? Why not just jump up and grab what you can while you can? They don't believe in goodness for its own sake. Chicken is its own reward.

We must also—alas—think about fat. As if we haven't a thousand times over. Chickens are fat. They have scrawny little feet, but plump little bodies. Chicken fat must be dealt with. It's easily recognizable—it's yellow and rests in pillowy blobs, mostly near the chicken's entrances and exits. It's easily removed—just pull it loose. Throw it away or use it to cook with—in which case you have to melt it down, or render it, and what you end up with is beautiful and golden and full of flavor. Once in a while, when a recipe demands it or when indulgence strikes, I melt down some chicken fat with several slices of onion and a bit of lemon, and I think of heaven. Does chicken fat bring you closer to that same heaven? Alas again, they say it does. Maybe you should just throw it away. But if you hold fast—heaven can wait—there's a recipe for rendering chicken fat on page 103.

Cutting Up a Chicken

We still have the whole chicken. Now is the time to explore it. We've washed it off, inside and out. There are still some superfluous things attached inside that if you want you can remove. There may be a few feather-ends sticking up from the skin; pull them out, with your thumb leaning against a knife and the end between them, or with tweezers.

This is how to cut it into parts, beginning with the wings: Rub your fingers over the chicken's shoulders; feel where the wing joints connect to the body of the chicken; there's a slight indentation there. That's the place to slice. Cut right through it. Once the wing is off, cut off the scrawny tip end—it's easy to slice away. (If it resists, bend it backwards; it'll crack, and then you cut where the crack is.) If you've started a soup collection with the innards, add the wing tips. Do one wing first and then the other.

Next: The thigh separates easily from the body—pull it away from the body and slice through the skin as it stretches from where the connection is; bend the leg back and away and you'll see the natural separation. Again, you can feel the joint, and you can slice right through it. Leave the thigh and the drumstick in one piece or sever them at what we'll call the knee, again by feeling the connection and slicing through it.

What's left is the torso. A chicken bust. The easiest way to deal with it is to bend the back (at about the level where the legs were connected) away from the breast, and cut through the backbone, which separates easily. Dividing the breast itself in half is more difficult than anything we've done so far because you have to cut across the breastbone, and that's harder than cutting through a joint or a connection of tissue. Poultry shears—or a sturdy and sharp pair of kitchen scissors—make it easier. If you don't have shears, use a good sturdy knife; position it; and then use your fist to give it more power—pounding down on the positioned knife as if your fist were a hammer and then slicing through the bone and the cartilage. If you want smaller pieces of the breast meat, cut each breast half in half again, this time horizontally—at a right angle to the breastbone.

You now have chicken parts. There are other ways to arrive at parts and pieces (aside from buying a chicken that way)—some people begin by slicing the chicken in a line on both sides of the backbone and leaving it in halves, or cutting into pieces from there. Either way works. And yes, you may buy parts if you wish and spare all the cutting.

But assuming that you've been working with a whole chicken, for the sake of economy or for the exercise, you now have a handsome collection of chicken pieces, and there's a final choice: to freeze the parts (by category, just as if you were buying them that way—a bag full of breasts, another of wings, another of thighs and drumsticks) or cook the whole in sections. What luxury!

How to Roast a Chicken

There are a thousand things to do with chicken, probably even a thousand and one, but the best—and the most classic—is the simplest: roasting.

A 3½- to 4½-pound chicken will serve 4 people (a pound on the bone per person is a reasonable guide), and there probably will be enough left for a sandwich or two or some chicken salad; certainly the leftover carcass will make a fine broth, to which you can add, if you like, the inner parts that you removed at the beginning, and a carrot, a stalk of celery, a wedge of onion (and a little onion peel for color), and salt and pepper. Secret ingredients: a few drops of lemon juice, and a little tiny bit of freshly grated nutmeg.

Now, it's time to roast. Rinse the chicken under running water if you haven't already, pat it dry with paper towels, and then get it ready for its destiny. First step is to tuck its wings behind its back, as if it were going for a stroll in Vienna. Hard to visualize? The wings are really in thirds. Put the last third—the tip—behind the chicken's back, from the top, folding it over its own shoulder, as it were. It's a hard bend, but when you make it, the other two thirds follow suit.

You can make a stuffing, if you want. When I stuff a chicken, I do it right in the roasting pan, so that anything spilled becomes part of the sauce. But I try not to spill because I like stuffing so much. Classic bread stuffing begins with cubes of good bread dried briefly in the oven at 275 degrees for 10 minutes; then turn off the heat and let it stand for another 5 minutes or so. (Life as we know it will not cease if you use a bag of stuffing mix.) Sauté diced onion in a truly generous amount of butter (my mother's recipe says, "lots!"); add chopped celery and cook until both are beginning to soften. Add to the bread cubes, with salt and pepper, a little sugar, chopped parsley, sage, thyme, if you like, and a beaten egg, if you like your stuffing extra moist. Moisten the whole thing with just a little chicken broth (not too much, or you'll have mush). Exact quantities don't matter, but in the end you'll need a little more than two cups of stuffing to fill a four-pound chicken—or a half to three-quarters of a cup of stuffing for each person you expect for dinner. You can add other things to the stuffing—nuts, including chestnuts, and sausage leap to mind—but it's so good just the way it is; sometimes plain is better than fancy. Stuff the cavity between the chicken's legs; close with skewers and cotton cord, or just cover the opening with a slice of bread, which works, though not as well. Pack it in lightly; stuffing expands, and you don't want it to spill out during cooking. The neck opening can also be stuffed; simply pull the flap of skin over the stuffing and skewer it closed. If you have any extra stuffing—or if you'd rather not stuff the bird itself—place it in a shallow, buttered baking dish, shallow in order to end up with more crispy surface. Dot it with (more!) butter, moisten it with a little broth or with some of the drippings from the chicken as it cooks, and bake it at 350 degrees for 30 minutes, or until it's crispy and browned on the top. (If you don't have room to cook separate stuffing and the chicken at the same time, bake the stuffing while the chicken is resting after it has finished roasting.) Stuffing temperature—baked in or outside the chicken—should be 165 degrees.

On the other hand, you may not want to bother with a stuffing—so rich, so delicious, so buttery, so expanding of body and soul. In that case, put a chunk of lemon in the cavity where the stuffing would be, perhaps with some onion, garlic, parsley, and herbs. For deeper flavor, make a paste of room temperature butter mixed with herbs (rosemary and thyme are good, as are several others), pressed or minced garlic, a bit of zested lemon peel, and salt and pepper. Squiggle your hands up under the front skin of the chicken at the end where the large cavity is. The skin pulls up fairly easily from the meat—just be careful not to tear the skin over the breastbone; leave that divisor alone. Use not quite half of the butter mixture, and push it under the skin on each side of the breastbone. Then pat the skin down again, and rub more butter or olive oil on the outside of the skin. Add the remainder of your butter mixture to the inside of the chicken along with the other herbs you've put there.

If you choose not to use a paste, simply rub the chicken with butter or olive oil, herbs, salt and pepper, and whatever you think would be good—orange or apple juice, for example—or don't add anything else at all. Additions add flavor—but ultimately, it depends on what you feel like and what you have in your refrigerator.

You can tie the chicken—truss it—if you want it to keep its nice plump little shape. You've already done the wings; now, using a piece of soft cord (really anything but plastic or a ribbon will do; cotton cord is best), tie the drumsticks together at their ends, just before the knobby part—call it their ankles, if you like. You can stop there, or you can continue to use the same cord to make an X around the back, come up across the wings, and knot in the front. It isn't hard, and you can really do it however you like—some people just tie the legs together—the general principle is simply to keep the chicken in a little bundle as it cooks. It isn't necessary at all, it's just nice. Keep in mind that there are those who say that chickens that have been left un-trussed cook faster and better, because their insides are better reached by the heat of the oven. They aren't wrong; it really doesn't make a great deal of difference. Trussing a chicken feels good to do, it makes a neat package—and the results cook nicely, too.

To Rack or Not to Rack

You need a roasting pan big enough to hold the chicken (and a little bigger if you want to add chunked pieces of potato and carrot as it cooks). Many people use a rack inside the pan; my mother taught me to use onion slices instead. They don't accomplish the same thing— keeping the chicken out of the fat and juices as it cooks—but as it turns out, I don't really want to do that anyway. The onions flavor the juices and flavor the chicken, and the chicken flavors the onion, and that's all lovely. What you lose if you don't use a rack is crisp skin—but we aren't supposed to eat the skin anyway. And the rest of the skin, the parts not in contact with the juices, does indeed stay crisp and brown and delicious.

You can add diced or chunked carrots and celery and potato in ad-dition to the onion in order to flavor the pan juices—and, having poached in the pan juices, they will be delicious as well. Garlic? Lemon? Rosemary? Thyme? Paprika? Curry? Honey? (All sprinkled over the vegetables as well as the chicken.) What do you feel like? Can you afford truffles?

Upside Down Is Right Side Up

Nearly everybody cooks the chicken with its breast up, bastes it (spoons the pan juices over it) frequently, or turns it from side to side as it roasts. This achieves a beautiful golden-brown color. As pretty as a picture. But cooking with the breast exposed dries out the breast meat, because the white meat cooks faster than the dark, and so when the dark is ready, the white is overcooked. As if that weren't enough, the white meat has almost no fat to keep it juicy, even if you've added butter under the skin. The butter melts fairly quickly in the heat of the oven; it flavors the chicken very nicely, and makes wonderful juices, but it doesn't act as continuous self-basting.

The solution is simple: Roast the chicken upside down. Flat back up; plump breast down. The dark meat will be in the hottest part of the oven—closer to the top—and thus it will cook faster. The lovely juices from the back melt into the breast as it cooks, and the whole chicken will be full of flavor when it's done. It won't be as beautiful as a magazine illustration of a roast chicken, but beauty is only skin-deep anyway. And the problem of beauty can be solved. Carve the chicken in the kitchen, not at the table, and discard the breast skin. The skin on the back will be crispy, deep golden brown, and delicious.

I learned this marvelous system of upside-down roasting from *Love, Time & Butter*, a lovely book by Joseph Hyde. When I read his way of roasting a chicken, I thought it sounded very odd. Because I liked so many of his recipes, I tried it, and the first chicken I roasted upside down was such a success that I have never roasted another chicken right side up. Turkey too. Chicken, by the way, often takes longer to cook than you think it will. Turkey never takes as long as you're told it should. That's why so many turkeys are dry and juiceless—they're overcooked. Pull out and discard the pop-up timer that comes with the bird—first of all, it's set for too long, and secondly, it works by melting when the turkey reaches a set temperature; the melting releases a spring, and the timer pops up. I don't want to eat melted plastic, or anything that resembles it.

Preheat the oven to 425 degrees so the chicken will start cooking as soon as you put it in. Roast it at that temperature for 15 minutes and then lower the heat to 350 degrees. You'll know when the chicken is done—it's really not one of life's great mysteries. It's done when the legs wiggle freely and when, if you pierce the skin between the body and the thigh with a fork or the tip of a knife, the juices will be golden yellow, not red, not rosy. The skin also begins to pull back from the knobs at the ends of the drumsticks. If you have an instant-read thermometer, place it into the meat of the thigh, avoiding the bone; the temperature should be 165 degrees. The chicken will continue to cook for several minutes after you take it out of the oven. In the worst possible case, if you cut into the chicken and find it's underdone—still rosy—simply put it back in the oven and cook it longer (even if you've started to cut it; that's not a deadly sin). The total time it cooks, of course, depends on how big it is. Start testing a small chicken after 45 minutes and a larger one after an hour. (I cooked my first roast chicken for my new mother-in-law. When I cut into it at the table, the joints were bright red, and the meat near them a boisterous pink. It went back into the oven, fast. It was fine, after it finished cooking, and she was lovely about it. I would have forgiven her anything after that.)

If you're roasting your chicken upside down on a bed of onion slices, you won't need to baste it (spoon up juices and pour them over the top to moisten the whole thing—this is done about every 10 or 15 minutes if you're roasting the chicken with its breast up, and if you are, you *must* baste it as it cooks). When the chicken is done, remove the pan from the oven, place the chicken on a platter, and let it rest for at least 15 minutes to give its juices a chance to settle.

Carving a Chicken

To carve the chicken, place it on its back. Pull the thigh and drumstick on one side away from the body, and cut between the thigh and the body to separate them. Feel for the joint between the thigh and the drumstick, and slice there to cut them apart, and then do the same with the other leg. At the other end of the bird, feel for the joint between the wing and the chicken's shoulder; cut there, taking a slice of breast meat along with the wing. Repeat on the other side. If you roasted the chicken upside down, cut away the breast skin—it isn't crisp or appetizing. Working first on one side and then the other, slice the breast meat away from the bone. Serve some of the crisp back skin with the chicken.

Skimming Off Fat, Making Gravy, and Deglazing the Roasting Pan

Skim off as much of the fat from the juices in the pan as you can—you do this just as you did when you made soup, by holding a large (serving-size) spoon flat just beneath the surface. The fat, which rises to the surface of the juices as they stand, will float into the spoon. If you have a juice and fat separator, pour all the juices into it, let them stand, and then pour from the bottom spout, which leaves the fat floating at the top.

Gravy isn't hard to make—it just requires patience and attention. And a whisk. To make a classic pan gravy, remove the chicken from the roasting pan, pour off (and save) the juices, and return three tablespoons of the fat to the pan. (If you don't have three tablespoons, add butter to measure.) Place the pan over medium heat on the top of your stove and scrape the bottom of the pan with a wooden spoon to release the browned bits—called the *fond* in French. When the fat is hot, add three tablespoons of flour, stirring constantly. A paste will form as you stir. Let it cook for about 3 minutes—this removes the raw flour taste—stirring all the while, and then begin whisking in (key word: whisking—*use a whisk!*) a cup and a half of the roasting juices and, if you need more liquid, chicken broth, a little at a time. When the first bit thickens, slowly whisk in the rest, reaching all the corners and sides of the pan. Let it cook a few minutes longer, whisking constantly, until it has thickened. Season with salt and pepper, and whisk in a teaspoon of Worcestershire sauce, and any juices that have accumulated under the chicken itself, but don't let the gravy get too thin; add juices judiciously. If the gravy is too thick, whisk in a tiny bit more broth—or wine—and let it cook a little longer. If you whisk in a tablespoon of butter at the end—off heat—the gravy will be that much richer and smoother.

Just as good—and less work—is serving the pan juices as a sauce. If you want the sauce to be thicker, pour the juices into a saucepan and boil over high heat until they become slightly syrupy or have reduced to the consistency you want. (If you roasted vegetables with the chicken, you can mash them into the sauce or leave them whole— they're a treat both ways.) If you're using the juices, and not making a separate gravy, finish by adding a little water, broth, or wine to the roasting pan and placing it over low heat; scrape the bottom clean, using a wooden spoon. Add this to the roasting juices. This process is called deglazing the pan, and it's remarkably easy—and at the same time that you scrape up the delicious caramelized morsels, your pan gets remarkably clean. Deglazing is done as a basis for sauce; getting the pan clean is gravy, so to speak. You see how it's all related?

A recipe for Roast Chicken begins on page 86. Stuffing and Gravy are on pages 87 and 92.

Chicken Breasts Three Ways

. . . .

Chicken breasts are a stunning marketing achievement—once upon a time (not so very long ago), if you wanted chicken breasts, you bought a whole chicken and cut it up. A breast was luxury food, and now it's served at McDonald's. One imagines that someday, chickens will be bred to be all breast, with a little pair of legs sticking out at the bottom and a tiny head at the top. Come to think of it, we're almost there. This is sad, because the dark meat is really better—it's juicier (because it's fatter, alas) and has more flavor. But that's another story. Chicken breasts hold the advantage: They cook quickly and they're low-fat, a winning combination. Even so, any of the following recipes can be made using chicken thighs, if you'd rather; just increase the cooking time.

Chicken Breasts with Spiced Yogurt

½ cup plain yogurt (preferably whole-milk; Greek yogurt is
    especially good)
1 tablespoon olive oil plus more for the baking dish
1 teaspoon fresh lemon juice
1 clove garlic, crushed
1 teaspoon grated fresh ginger
1 tablespoon curry powder
1 teaspoon ground cumin
½ teaspoon ground coriander
¼ teaspoon allspice
Salt and freshly ground black pepper
2 skinless, boneless chicken breasts
Optional garnish: mint leaves

1. Whisk together in a large bowl yogurt, oil, lemon juice, garlic, ginger, spices, and salt and pepper. Cut the chicken breasts into large
   cubes, and add to the marinade, turning until all pieces are well
   coated. Marinate at room temperature for 20 minutes, or in the refrigerator for 3 hours.
2. Preheat oven to 375 degrees.
3. Remove the chicken from the marinade and place it in a lightly
   oiled baking dish. Roast at 375 degrees for 12 to 15 minutes, cutting into a large piece to be sure the chicken is done. Garnish, if
   you like, with mint leaves. Raita, on page 256, makes a good sauce
   with this, and both go well with buttered rice (page 170).

SERVES 4

Sautéed Chicken Breasts with Thai Sauce

1 tablespoon wine vinegar

2 teaspoons lime juice

2 teaspoons brown sugar

1 tablespoon soy sauce

Optional: 1 teaspoon Asian chili paste or to taste

½ cup peanut butter

¼ cup boiling water

1 tablespoon olive oil

2 skinless, boneless chicken breasts, halved

Optional garnish: cilantro, chopped or whole

1. In a small bowl, combine the vinegar, lime juice, brown sugar, soy sauce, and the chili paste if you're using it. Add the peanut butter and the boiling water and mix well—the water will melt the peanut butter as you stir.

2. Heat the oil in a skillet. When it's hot, add the chicken, former skin side down, and cook for 5 minutes; turn and continue cooking for another 5 minutes.

3. Pour the sauce over the chicken and cook for 3 or 4 minutes longer. Garnish, if you like, with cilantro.

SERVES 4

Jil's Honey-Mustard Chicken Breasts

2 tablespoons Dijon mustard

¼ cup honey

2 tablespoons olive oil

1 tablespoon capers

2 skinless, boneless chicken breasts, halved

1. In a large bowl, combine the mustard, honey, oil, and capers. Add the chicken breasts, turn, and marinate for 20 minutes.
2. Preheat the oven to 375 degrees.
3. Add the chicken, former skin side down, and the marinade to a baking pan and bake at 375 degrees for 7 or 8 minutes. Turn the breasts over and continue baking for another 7 or 8 minutes, or until an instant-read thermometer poked into a thick spot reads 160 degrees and the sauce is bubbling and lightly browned. Let stand for 5 minutes before serving.

SERVES 4

Chicken in Peanut Butter Barbecue Sauce

We don't think of peanut butter as a savory, but it is. Take peanuts back to their South American and African roots—or think of Thai food—and you'll see that peanuts (from soup to sandwiches) are fairly magical little things.

¼ cup hot water
¼ cup peanut butter (smooth or chunky)
¼ cup onion, chopped
2 tablespoons lemon juice
2 tablespoons unsalted butter, melted
2 tablespoons dark brown sugar
2 tablespoons vinegar
2 tablespoons Worcestershire sauce
1 chicken cut into serving pieces

1. Preheat the oven to 375 degrees.
2. Whisk together the water and peanut butter. Add all the remaining ingredients except the chicken.
3. Place the chicken pieces in a roasting pan, skin side down. Spread with half the peanut butter mixture. Roast for 20 minutes. Turn the chicken pieces, coat them with the remaining peanut butter sauce, and continue cooking for another 20 minutes. Test for doneness; chicken should read no higher than 165 degrees on an instant-read thermometer poked into the thigh, away from the bone; the sauce should be thick and slightly browned.

SERVES 4 TO 6

Chicken and Peppers

Here we have a sort of resemblance to Sausage and Peppers, a hero sandwich favorite. In the old days, when fat was not yet unhealthy and immoral, I added Italian sweet sausage to the mix. Two proteins! Two fats! It was awfully good, though. I could be talked into doing it again. Whether or not you choose to do it is surely something we don't need to discuss.

3 tablespoons extra virgin olive oil

1 chicken, cut into serving pieces

2 red onions, sliced

2 cloves garlic, minced

2 red bell peppers, peeled (with a swivel-blade peeler) and chunked

2 tomatoes, quartered

¾ teaspoon dried oregano

Salt and freshly ground pepper

1. Preheat the broiler.
2. Spread a large baking pan with one tablespoon of the olive oil. Add the chicken (skin side down), onions, garlic, red peppers, tomatoes, oregano, salt, and pepper. Sprinkle with the remaining olive oil.
3. Broil for 15 minutes. Turn the chicken, mix the vegetables, and continue to broil for another 15 minutes. (If the chicken begins to char, lower the heat.) Mix again and broil 10 minutes longer, until the peppers are browned and soft and the chicken is done.

SERVES 4 TO 6

Note: if you want to use sausage (sweet or hot), sauté it separately, slice, and add before serving.

You may also want to add ½ to 1 cup of marinara sauce, sautéed mushrooms, or both.

Honey Orange Chicken with Rosemary

When it's finished, this dish looks beautiful—what with the orange of the carrots and sweet potatoes. You can add quartered red onions (or shallots), too, if you'd like. Not to mention unpeeled cloves of garlic along with the vegetables so that the soft, nutty garlic can be spread on bread. You don't need anything else with this; it's a celebration all by itself.

1 3- to 4- pound chicken, washed and patted dry

2 tablespoons fresh rosemary, chopped

2 cloves garlic, chopped

2 tablespoons honey

1 tablespoon extra virgin olive oil

½ cup orange juice

1 tablespoon Dijon mustard

Optional: ¼ cup white wine

Salt and freshly ground black pepper

2 sweet potatoes, peeled and chunked

2 white potatoes, chunked

6 carrots, scrubbed and chunked

Optional: whole unpeeled cloves of garlic

2 to 3 tablespoons of chopped flat-leaf Italian parsley

1. Preheat the oven to 425 degrees. Place the chicken in a roasting pan large enough to surround the bird with vegetables.

2. Mix the rosemary, garlic, honey, and olive oil. Work your fingers under the skin of the chicken, from the large cavity end, between the drumsticks. The membrane separating the skin from the flesh pulls apart easily. Distribute half of the herb mixture under the skin on both sides of the breastbone. Use part of the rest to rub the chicken's outer skin, back and front, and place the remainder in the chicken's cavity. Turn the chicken breast side down.

3. Roast the chicken for 15 minutes. Mix the orange juice, mustard, wine, if you're using it, and salt and pepper. Reduce the heat to 350 degrees. Surround the chicken with the potatoes and carrots. Add the unpeeled garlic, if you're using it. Pour the orange juice mixture over all.

4. Roast until the chicken is done, about another 45 minutes. The chicken is done when its legs wiggle easily and its juices run golden when a knife is poked into the skin between the legs and the body (no higher than 165 on an instant-read thermometer poked into the thigh, away from the bone). Check the vegetables; if they're not done, remove the chicken to a platter, stir the vegetables, and continue to roast them at 400 degrees until they're browned and tender.

5. Let the chicken rest for 15 minutes before serving. Carve the chicken in the kitchen (see page 92 for how to carve a chicken), discarding the breast skin. Use a large spoon to remove as much of the fat from the juices as you can (the fat will rise to the surface as the chicken rests); if you want to thicken the juices slightly, mash a few potato pieces into the juices and stir. Serve the chicken and vegetables on a platter with some of the sauce spooned over them, and the remainder of the juices separately. Or you can leave it all in the pan, in its glory. In either case, sprinkle with the chopped parsley.

SERVES 6

Classic Chopped Chicken Liver

Chopped Chicken Liver is terribly unhealthy, unless you use organic chicken livers, and don't need to worry about cholesterol. But it's also wonderfully good. Don't have it often, but when you do, enjoy it.

5 tablespoons rendered chicken fat (see Note below about how to
   render chicken fat)
2 cups chopped onions
1 pound chicken livers, trimmed of connective tissues and
   membranes
2 hard-cooked eggs, peeled
Salt and freshly ground black pepper
Optional: cracklings from rendered chicken fat

1. Melt 4 tablespoons of the fat in a large skillet. Add the onions and sauté over medium heat, stirring occasionally, until they are soft and golden. Remove the onions to a dish and drain as much of the fat as possible back into the pan. Add the chicken livers to the pan and sauté until lightly browned. Cut into one of the livers; it should be barely pink in the middle.

2. Use the pan or a mixing bowl to combine the livers, pan drippings, and onions. Chop everything together. (You can pulse in a food processor, but be careful: You don't want a paste, but rather a coarsely ground mixture.) Add the eggs, chopping them in by hand. Season with salt and pepper. Stir in the last tablespoon of chicken fat, and, if you can bear it, sprinkle the top with cracklings. Serve with crackers, toast, or rye bread, or cover closely with plastic wrap and refrigerate. Serve at room temperature.

SERVES 8

Note: You can buy chicken fat in little tubs (because it's tubby?), but it's much better to make your own. Save blobs of chicken fat in a package in the freezer, and when you have enough, cut the blobs into rough cubes. In a frying pan, cover them with water, bring to a boil, lower the heat, and simmer until the water has evaporated and the fat is cooking in its own juices. Add a sliced onion, a few drops of lemon juice, a small pinch of freshly grated nutmeg, salt and pepper. Cook over low heat until the onions are browned and crisp. Strain. The onion and crisp bits of fat are the cracklings, or, in Yiddish, the *grivenes* (pronounced griv-eh-ness). Pour the fat into a clean jar; refrigerate. Use the cracklings (with a little salt and pepper) as a spread for crackers or bread or to garnish mashed potatoes. Use the fat to brown potatoes or onions. Use both in chopped liver.

6

AND THEN THE EGG

If Chickens Came First

... it was comfort ... to sit up and contemplate the majestic panorama of mountains and valleys spread out below us and eat ham and hard boiled eggs while our spiritual natures reveled alternately in rainbows, thunderstorms, and peerless sunsets. Nothing helps scenery like ham and eggs.　　　—*Mark Twain,* Roughing It

Do you need to ask the classic question: Which came first, the chicken or the egg? You don't need to turn the page upside down or to wait until the end of the chapter for the answer. It's right here: Neither. The dinosaur came first.

The really important thing to know is that eggs came before people. So nobody made a note of when the first egg happened, or how, or by whom. But somebody had to be responsible; somebody always is.

Birds have little birdbrains, but they're much smarter than we think they are. Except for chickens. Chickens are not smart. They're silly little things, with wings but unable to fly, ready, like turkeys, to drown in the rain just by looking up with their mouths open, suspecting the sky is falling every time they are bumped on the head by an acorn. But chickens make eggs, and that is their miracle, and it is enough.

It takes a hen about twenty-four hours to make an egg, and after the egg is finished and comfortably nestled where it should be, the hen looks around, rests for half an hour or so, and then starts right in on the next one. And each of those eggs is a perfect package—full of essential proteins and vitamins and a host of other good things, all contained in a thin but sturdy protective shell. Not to be overly poetic, eggs are beautiful things.

And you can do such beautiful things with them, everything from a simple hard-cooked egg to a soufflé. They can accompany either sausage or caviar; they can sit next to a slice of ham, or under a bit of truffle. Eggs star in custards and omelets and frittatas and have supporting roles in hundreds of other wonderful things that wouldn't exist without one or two beaten in. They are a kitchen cornucopia: Keep a dozen eggs in your refrigerator, and you will always eat well.

Buying and Storing Eggs

There's another classic question about eggs: Which are better, brown-shelled eggs or white? Same answer, this time without the dinosaurs: Neither. The breed of the hen determines the color of the eggshell, but the contents of the shell are the same no matter what its color is. Even so, by and large, Americans traditionally prefer white eggs, except in New England, where the preference is for brown. Brown eggs tend to be more expensive—because the breeds that lay brown eggs are larger, and cost more to keep and feed, and perhaps partly because brown eggs look to many of us as if they're more natural and thus healthier, and on the assumption that people are willing to pay more for something natural and healthy, they cost more.

I'm just as gullible as anybody else; given a choice, I choose brown eggs. But organic and cage-free. I'm willing to eat an egg that was mass-produced in an incredibly crowded factory space where the lights are never turned off and the chickens are always turned on—but I'd much rather have one whose mother saw the sky, felt the earth beneath her feet, and felt good when her egg was born. Not to mention all the stuff that caged chickens are given to eat. I may not be nuts about the idea of all the worms and bugs that chickens naturally prefer, but nature does amazing things, and those buggy meals turn into beautiful eggs, given half a chance, and I can concentrate on the result quite happily and ignore the cause.

The point is that you can buy a brown egg or a white one; blue ones are harder to find unless, like Martha Stewart, you raise your own. Most important is that the egg be fresh, that its mother was raised organically and cage-free, if possible; and that it's well refrigerated when you buy it, and again right after you bring it home.

About the size of eggs: The standard is large. I like extra-large, and that has never made any difference in any recipe I've used. But we're told that for baking, it's best to use the standard large eggs.

In any case, it helps to remember that the egg, as far as nonvegans are concerned, is here not only to make more chickens, but also to serve, savor, and enjoy. We are very lucky in that way. This world is full of amazing things, and not least among them is the egg.

Hard- and Soft-Cooked Eggs

I would love to recommend soft-cooked eggs, but in good conscience, I can't. They're soothing and comforting, but they aren't safe for everybody. A runny egg may present only a very small risk—as does crossing at the corner against the light—but the risk is there, and I advise against it. I'd much sooner jaywalk than eat an undercooked egg. A salmonella infection is less fun than the flu. A hard-cooked egg is perfectly delicious, not a sacrifice at all, and so that's what I'd rather eat. (If you must soft-cook an egg, follow the directions below for hard-cooked eggs, but cook them for only three minutes.)

Avoiding the pitfalls of hard-cooking an egg is remarkably simple, but even so, an awful lot of people don't manage to do so. The pitfalls are three: One, that the egg will crack and its substance leak while it's cooking; two, that there will be an unpleasant greenish ring around the yolk; and three, that it will be so hard to peel that you'll have egg salad between your fingers whether you mean to or not.

To take them in order:

First: Take a thumbtack, pushpin, hat pin, anything like that; the pin on the back of your grandmother's brooch will do. Hold the tack firmly in your strong hand, and hold the egg firmly in the cup of your other hand, with the broad (wide) end up. (One end is noticeably narrower and more pointed than the other. Narrow end down.) Fearlessly push the point of the tack into the top of the broad end of the shell. The reason for this is that there is a small cushion of air at the wide end of an egg, and when the air is heated (while the egg is cooking, silly), it expands, and if it can't get out any other way, it cracks the shell and leaves thusly. If you've made a hole for it, it doesn't need to resort to violence and it responds with gratitude.

Second: The way to avoid that unappetizing green ring is to gently place the raw, hole-poked eggs into a pot of water (I use the hottest water I can get from the tap), bring the water quickly to a boil over medium high heat, lower the heat immediately, and let them simmer for eight minutes. (We've already discussed simmering, on page 29.) Then quickly drain away the hot water from the eggs (you can use a pan lid to keep the eggs from falling out—but if, despite your best efforts, one does, simply pick it up and put it back in the pan). Rattle the eggs around in the pan so their shells crack, fill their pan with cold water and ignore them for a while. When the cold water warms, as it will, replace it with more cold water until the eggs themselves are cool.

Third: With any luck, by the time the eggs are cool, they should be easy to peel. Begin peeling at the broad end—the one you pricked with the thumbtack. Bonk it on something hard—I use the side of the sink, because I peel eggs in the sink, for a reason we'll come to in a minute. Use the side of your thumb to pull away the shell, and try to keep the pieces large as you peel them—not because you want big chunks of eggshell, but because it's easier that way.

If it isn't going well, try peeling the eggs directly under a stream of running water (you see why I peel eggs in the sink?). The water plunges into the eggshell and divides the membrane just under the shell from the egg itself, and usually makes peeling so easy that you wonder what all the fuss was about. Once in a while, an egg resists, and there's nothing you can do but carry on as best you can. Remember that the fresher an egg is, the harder it is to peel, so if you're having a hard time even after following all these remarkably vivid instructions, think of its freshness and take comfort in that.

If you want to make stuffed eggs (and how delicious they are!), it's said that the way to get the yolk perfectly centered is to place a carton of eggs on its side (rather than its bottom) in the refrigerator the day before you cook them. (The virtues of planning ahead are many.) The rumored explanation is that this moves the yolk away from the large end of the egg, which is where it tends to settle after it has been in the carton a while. To stuff the hard-cooked eggs, cut them in half the long way, remove the yolks, mix them with mayonnaise and whatever suits your fancy—chopped shrimp, mustard, curry powder, chopped olives, capers . . . and mound the mixture back into the waiting egg whites.

The end result of all the pricking, cooking, and peeling of eggs is— most of the time—a beautiful oval egg, perfectly complected, both luxurious and enormously practical. You can eat it just as it is—what pleasure!—or you can stuff it (the egg, I mean), as above, or quarter, halve, or crumble it into a variety of salads, from chef salad to its own egg salad, use it to make a sandwich, slice it to decorate almost anything (well, not apple pie), cover it with sauce, or drop it into a bowl of borscht. Oh, the things you can do with a hard-cooked egg!

Cracking the Egg

Before we go any further, you need to know how to open a raw egg. Tap (gently but firmly) its middle against an edge (like the top of a glass or a bowl) or on a flat surface. Holding it so that your thumbs are next to the crack, one on each side, pull the sides gently apart. If a bit of shell comes along with the egg, use a remaining half-shell to fish it out. Be patient. When you need more than one, it's helpful to crack each egg into a cup; pour the egg into a mixing bowl, and crack the next egg into the cup again. That way, if a piece of shell comes along with the egg, it's easier to retrieve.

Scrambled Eggs

The very best (not to say perfect) scrambled eggs are cooked incredibly slowly. If you have the time and the energy, the way to go is to use a double boiler, if you have one. Place a large chunk of butter (about one tablespoon for every two eggs) in the top pan, and when it's melted, add the eggs, which you've already cracked and mixed well with a fork. Don't add anything but a bit of salt and freshly ground black pepper; pure egg is sufficient for now. Every few minutes, give them a stir. Patience in the kitchen, as nearly everyplace else, is a virtue.

If you don't have half an hour or so to stand and stir eggs, use a frying pan (nonstick works best) and medium-high heat. Crack the eggs into a bowl; beat them well, and add salt and pepper. Again, no cream or milk or anything else: pure egg. Melt the butter and let it foam, add the eggs, let them set for a minute or two on the bottom, and then stir—keep the curd large if you like it that way by stirring less frequently; if you want a smaller curd, stir often. If you want very creamy eggs, which for me is almost the point, remove the pan from the heat *before* the eggs are done; residual heat will finish the job. Important: If they're going too fast, and you, too, like your eggs creamy, stop the cooking by adding a chunk of butter or a generous spoonful of sour cream—or both—and stir. Or, you can plan ahead and save a bit of raw egg to add at this point, thus slowing down the cooking and maintaining the taste of pure egg. These eggs are so close to perfect that it seems pointless to spend a half hour cooking them any other way.

Fried Eggs

Frying eggs is another art form. It seems so simple—but the world is full of badly fried eggs. Why add more? Melt a chunk of butter (or olive oil, but I believe eggs prefer butter) in a small nonstick frying pan (to make two eggs), let it foam, and, having neatly cracked the eggs, slide them in. Let them cook over gentle heat until the whites are almost set; if you must turn them over, do so with extreme care, using a wide spatula. Essentially, this is a task that requires both practice and luck, mostly, thank goodness, the former. (Unless, of course, you're good enough to turn them directly in the pan with a flip of your wrist, but that seems, I'm sorry to have to say, unlikely.) If you're not going to turn them over—and, in truth, I believe the whites taste better unturned—a particularly nice way to finish them is to add a teaspoon of water to the pan and cover it. Cook for another minute or two. There will be a soft film over the yolks, the whites will be well cooked, and all should be well. (If you want more than two eggs, of course, just use a larger pan and a bit more butter.) How long you cook the eggs depends on whether you want the yolks runny or firm. In a way, it seems to me that if you don't want to take the small risk that comes with having blissfully runny yolks, you're better off cooking scrambled eggs.

Poaching Eggs

Poaching eggs (cooking them in a water bath) is a nice thing to know how to do, but you probably won't need to do it very often. Poached eggs are seen most often sitting on an English muffin and a slice of ham with some hollandaise sauce on top: eggs Benedict; but they can also perch on an artichoke heart or a steak.

How often, you may ask, does one eat steak with an egg? Or, for that matter, whip up a batch of eggs Benedict on a Sunday morning? Topping buttered toast with a poached egg is much simpler, and a nice change from what we usually do. Egg poaching starts off seeming hard and tricky; it gets easier as you learn how to do it—the same old story, another kitchen lesson. To poach eggs, fill a (non-iron) skillet with about two inches of water (enough to generously cover the eggs); add a teaspoon or two of white vinegar (to help the eggs hold their shape), and bring to the boil. Turn down the heat, so that the water is just simmering. Julia Child recommends precooking the eggs, in their shells with a thumbtack-sized hole poked in their broad ends, in boiling water for just ten seconds. If you've done this, next crack each egg, hold it just over the water, and gently drop it in. If you haven't preboiled them, crack each egg open into a cup, and, holding the cup just above the water, gently slide the egg in. Work as quickly and gently as you can. Keeping the water at the simmer, cook for four minutes—until the whites are set and the yolks are still runny. Remove the eggs (again, working as quickly as you can) with a slotted spoon, and rinse them— to get rid of any vinegar taste—by placing them in a bowl of hot water. Eggs can be poached before you need them—keep them covered with cold water, and when you need them reheat them in lightly salted simmering water for just a minute. If you like, and if you've made the eggs ahead, hold each egg lightly in your hand and trim its ragged banners with a knife or a pair of kitchen scissors.

Separating Whites and Yolks

Sometimes you need the yellow and sometimes you need the white. Since eggs only come mixed, it's up to you to do the work. It isn't hard—you'll get the trick very quickly. Work over a bowl; everybody, no matter how experienced, should crack eggs over a bowl. Separate the white from the yolk over a small bowl and then add the separate contents to larger bowls so that if things don't work, you won't have destroyed all that went before. Whites won't whip—for chemical reasons of their own—if there's even the smallest bit of fat in them; yolks contain fat; ergo: If there is any yolk at all in the whites, they won't rise. Do them one at a time, and add each successful white to a larger bowl as you go along.

Now, given three bowls (one for the whites, one for the yolks, and one to work over as you deal with each egg), crack open the egg. If you don't want to get your fingers into your food, simply pour the contents of one half of the eggshell into the other half shell, and then go back and forth, over the smallest bowl you're using (it can be a cup), letting the white drop into the bowl and keeping the yolk inside the shell. Do this until there's no white left; add the yolk to the yolk bowl and the white to—well, you know what I'm going to say. Or you can hold a slotted spoon over the bowl or cup and slide the whole egg into the spoon; the white should pour itself through the slots into the bowl.

If you're willing to use your fingers, it's very easy to pour the whole egg into your cupped hand and let the white ooze through your fingers into the cup. You'll end up with just the yolk in your hand; it goes into its proper bowl. Be sure to wash your hands first, yes? And after, too.

However you do it, don't worry about the ropy band attached to the yolk. It has a name and a purpose: it's the chalaza, and it centers and anchors the yolk inside the white. The fresher the egg, the larger the chalaza; it grows old and wanes as the egg ages.

Whipping Egg Whites

Egg whites whip best at room temperature. Once they've been separated, and are completely free of any trace of the yolks, you need a completely clean and dry bowl (stainless steel or—lucky you!—copper) and beaters. Using an electric mixer at moderate speed, begin beating the whites, and when they start to foam, add a pinch of salt. Keep going (if you're beating by hand with a whisk or a rotary beater, you'll start getting tired soon), and add a pinch of cream of tartar to stabilize the foam. Keep going (that's the mantra); increase the mixing speed. Soon you'll have soft, floppy peaks; keep going, and soon you'll have firm peaks. They shouldn't look dry or grainy—if they do, you've gone too far. The reluctant remedy is to add a tablespoon of sugar, and beat briefly again. Then: Stop! And use the beaten whites very quickly—you have made bubbles, and you know bubbles don't last.

Emptying Eggshells

Undoubtedly, not long after they came down from the trees, and probably well before, considering where birds build their nests, human beings discovered that eggs are good to eat. And once they knew that, undoubtedly they also wanted to guarantee a steady supply and therefore learned how to raise chickens.

Outside the coop and the kitchen, eggs have had an entirely separate and successful life as symbols. That seems inevitable. They are perfect packages spiritually as well as physically: From our earliest days, the world around, eggs symbolized fertility, creativity, rebirth, renewal, hope, and abundance. They figure in creation myths, legends, and ritual. Oh, after all, clever chickens!

It's for all those reasons that eggs are so important in our springtime rituals of Easter and Passover. A hard-cooked egg sits on the Seder dish along with a roasted lamb bone and bitter herbs. Easter, of course, is filled with eggs and their symbols—the poor Easter Bunny is called on to tote a basket full of eggs; presumably Mama Chicken is too exhausted to wake up for breakfast. The Easter Bunny doesn't even get a carrot for his trouble—he's just turned into chocolate and eaten.

To me, the most magical eggs have always been the empty ones— they last forever, not as reminders of what was but as evidence of secret skills, the shell of an egg like the surface of a bubble, a memory, a breath, still here when all reason tells you it should be gone.

Is it disappointing to discover that it's easy to empty an eggshell? Where does the magic go once you know that all you have to do is wash the egg, and stick a long needle inside it, and blow? That's all you do. Wash and dry; poke the needle in (let the symbolism go!) and make a small hole in the small end of the egg and a large hole in the large end of the egg. Stick the needle far enough into the egg to break the yolk. Either blow as hard as you can through the small hole—over a bowl, please!—or, if you feel especially hygienic, use the tip of a baster (if you can find one small enough—you can find egg blowing tools online) to pull out the contents. (But really, if you feel especially hygienic, maybe you shouldn't do this at all.) Press the bulb of the baster to expel the air it contains, then insert the tip into the larger hole. Release the bulb to pull out the contents. If the eggy insides don't come out easily, use the needle again to be sure both the egg's membranes and yolk are broken. Rinse and dry again. You can make scrambled eggs out of the mess in the saucer if you like—you don't have to say where the meal came from—or you can be profligate and throw it away.

The rest of springtime egg magic comes on the vernal—for green—equinox. That's the time when—supposedly—you can stand an egg on its small end and it won't fall. There are those—O! alas for poetry?—who say it's all baloney and you can't do it ever. I'm not sure that I want to spend an otherwise happy day in March (the first day of spring is usually on or near March 21) going through a dozen eggs on the sidewalk. I can't stand on my small end, either.

A recipe for Scrambled Eggs is on page 109; Hard-Cooked Eggs, on page 106, Stuffed Eggs, on page 108; Fried Eggs, on page 110; and Poached Eggs, on page 110.

Swiss Baked Eggs

Here we have a simple and satisfying egg dish—almost a deconstructed quiche. Faster. And good for brunch or supper.

Unsalted butter for the baking dish
¼ pound Gruyerè cheese, grated
8 eggs
Salt and freshly grated black pepper
½ cup cream or half-and-half
Freshly grated nutmeg

1. Preheat the oven to 350 degrees. Generously butter a baking dish.
2. Spread half the cheese over the bottom of the baking dish. Carefully break the eggs over the cheese. Top with the rest of the cheese. Sprinkle with salt and pepper. Pour the cream over all, and lightly sprinkle with the grated nutmeg.
3. Bake at 350 degrees for 15 minutes, or until the yolks are as you like them, soft and runny, or firm.

SERVES 4

Serve with toast or good bread.

June's Shakshouka

Shakshouka, essentially eggs poached in a tomato sauce, is a nomadic kind of dish. It may have come originally from Italy to northern Africa by way of Tunisia; it has spread throughout the Middle East, and is especially popular in Israel—it travels well. My sister gave this version to me, pointing out that Tunisia and Italy almost touch in the Mediterranean and that marinara sauce and shakshouka are equally close. Huevos rancheros, the Mexican dish of fried eggs with tomato sauce and tortillas, is in the same family, an ocean away. Only connect, said E. M. Forster, and tomatoes and their sauce have connected around the world. If only the rest of us would . . .

According to the Israeli Foreign Ministry, the name shakshouka is partly from leshakshek, *a Hebrew word that means to shake. I've also read that it's a blend of Hebrew and North African words that mean all mixed up. Either way, shakshouka can be made with canned tomatoes, as it is here, or with fresh tomatoes—use 5 or 6 tomatoes, peeled and chunked, instead of the canned.*

3 garlic cloves, chopped

2 tablespoons extra virgin olive oil

1 28-oz. can whole tomatoes, crushed with your fingers, or 5 or 6
   ripe tomatoes, peeled and chunked

Large pinch of sugar

Salt and freshly ground black pepper

Optional: to taste—Tabasco, red pepper flakes, chopped chili pepper,
   or harissa

Optional: sweet paprika or powdered cumin to taste

2 eggs per person (see Note below about the dangers of eating eggs
   with runny yolks)

Good bread or pita

1. Sauté chopped garlic in oil until it softens. Don't let it brown—garlic becomes bitter when browned. Add tomatoes and sugar. Simmer over low heat for 45 minutes, or until the sauce is thick.
2. Add salt and pepper and optional ingredients to taste. Mix well.
3. One at a time, carefully slip the eggs into the sauce. Cover and poach over low heat until the whites are firm. (See Note below.) Serve hot, with bread.

SERVES 4

Note: When the whites are firm, the yolks may still be runny. Young children, pregnant mothers, and those with impaired immune systems are warned to avoid eating eggs with runny yolks. If that's a worry for you, simply poach the eggs until the yolks are well cooked. They'll still be delicious. The eggs and sauce are very good eaten inside a pita—with several napkins on the side.

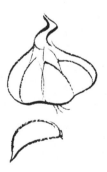

Crustless Quiche

Is a quiche without a crust still a quiche? It is if you say it is. The word quiche is apparently derived from the German Kuchen, cake—*through French-German dialects in Alsace-Lorraine; from* Kuchen *to* Küche *to* kische *to* quiche. *We are not pedantic, heaven knows, and in any case the original cake could have referred to the overall shape of a quiche, rather than to its crust. So say I. In any case, for most of us, the crust is not the best part of a quiche—it's just what it's inside of. How much easier it is to mix eggs and whatever we choose, bake, and serve. Healthier, too. And more likely to be made more often. Onward! So say I.*

The crustless quiche works well for brunch, lunch, or the first course of dinner. Crustless, the quiche reveals its kinship to the Italian frittata—kitchens without borders, in a way.

Mix together:
    4 eggs
    2 cups half-and-half
    1 tablespoon flour
    Pinch of freshly grated nutmeg
    Salt and freshly ground black pepper

This is the foundation of the quiche. To it, you can choose from many possibilities. A cup of onions sautéed in 2 or 3 tablespoons of butter and mixed with a half-cup of diced cooked ham or bacon and grated cheese (about one cup of Gruyère, Swiss, or Parmigiano Reggiano, or a combination) makes a classic quiche. My friend Joan uses slices of smoked salmon and canned artichoke hearts and about ½ cup grated feta cheese; she pours the egg mixture over this and then tops the whole thing by floating over it sliced shallots that have been sautéed in butter. Her grandson Sacha likes his quiche mixture over steamed broccoli florets and grated Cheddar cheese, with the same sautéed shallot topping. She also notes that the quiche can be baked ahead, refrigerated overnight, and reheated for ten minutes in the oven at 350 degrees.

1. Preheat oven to 350 degrees.
2. Generously butter a 9-inch quiche or pie dish or an 8-inch square baking dish, and sprinkle it with bread crumbs. Spread the filling—onions and ham, or salmon and artichokes, or whatever you choose—in the dish. Sprinkle cheese on top. Pour the egg mixture over all.
3. Bake at 350 degrees for 25 minutes, or until the top is golden and the custard is almost set in the middle—it should have a tiny jiggle; it will continue to set after it has been removed from the oven. (Don't overcook it; this makes moisture ooze and form on the custard—cooks call this "weeping," sadly enough.) Cool on a rack; serve warm or at room temperature.

SERVES 4 TO 6

Salzburger Nockerl

. . . .

Salzburger Nockerl is on its way to being a soufflé. Its base is simply sugar and egg yolks mixed into stiffly beaten egg whites; the base of a soufflé is a cream sauce with egg yolks and another flavoring—anything from cheese to chocolate—again blended with stiffly beaten whites.

The Nockerl are a sweet cloud of eggy air, and, as a song from an operetta has it, "Sweet as love and tender as a kiss." (If God arranged a feast, the song goes on, Salzburger Nockerl would be served for dessert.)

The Nockerl are arranged to look like the mountains around Salzburg, the city where Mozart was born. The city's residents are proud of both, but you just can't make egg whites look like Mozart.

Unsalted butter for the baking dish
5 egg whites at room temperature
Pinch of salt
2 tablespoons sugar
4 egg yolks
1 tablespoon flour
½ teaspoon grated lemon rind or 1 teaspoon pure vanilla extract
Optional: to make a creamy, jammy finished dish, pour ½ to 1 cup
    cream into the bottom of the baking dish and dot the cream with 2
    or 3 tablespoons jam or cranberry sauce.
Optional garnish: powdered sugar

1. Preheat the oven to 375 degrees. Generously butter a baking dish.
2. Beat the whites with an electric mixer in a clean, dry bowl; when they foam, add the salt. Continue to beat until they're stiff; gradually add the sugar, and beat for two minutes longer.
3. Beat the yolks with the flour and lemon rind or vanilla, and then use a broad spatula to gently fold them into the whites (not the other way around, as is usually done). The two should be well mixed, but

the whites must not lose their lift. Use the spatula to turn the mixture into the baking dish, and form 3 or 4 mounds, higher than they are wide (the mountains). It's fine if the mountains touch each other; they'll be separated for serving, in any case.

4. Bake for 10 minutes, until the Nockerl are golden brown. The inside should still be moist and creamy, but not runny. Serve immediately.

SERVES 4

Optional: The finished dish can be sprinkled with powdered sugar (snow on the mountains?), but that seems like gilding the lily to me. I've never understood why there isn't any whipped cream—this is Salzburg!—with Salzburger Nockerl; serve it on the side, if you want to. The lily is gilded.

Cheese Strata

. . . .

There are dozens—no, hundreds—of variations of cheese strata, but I like best the one I learned first. It's pure; embellish it at will. Just remember that good bread, butter, and cheese are essential to a good strata. They're what it's all about.

4 large eggs

2 cups milk

1 teaspoon Dijon mustard or ½ teaspoon mustard powder

½ teaspoon paprika

Salt and freshly ground black pepper

Unsalted butter at room temperature

8 slices good, firm bread

½ pound sharp Cheddar cheese, sliced

1. Preheat the oven to 375 degrees. Butter an 8×8-inch baking pan.
2. Beat the eggs and milk together. Add the mustard, paprika, salt, and pepper, and mix well.
3. Butter bread slices on one side. If you've used bread like Arnold's or Pepperidge Farm, halve or quarter it. Cut other bread to roughly that size.
4. Layer the bread on edge (each piece leaning on another) with slices of cheese, so that each piece of bread has a piece of cheese. Pour the egg mixture slowly into the dish, making sure all the bread is soaked. Let it stand for a few minutes, pressing the bread into the milk with a fork or the back of a spoon.
5. Bake at 375 degrees for 30 minutes, or until the strata is browned and puffed and its middle is firm. Serve immediately.

SERVES 4

7

PASTA NOW AND FOREVER

A Basketful of Macaroni

No man is lonely while eating spaghetti. —*Robert Morley*

Pasta—Italian for paste or dough—is a category, a generic. One of the best-known pasta shapes, without taking a scientific poll, is undoubtedly spaghetti. In Italian, the word spaghetti is plural. Should you ever have the opportunity to address a single strand of spaghetti, please call it spaghetto.

Spaghetti—the word—comes from the Italian word for string, *spago*; in the plural, *spaghi*, strings; adding "ett" makes them little. Little strings are thus *spaghetti*, and spaghetti is just one of the hundred of shapes and sizes of pasta. That almost miraculous stuff adapts to equally numerous sauces, from the simplest drenching of oil and garlic to the layering of lasagna, among other things—complicated, but still not difficult, and almost inevitably delicious.

Pasta can do almost anything. It can be added to soup; it can be stuffed and plumped like a little pillow; it can be a meal unto itself or just a beginning or it can be something to the side; it can be—as the word tells us—Italian, but it has many relatives around the world, one way or another, and for at least one cousin, it can be dessert. Think of sweet noodle kugel as Jewish pasta.

For dinner on another day are the buckwheat noodles of Japan, the rice noodles of Thailand, the pot stickers and wontons of China. But they all do the same thing as Italy's ravioli and penne: They take a basic substance—rice or wheat—change it to preserve it, and when it's ready to cook, they elaborate it with vegetables and meat (thus stretching the more costly foods with the less expensive starch). In doing so, they lift the starch from its earthbound roots into the clear skies of delight. Pasta almost means a kind of love. (It was Sophia Loren in her prime who said, "Everything you see I owe to spaghetti.")

Italy's packaged pasta, which is what we think of first when we think of pasta, is made from semolina, a durum wheat flour, which has been moistened with water, kneaded, rolled and cut or extruded into a variety of shapes, and dried. That's pasta at its most basic—and there are enough variations of that simple concept to provide a different meal for every night of the year. Almost—almost—anything you can think of is good with pasta. It's one more of those wonderful kitchen substances: If you have it, and you know what to do with it, you'll eat like royalty. Or more likely, a whole lot better. I don't know that kings and queens get to have a bowl of spaghetti marinara of a Tuesday night.

For a long time in the United States, the generic word was maca-roni, not pasta. Spaghetti was one of macaroni's best-known shapes—usually with meatballs or with tomato (marinara) sauce. That's what you ate in the little Italian restaurant with the red-and-white check-ered tablecloths and the two bottles of Chianti—one to drink and one with a candle stuck in it, both nesting in their attached woven straw baskets. That little restaurant was where you fell in love—or went to eat while you were falling. It was your place, as romantic as your song. But even so, it wasn't very adventurous. Just enough so to make you feel you were doing something special.

Things began to change after World War II, when soldiers came back from the beaches of Italy with the taste of pizza and pasta in their memories. American food embraced those memories until pizza became as American as apple pie—though first we had to learn to stop calling it pizza pie. Pizza *means* pie. Pizza pie is pie pie.

Pasta is a matter of national pride for Italians, who still feel strongly about the Italian chefs who accompanied Catherine de Medici (a Florentine princess) to France when she married the future King Henry II in 1533. Her food evolved into what we now call French food. No matter how that heated discussion is carried on, pasta is universal—there's probably an Italian restaurant in Kathmandu.

Who were the first to eat pasta? The mythology is that Marco Polo brought pasta back from China in the thirteenth century. No. There was pasta in Italy long before that Venetian explorer headed east. The Etruscans were eating pasta before Romulus and Remus founded Rome, and the Romans went on to eat bowls of pasta for several centuries before the empire fell. Pasta is made mostly of wheat, so it seems only reasonable that wherever there was wheat farming, sooner or later there were ways found to preserve wheat for a rainy day. Bread is wheat's tomorrow; pasta is wheat's future. The first recorded mention of a noodle—remember, Jewish pasta—was in the Jerusalem Talmud. And not long after the birth of Jesus, a recipe for something very much like lasagna appeared in one of the world's first cookbooks. *The Art of Cooking Sicilian Macaroni and Vermicelli* was another book of recipes, compiled in about 1000 A.D. by Martino Corno, chef to the Patriarch of Aquileia, an ancient Roman city at the head of the Adriatic. Two centuries later, in 1279, someone thought highly enough of pasta to list a basket "full of macaronis" in his will.

There are several stories about the derivation of the word macaroni. Least likely is that it's descended from a Greek word for a kind of soup. There's an Italian word—*ammaccare*, to bruise or crush, as in the process of making pasta.

Then there's a story about a traveling friar who tasted a dish of rigatoni served near Naples, and liked it so much that he exclaimed, "Oh, the dear things! The great big dear things!"—in Italian, *"Ma cari! Ma caroni!"* Probably not true, but still nice.

As to Yankee Doodle, who stuck a feather in his hat and called it macaroni, one theory is that this was a reference to the Macaroni Club, a London spot frequented by young dandies—that the colonials were so rural and unsophisticated that they would call a feather something fancy. Supposedly the song was sung first by the British to make fun of the Yankees—and then the victorious Yankees made it their own.

Then there's Thomas Jefferson, who, like many Americans to follow, fell in love with the pasta he tasted while touring in Italy. (He was the American ambassador to France, and learned to love French food too.) He sent a pasta-making machine home to Virginia, along with several crates of *maccheroni*. (While he was in Europe, Jefferson also tasted his first ice cream and his first French fried potatoes—he brought home recipes for all, pasta, French fries, and ice cream.)

Today, in Jefferson's United States, macaroni is a specific shape of pasta—little narrow tubes. But there are hundreds of different shapes, from twirly fusilli to flat sheets of lasagne. Flat, long strips—like fettucini—go well with cream sauces; chunky sauces go well with sturdy shapes like oriecchiette. Simple sauces and tomato sauces are universals; they go with everything. All those shapes, in the two basic kinds of pasta (fresh and dried), give us the alphabet of pasta—an almost limitless language of food.

How to Cook Pasta

Back in your own international kitchen, there are only a few important things to remember about cooking pasta. First of all, it needs to cook in a large amount of water. Use a big pot. Use four quarts of water to cook one pound of pasta. (And one pound of pasta is enough for four people as a main dish.) When the water comes to a boil, add salt—between one and two tablespoons of salt for the four quarts of water—then add the pasta. Don't add olive oil—oil prevents sauce from sticking to the pasta later. Stir once, right away, partially cover, and lower the heat slightly so that it stays just below a hard boil. Let the pasta cook for nine minutes and then taste it to see if it's done.

Al Dente

Done, it must be said immediately, means al dente—literally, to the tooth, which means that it isn't mushy; it offers just a bit of resistance to your teeth as you chew it. Not too much. Just a little. The line is easily crossed—from al dente to mush—and realizing when the pasta is done is a triumphant moment of vigilance. Pasta is the only food I can think of that isn't cooked until it's done; when it's *almost* done, that's when it's done. I don't know where the myth about tossing a strand of spaghetti onto the wall came from (if it's done, the myth goes, it'll stick), but spare your wall. You yourself, standing there, waiting patiently or otherwise, are the best judge. Find out whether it's done to the tooth by tasting a bit; if your teeth recognize a bit of resistance—just a bit—it's done. You may have to taste it more than once; you can deal with that.

Draining and Saving Some Cooking Water

When the pasta is done, drain it thoroughly—and, Jack Lemmon movies aside, tennis rackets don't work; use a colander or a large strainer or a large Chinese mesh scoop. Don't rinse the pasta—more sauce-resistant problems if you do. It's an excellent idea to do two things: First, save some of the cooking water. Just catch it in a mug or a cup set beneath the colander and put it to one side, because you might need it later, or scoop it out of the pot before you drain the pasta. Two, warm up the bowl in which you're going to place the pasta. You can just put the bowl briefly over a pot of boiling water; or you can simply empty the boiling cooking water into it, let it sit a minute, and then pour out the water (saving a cupful as you go)—that's sufficient, and will do the job at hand.

It's a good idea to make sauce in a wide pan, like a skillet, so you can add the hot, drained pasta right into the sauce. Stir, cover, and let sit for just a minute. Remove the lid, stir again, and serve immediately. Finally, when appropriate, add some freshly grated (freshly grated) (yes, she said freshly grated) Parmigiano Reggiano cheese. If there's any extra sauce, serve it on the side, to be added at the table. The feast begins.

Parmigiano Reggiano

The thing about the cheese is that Parmigiano Reggiano is the best. Don't buy it pregrated; it loses flavor quickly that way. Make sure that the rind is stamped "Parmigiano Reggiano," and buy a small wedge (unless you're feeling flush—it's expensive). Keep it a bit loosely wrapped, so it can breathe. Treasure it, but use it generously, and don't throw away the hard rind when its glory days are over—the next time you make sauce or soup, drop the rind in early on. It adds a certain something (rather hard to define, but there it is) and makes you feel enormously wise and providential. After the cooking is done, you can cut it into small cubes—it's still nicely cheese-flavored. Otherwise, take the rind out before serving—you could save it for the next pot, if you liked, but I think it has probably given its all, and the next step after providential could turn out to be cheap and stingy. Start over with a new piece—you'll be glad you did.

There are other kinds of cheese used in Italy for grating—romano, Asiago, Grana Padano, pecorino, all very good—but Parmigiano is, for my money, unequaled, unless it's first among equals. Some say that Parmigiano is filled with umami—the fifth taste, the perfect one, the one beyond salt, sweet, bitter, and sour. Umami is a Japanese word meaning deliciousness, and while the other four tastes may also feel (and be) delicious, umami is different, umami is more, umami is beyond. Because of that, it adds savor to whatever you're cooking. That may be. Parmigiano certainly does.

Olive Oil

A full meal could be, and sometimes is, made of nothing more than pasta and butter or olive oil, with a coating of Parmigiano. And olive oil is right up there with the other two, the pasta and the cheese—and then some. You can eat it, you can make soap out of it, you can use it as a lotion, it can be medicine, and in a pinch you can put it in an oil lamp and light the light. Homer called it "liquid gold," and he was right—except that extra virgin olive oil is sometimes green.

What does all that mean, that "first cold pressed extra virgin" stuff? How can a virgin be extra? Isn't it like being pregnant, or being unique? You can't be just a little; you either are or you aren't. Is there a condition known as extra-pregnant? (Twins, perhaps?) We do say "very" unique, but we're wrong when we do. Unique is its own condition. You are or you aren't. And the same is true for virgin. So why does the label say *extra* virgin? Does that mean there's more than one? How many does it take to make a bottle?

Cold pressed extra virgin olive oil is label talk—something like giant shrimp, but not an oxymoron. It means two things: First, the olives have been cold pressed. Using heat in the pressing process affects the chemistry—thus the taste—of the resulting oil. (First cold pressed means that the oil came from the first pressing, which is better than later pressings.) Second, the oil has a very low rate of acidity—again, affecting the taste. Virgin olive oil is produced without any chemicals—the olives, in that sense, are indeed virgins. Extra virgin means this is the best possible oil. The taste of cold pressed extra virgin olive oil speaks directly to the olives, the trees, the summer sunshine, and the earth. It has a sweet mellowness, and an earthy bitterness. It's a beautiful golden green color—the color of growing things. It's a question of good, better, best, and extra-best.

How marvelous it is that somebody put them all together: pasta, olive oil, and Parmigiano Reggiano. It ranks right up there with the discovery of how good chocolate is when sugar is added to it. In the annals of food history, someone tasted the first oyster (perhaps after watching a sea bird?), someone stuck a finger into a (fallen, let's hope) beehive, and someone noticed that milk, if you jostle it long enough, turns into butter; someone else went one step further and turned milk into cheese. And in Italy, and perhaps in other places as well—or not quite as well—someone mixed wheat and water and salt and pushed the resulting paste through a hole and let it dry, and later cooked it, added olive oil and cheese, and the world shouted "Hurrah!" forever after.

Directions for cooking pasta are on page 126.

Anchovy Sauce for Pasta

Anchovies do not grow in long, flat pieces. Neither do they grow wrapped around capers. Left to their own devices, anchovies are small fish with very sharp little teeth. They eat plankton and tiny young fish, and they, in their turn, are eaten by larger fish. They're abundant in the Mediterranean, and that's undoubtedly why they are served so often—in so many ways—in countries bordering that sea. It's the way they're preserved—in brine, and packed in salt or oil—that gives them the strong taste so many of us dislike on pizza. That's the thing about anchovies: You have to be careful where you put them. The other thing is that they're the secret ingredient in a wide variety of things we love, like Worcestershire sauce and Caesar salad.

This pasta sauce is all about anchovies—and it is much better than you expect it to be. It resembles bagna càuda, a warm garlicky dip for raw vegetables. Both the sauce and the dip are simple and wonderful. And pasta with anchovy sauce is unexpectedly good on a hot day.

¼ cup extra virgin olive oil

1 2-ounce can flat anchovies (there are those who use 2 cans, and then scatter a few more anchovies over the completed pasta; I'm not one of them)

2 cloves garlic, finely chopped

Freshly ground black pepper (no additional salt is needed)

⅛ teaspoon hot red pepper flakes

1 pound pasta, cooked

Optional: 2 tablespoons unsalted butter

¼ cup chopped flat-leaf parsley

1. Heat the olive oil and add the anchovies and garlic, stirring. The anchovies will melt into the oil; encourage them with the back of your spoon. Cook for a few minutes, until the garlic is soft, fragrant, and very light gold. Don't let the garlic burn—burnt garlic is bitter.
2. Add black and red pepper; stir.
3. Add the hot pasta, cooked according to package directions, and drained. Mix well. If the sauce is too dry, add a little more olive oil (or 2 tablespoons of butter). Garnish with chopped parsley. Serve immediately.

SERVES 4

Variations: Omit the anchovies and serve as classic oil and garlic sauce. Or, add broccoli florets to the cooking water with the pasta.

Marinara Sauce

The marine in marinara sauce doesn't mean seafood; it means the sauce of sailors—a quick, simple sauce made by sailors in Naples in the sixteenth century, after Spanish ships first brought tomatoes to Italy and then to the rest of Europe. Marinara sauce did well before refrigeration— unlike more complicated meat sauces, it can be made quickly from tomatoes, it keeps well, and it lends itself to variations, all of which make it especially good for shipboard food.

A word about onions and garlic in marinara sauce: Many Neapolitans  *use either onion or garlic in their sauce, but not both—and they feel very strongly about it. I like both—but fair's fair; you've been warned. And the classic sauce, which is meant to be quickly made, doesn't have tomato paste in it—without the paste, it can cook for only twenty minutes or so. I like adding tomato paste for the body it brings to the sauce; it also intensifies the flavor—but that means cooking it a little*

*longer than would be necessary otherwise. The sauce, either way, is basic,
and as wonderful each time you have it as it was the first time you tasted
it. There are a few good bottled sauces (or maybe only one?), but this is so
fast and easy, bottled sauce seems hardly necessary.*

1 28-ounce can whole tomatoes; rinse the can with a little water
to add to the pot (don't use cans labeled San Marzano—they
probably aren't the real thing but will be priced as if they were;
Muir Glen tomatoes are organic, good, and cook to a workable
thickness; Redpack whole tomatoes with tomato purée are my
second choice)

2 tablespoons olive oil

½ medium onion, chopped

1 clove garlic, minced

1 to 2 teaspoons dried oregano

¼ teaspoon red pepper flakes

1 healthy pinch sugar

Salt and freshly ground pepper

1 can tomato paste (more can rinsing with a little water to scrape up
the bits)

1 tablespoon flat-leaf parsley, chopped

2 tablespoons basil (fresh and chopped or preserved in oil; see page
137)

Parmigiano Reggiano cheese, grated

1. Crush the tomatoes with your fingers, or, if you don't like doing that,
use a potato masher. (Just don't use canned crushed or diced
tomatoes—they aren't as good.) Sometimes a tomato will spatter—
the best way to crush each tomato is to make a hole or slit in it (with
your fingers or a knife), and then crush it over a bowl, or into the pot
when you reach that point in the cooking. If you want to crush the
tomatoes directly into the pot, drain their juice into the pot first
when things reach that stage, number 3 below.

2. Film the bottom of a large, wide pot with olive oil over medium heat. (Be sure to use a *wide* pot—a skillet works well; this helps water to evaporate as the sauce cooks.) Add the onions and sauté them for several minutes, until they become soft and translucent; then add the garlic and cook for one or two minutes longer. Add the oregano, red pepper flakes, sugar, salt, and pepper, and stir.

3. When everything is good and hot, pour in the tomatoes and the tomato paste; as noted, rinse the cans with a little water, and add that too. (There should be a sizzle when the tomatoes or their drained juice hit the hot pan.) Add the parsley, lower the heat, and simmer for 30 to 40 minutes.

4. If the sauce is too thin, raise the heat slightly and continue to cook, stirring often, until it's the consistency you want. Add the basil; cook a few minutes longer; taste; adjust seasonings, and serve.

YIELD: THIS MAKES ENOUGH FOR FOUR SERVINGS OF PASTA
AND THEN SOME.

Refrigerate whatever is left, or freeze it. Use frozen sauce to flavor soups, stews, or other sauces instead of canned tomatoes. Once thawed, the sauce keeps for up to three days. To make larger batches, increase ingredients proportionately.

Cheese: Again, my preferred grating cheese is Parmigiano Reggiano (though I've been told that southern Italians use a mixture of romano and Parmigiano). (Parmigiano Reggiano should have some of those letters stamped on the rind if it's the real thing.) Grate it yourself a few minutes before you need it.

Broccoli and Penne

It was the first President Bush who said he didn't like broccoli, and that he was president, and he damn well wasn't going to eat it anymore. Well, I don't think he said damn, but that was definitely the message. I suppose there are children who suffer through broccoli before they grow up to be president, but maybe they've never tasted broccoli at its best. This is sad—broccoli is delicious and it is enormously nutritious. It's loaded with vitamins, minerals, antioxidants, glucosinolates (cancer fighters), fiber—all the good stuff—and has very few calories. Almost none, by the time you've chewed it. Thomas Jefferson, a different sort of president altogether, planted broccoli seeds in his garden at Monticello. Does that mean that if you like the Declaration of Independence, you'll like broccoli? No. But it gives hope.

1 bunch broccoli—stems peeled and sliced, and florets cut from stems

1 pound penne, or mezzi or plain rigatoni

1 onion, chopped

3 tablespoons extra virgin olive oil

1 clove garlic, minced

2 flat anchovy filets

1 tablespoon tomato paste

Broccoli cooking water

¼ cup dried currants

¼ cup toasted pine nuts

> Toasting nuts intensifies their flavor. Roast pine nuts by placing them on a flat tray and cooking in the oven at 325 degrees for between 5 and 10 minutes or until they're lightly golden, stirring halfway through. Or cook them in a heavy pan on top of the stove, stirring often, until they're lightly golden.

Salt and freshly ground black pepper

Asiago, pecorino, or Parmigiano Reggiano cheese, grated

1. Add the broccoli to a large pot—suitable for cooking pasta—of salted water. Bring to a boil and cook for 5 minutes. Add the penne to the boiling water to cook according to package directions, until al dente—about 9 or 10 minutes longer.

2. While the broccoli and pasta are cooking, sauté the onion in olive oil until soft and golden; add the garlic and anchovies and cook 2 minutes longer, or until the anchovies have melted into the sauce (encourage them with the back of a spoon). Add the tomato paste, and scoop up a half-cup of water from the broccoli pot to add to the onion mixture; stir until combined. Add the currants and pine nuts.

3. Drain the pasta, saving a cup of its water in case the sauce needs more thinning; while the broccoli is in the colander or the strainer, cut up any large pieces. The goal is to have some small pieces of broccoli inside the penne when the dish is finished. Add the broccoli and pasta to the onion pan; mix, and let cook for a minute or two. Serve hot, with grated cheese.

SERVES 4 TO 6

Pesto

There are reasons why pesto is nearly ubiquitous in the summer. First, it's because pesto tastes so good. Then it's so easy to make. It keeps well, and it goes with many things. Furthermore, it's pretty. We are lucky to have nearly ubiquitous pesto.

Note: Exact quantities don't matter. Use this listing as an initial guide, and fly from there.

2 cups loosely packed basil leaves (no stems—they don't purée, and tend to be bitter), washed and dried (in a salad spinner, or simply shaken dry)

Optional: small handful of parsley leaves

1 or 2 cloves garlic, chopped

2 tablespoons pine nuts, lightly toasted in a dry skillet (see page 135)

¼ to ½ cup extra virgin olive oil, as needed

½ cup freshly grated Parmigiano Reggiano cheese

1. Combine the basil, parsley, garlic, pine nuts, and ¼ cup olive oil in a food processor. Pulse, stopping to scrape down the sides of the bowl once or twice. Add additional oil if it seems dry. Scrape into a bowl, and add cheese just before serving.

YIELD: ABOUT 1 CUP

Important Note: Basil can be kept for weeks—even months—in the refrigerator by processing the leaves with just enough extra virgin olive oil to chop them. Pulse briefly. Scrape into a clean jar, and cover with a ½-inch layer of olive oil. Keep refrigerated. Spoon out basil as needed, replacing the oil as you go. The oil can be used for sautéing or flavoring. The basil can be used in pasta sauces, soups, chicken, stews . . . and in a pinch, it can be used to make pesto, if you have no fresh basil available.

Things to do with pesto:

1. As is, use it as a sauce over pasta.
2. Even better—and just a bit more unusual—cook potato chunks (about 2-inch pieces) in salted water for 10 minutes before adding pasta; add stemmed and washed string beans, left whole, at the same time as the pasta. Cook 10 minutes longer, or until the pasta is al dente. Drain and mix with pesto before serving.
3. Add dollops of pesto to vegetable soup—in the pot, or to taste in individual bowls.
4. Arrange slices of fresh ripe tomatoes on a plate, and dot with pesto.
5. Make little tarts, using preformed phyllo or puff pastry tartlets. Add a layer of goat cheese to each, then a layer of pesto, a thin slice of tomato, and some grated Parmigiano Reggiano or Gruyère on top. Bake at 350 degrees for 10 minutes, or until the cheese is brown and bubbling.

Summer Sauce for Pasta

Pasta Primavera is springtime pasta, usually mixed with early vegetables, or topped with an uncooked sauce. This sauce is for the summer, though I use canned corn to make it all year long. By August, I can't really think why I should make it any other way. I like to use Green Giant Niblets Extra Sweet Corn Kernels. But they can be hard to find and other varieties work too.

2 tablespoons olive oil

¼ large onion, chopped

1 clove garlic, minced

1 cup corn kernels, freshly cut from the cob, or 1 11-oz. can corn
    kernels

2 tomatoes, peeled and cut into small pieces (see page 272)

2 teaspoons preserved basil (see page 137), or 2 tablespoons fresh
    basil, chopped

Salt and freshly ground black pepper to taste

Optional: ½ cup marinara sauce

1 pound pasta, cooked

1. Heat the olive oil in a sauté pan; add the onion and cook for 4 or 5 minutes, until they become translucent and soft; add the garlic, and cook 2 minutes longer.
2. Add the corn and tomato, and cook, stirring occasionally for 8 minutes longer. Add the basil, salt, and pepper, and stir. If using, add the marinara sauce and stir.
3. Add freshly cooked pasta (small shapes work best) to the pan, stir well, and serve.

SERVES 4

Note: A good uncooked summer sauce can be made with thinly sliced onions that have been briefly sautéed in extra virgin olive oil with a little minced garlic, chopped fresh parsley leaves, fresh and dried oregano, shredded fresh basil, peeled and chopped ripe tomatoes, and salt and pepper. Let stand for an hour or two; taste to adjust the seasoning, adding more salt and oregano if you like; and serve over hot pasta.

David's Pasta with Celery and Tomato Sauce

The myth about celery is that it takes more calories to chew than the celery itself has, so the result of eating celery is negative calories. Alas, no. According to Snopes.com, the Web site that debunks (or verifies) urban legends, rumors, and old wives' tales, chewing celery won't make you thin ("it burns about the same amount of energy as watching paint dry"). Digesting celery might result in the valued negative, but by such a tiny amount that it isn't worth bothering with. On the other hand, celery is good for you, it feels virtuous, and—in this recipe, originally a Roman sauce—it's just delicious.

1 onion, chopped

2 tablespoons extra virgin olive oil

1 heart of celery—several inside core stalks, with leaves, diced

Salt

1½ to 2 pounds ripe tomatoes, peeled (see Note below, about using canned tomatoes) and crushed with your fingers or a potato masher

1 pinch sugar

Freshly ground black pepper

1 pound spaghetti, spaghettini, or fresh fettuccine, cooked (save 1 cup of the cooking water)

Freshly grated Parmigiano Reggiano cheese

1. Sauté the onion in olive oil until lightly browned. Remove the onion with a slotted spoon (draining as much oil as possible back into the pan) and reserve. Add the celery and a little salt to the remaining oil, and cook for 4 or 5 minutes. Remove, again with a slotted spoon, and reserve with the onion.

3. Add the crushed tomatoes to the remaining oil. Add the sugar and pepper to taste; stir. Cook for 40 minutes over medium-high heat, stirring frequently, or 1 hour over low heat. Taste for seasoning.

4. Add the reserved onion and celery to the sauce, and add cooked pasta. Add a little of the saved water if the sauce is too dry. Stir well. Serve immediately with grated cheese sprinkled on top.

SERVES 4 TO 6

Note: David says that this should be made only in the summer, with fresh ripe tomatoes. I've made it with canned Muir Glen tomatoes, and while it wasn't the same, it was still very good.

8

THE BIG DISH

The Traditional Center

Show me another pleasure like dinner which comes every day and
lasts an hour.   —*Charles Maurice de Talleyrand*

Vegetarians have long since proved that you can get through the
day quite happily without eating meat. But for those of us who
aren't vegetarians, meat seems to offer psychological substance, as if it
were the center of the meal while everything else is the framework.
Most of us have been raised to think of meat that way—meat and potatoes and all that—which is unfortunate, because meat is probably
the least healthy and most wasteful part of dinner, not only in terms
of body fat but also in the way animals are raised, slaughtered, and
shipped, all at great cost to the world's economy and to global warm-
ing, to say nothing of simple morality.

Still, the psychological proof of the pudding, as it were, is that the
word meat comes from an Old English word (*mete*) that meant food—
all of it, from soup to nuts, everything we eat except what we drink.

Food, then, was *mete* and drink. The modern sense of meat has only been with us for a relatively short while; thinking of meat as an essential part of the meal began at around the turn of the last century. (Dark meat and white meat, by the way, were supposedly the Victorian way of avoiding having to say "leg" or, worse, "breast.") Maybe the first step on the road to eating less meat is recognizing its relatively short time in the limelight, as well as its psychological baggage.

For our purposes here, meat means beef, pork, lamb, and—strangely enough—fish. (Chicken and turkey are discussed in chapter 5.) Fish isn't usually thought of as meat; we tend to keep it in a category of its own, under the label seafood. That fishy idea is partly of religious origin. Jews who keep kosher kitchens, for example, have three categories of food: meat, dairy, and neither, or *pareve*. Dairy is milk, butter, and cheese, none of which may be eaten in the same meal as meat, but fish is one of the *pareve* foods that can be eaten with both meat and dairy. Catholics who can't eat meat on certain days may eat fish—again, it's not considered to be meat. (Pork is forbidden food for Jews who keep kosher, and to all Muslims. How strange we all are! Especially to each other.)

Religious or not, we can safely assume that the center of the meal, whether or not it's meat, can be thought of as big. Big doesn't necessarily mean impressive, though of course it can be. Big doesn't mean huge (huge means huge, after all; it doesn't need a synonym). Big doesn't mean complicated or difficult; big can be beautifully simple.

Big, then, in this sense, means satisfying, central, and perhaps even large enough to have serious leftovers. Big, in fact, can be the introduction to leftovers, made almost on purpose to come back again, a culinary reincarnation proceeding day by day to nirvana. (Culinary reincarnation, though, can only last so long. If you put something in a jar and the jar finds its way to the back of the shelf in the refrigerator, sooner or later, it'll turn green and things will grow out of it. Say goodbye, and begin again.)

Browning or Searing

There are a few basic procedures involved in cooking meat. Perhaps the place to begin is with the process of browning (otherwise known as searing). For a long time, it was thought to be essential to brown meat (cook it over high heat until it completely loses its outer red color and develops a brown crust). Browning was believed to seal in the meat's juices; they wouldn't ooze out through that cauterized crust. Then it turned out—science having been turned loose on cooking—that the juices could indeed ooze out, and that the imprisonment of juices was not the True Purpose of browning. Caramelizing—adding the flavor of the crust—to the finished dish was the True Purpose. That may be so, but once you've been exposed to the "Seal in the Juices" theory, it's hard to abandon it. Either way, almost always the first step when cooking meat is to brown it. Use high heat, a bit of oil (the kind of oil you use depends on the flavor you're after in the finished dish), and, when the oil is hot, add the meat.

That's the first of three important things: The oil needs to be hot when you add the meat. And that's a reason for using oil rather than butter. Butter burns at high temperatures, and that affects flavor badly. Oil (olive, vegetable, safflower, canola, peanut), or meat or bacon drippings can stand higher temperatures without burning. If you want a buttery flavor, use a mixture of oil and butter and watch carefully to be sure that things are under control.

The second important thing: Don't crowd the pan—crowding means that the meat will steam and get gray instead of brown. Give it room and let it rip. Do more than one batch if you have to.

Finally: Don't rush things; the kitchen is an excellent place for the learning of patience. The meat will have a better crust if you let it stay in one place and develop its color before you turn it, but when the meat is—finally—brown on one side (you can tell by lifting up a corner and peeking), turn it and let it brown on the others. (Steak has essentially only two sides, but cubes of meat, like those for stew, have several. You don't need to be a mathematician to figure out how many sides there are; just look.) On the other hand, don't wait too long—the meat should brown, not burn. Lift up a corner from time to time to see how things are progressing, and turn the meat—or remove it—as soon as it arrives at where you want it to be. A bit of practice is all you need; you'll be good at this very quickly.

A postscript: Start with the best side down. The first side that browns looks best at the end, so put the good side (if there is one) down first. Skin side down, for instance, with chicken. Fish steaks or filets want the bone side—the side that was closest to the bone, or less positively, *not* the skin side) down first. Some meat doesn't matter as much—just start with the best side, the one that, given your druthers, you'd put face up on the plate.

And another: Dredging meat lightly in flour (dredging means creating a light covering—achieved by putting seasoned flour and meat in a plastic bag and shaking, or by putting the flour on a dish and patting the meat down on top of it and then turning the meat and patting again) gives the finished meat a crisp covering, if it continues to cook without liquid. If there is a liquid, as for stew or a braise, the flour helps to lightly thicken the sauce. It's not essential to use flour; you're the driver and you make the choice.

Sautéing

Essentially, what you're doing in the browning process is sautéing the meat over high heat. *Sauté* is a French word that means literally to jump. It isn't exactly that the food jumps around while it cooks—it tends to stay in one place; rather, it's that the cook (that's you!) stirs and tosses the sauté pan as the food cooks, and thus the food jumps. It's that dramatic thing that you've seen on television, if you've watched anybody cook—a jerk of the wrist, and presto! the food is

stirred without having been touched. That's lovely, and you can practice the motion if you want with a cold pan and a handful of beans
(maybe somewhere where you don't have to pick up all the spilled
beans), but if you don't want, by all means feel free to use a spoon or a
fork. I do.

If you're not cooking the meat in the same pan you browned it in (or
if you're adding other ingredients), the next step is usually one of three
things: Take the meat out and put it on a dish so you can go on to the
other steps, like sautéing onions and vegetables; deglaze the pan (below); or carry on as you are.

If you're not putting meat in your big dish at all, you still want to
start by sautéing, or sweating, the vegetables: their water evaporates as
they sauté and their flavor thus intensifies. Onions usually need to be
sweated until they're translucent and soft; other vegetables, too, take
on a slightly cooked look.

Deglazing

Deglazing the pan is a kind of kitchen magic—oh! There is so much
magic! After you remove the meat, you'll see little bits of things that
are stuck to the bottom of the pan, the flavorful *fond*. Pour a few tablespoons of wine, or broth, or juice, or even water into the pan, turn up
the heat, bring the liquid to a boil, and at the same time, with a
wooden spoon or a wooden spatula, stir and scrape so that the *fond* is
loosened and dissolves. This is the beginning of a sauce. If you've
deglazed with wine or good broth and used just enough to cover the
bottom of the pan and a bit more, you're almost finished (and if you
have too much liquid, let it bubble until it has evaporated and reduced
to the consistency and amount you want). Stir in a pat of butter, and
you have a sauce right there. It'll be even better if you sautéed a few
chopped shallots or a bit of minced onion in the pan before you added
the wine.

Slow Cooking and Casseroles

That's the beginning (the searing) and the end (the deglazing of the pan) of one kind of big-dish cooking. But, oh yes, there's more. There's the middle.

Look at it this way: Before—way before—there were slow cookers, there were casseroles. Consider the caveman, with his new, and enormously valued, fire. Did he and the woman he cooked with quickly sear the mammoth roast while the plants grilled? Not likely. In all probability—and for a very long time after the cave had been left behind—everything simmered and baked in one earthenware pan, over a slow and steady fire.

That's probably why casseroles and Dutch ovens and the like are fairly universal. The word *casserole* comes from the French word for stew pan, a large, deep covered pot that doubles as a cooking pot and a serving dish—*en casserole* means served in the cooking dish. Dutch ovens are thick, heavy pots, good for slow cooking, for making braises and stews. There are big dishes—cooked in casseroles or Dutch ovens or stew pans—in just about every culture, from the tagines of Morocco to the stovetop pad thai of Thailand, the paella of Spain, the curries of India, and the moussaka of Greece. None of those is a casserole in the classic American sense; they aren't string beans with cream of mushroom soup and canned fried onions. But they are all the amazingly varied combination of vegetables, meat, starch, and a sauce or liquid, all cooked together, that is the essence of this kind of cooking. The big dish. Out of many, one. Or, if you prefer a different slogan, all for one and one for all.

Doing the Prep Work

Get everything ready before you turn on the heat. In French cooking this is called the *mise en place*—a phrase that means the prep work.

(Of course, you've read the recipe before you begin to cook. You have, haven't you?) You've seen this on television—little dishes with things in them, a half-cup of onions in one, a teaspoon of minced garlic in another, a bowl of carrots and celery, and herbs and spices in a collection of little containers surrounding the chef. It's nice to chop as you go, and the more time you've spent as a cook, the easier it is to do this, to enjoy the onions sautéing while you mince the garlic, for instance, but if you're in the middle of a recipe and suddenly have to stop while you find that piece of ginger you've had for so long in the fridge, and it turns out to be somewhere behind the carrots and under the celery and it takes you an awfully long time to find that out, in the meantime, back on the range, things are cooking—and burning—and getting too well done, or have come to a horrible halt. It's best to think ahead and be ready for whatever comes next. Television chefs have other people to do the prep work, but for the rest of us, very often one of the best parts of cooking is the idiot work. Good things—thoughts, ideas, daydreams, premonitions—happen while you're cutting the carrots.

Everything you prepared ahead gets layered with the main ingredients in a baking dish, or it's mixed into a stir-fry or a braise, and then it all simmers over the heat or roasts in the oven—slowly or quickly, as the case may be—and is brought to the table at last in all its glory. That makes it sound perhaps simpler than it is, but no matter: Those are the steps, and there's no need to make a fuss over them. Unless you like making a fuss just to show that you did. That's always possible.

Braising

To braise something (usually, but not always, meat) means to cook it with some liquid in a covered pot over medium-low heat. Roasting, on the other hand, means cooking in the oven in a pan without a lid. Braising can be done on the stovetop or in the oven; roasting needs an oven. Braising keeps ingredients moist, and there's an exchange of fla-vor between the liquid and the other ingredients. Roasting is dry—not without humor, of course, but dry.

French anthropologist Claude Lévi-Strauss wrote that roasting meat is a status meal in every culture, because roasting means, when it's done, less food. When meat is roasted, some of its juices are lost, and it shrinks slightly. If you can afford for that to happen, you had more than enough to begin with. Braising or stewing, on the other hand, means conserving the juices—they become part of the meal. The folk eat stew; the upper crust eats prime rib. Let's hear it for the folk! It's their bread—crusty peasant bread—that we love, among a host of other things that have made it to the top. The food of the peo-ple rises, just like cream.

Braising also involves less expensive cuts of meat; no prime rib here—rather, the best choices for braises are chuck roasts, brisket, and shoulder roasts. And braising is a cook's friend—after everything is in the pot, it cooks happily and slowly without much more than a peek and a stir every now and then. And last, yes, last, braises make for excellent leftovers.

The method is similar in most recipes: brown the meat, sauté the aromatics (onion, garlic, carrot, celery), combine, add a liquid—broth, a little wine, tomatoes with their juices—and cook on the top of the stove or in the oven until tender. There are things that can be added—a bay leaf, herbs, some potatoes, other vegetables—but the principle remains the same.

Is there a difference between braising and stewing? Not exactly. Both mean cooking in a covered pot with a small amount of liquid; stew tends to be meat, and anything can be braised. On the other hand, many foods can also be stewed. Braise is a French-derived word; a *braise* was the live coals on which a lidded pan—a *braiser*—was placed; stew may also come from the Old French: *estuver*, to heat in steam or smoke. Many of our English food words derive from French words—the animals are Old English words but the food they provide is French (instead of saying cow, we say beef, from the French *boeuf*, pig becomes pork, from *porc*, and sheep is mutton, from *mouton*), a legacy of the Norman conquest of England and a reminder of the niceties of the table. We'd rather not think about cows when we eat steak.

Lamburgers and Hamburgers

....

Hamburgers aren't made with ham, but lamburgers are made with lamb. Lamburgers are thus a truth in cooking recipe. Lamburgers are a fine way to make a change, but let it be known that hamburgers remain the classic. And this is also a new way to serve the classic.

1 pound ground chuck (85 percent lean) *or* ground lamb
  If you can't find ground lamb, buy shoulder lamb chops and pulse them briefly (with fat, yes, but bone, no) in the food processor.
1 tablespoon olive oil or butter
Optional: four pieces of cheese
  Use cheese that melts nicely for the stuffing: feta, mozzarella (plain or smoked), Gruyère, Cheddar, even blue cheese all work well.
Salt and freshly ground black pepper
8 slices good white bread, like Arnold's or Pepperidge Farm
3 to 4 tablespoons Hellmann's mayonnaise (regular or light, *not* nonfat)
1 tomato, sliced
4 slices red onion
4 slices dill pickle

1. With wet hands—to handle the meat more easily—lightly shape the meat into four patties. Be as quick as you can, and be gentle: The more you handle raw ground meat, the tougher the cooked meat will be. Make a slight indentation, with your fingertips, on one side of each patty; in theory, this helps to keep them flat. If you like, stuff the patties with pieces of cheese, forming the meat into balls, poking the cheese into the middle, then shaping the meat around the cheese so that it's well covered, and finally making the meat flat rather than ball-shaped.

2. Heat the olive oil in a frying pan. Lightly sprinkle the patties with salt and pepper and add them to the pan. Cook on the first side for 3 to 5 minutes. Don't press down on the patties with a spatula: Yes, I know you've seen cooks do that, but that's really just a good way to push the juices out of the meat. It's much nicer to keep them in! Turn the patties over, and cook for another 3 to 5 minutes. (Three minutes for each side is for medium rare; five, well done. But check by cutting into one to be sure.)

2. While the burgers are cooking, toast the bread slices. Coat one side of each toast slice with mayonnaise, and to four of the slices add tomato, onion, and pickle. Top with a meat patty and the second slice of toast, mayonnaise side down. Cut in half with a serrated knife; serve immediately.

SERVES 4

Lamb and Beans Provençal

In his lovely first book about fast cooking, Fast Food My Way, Jacques Pépin gives a recipe for lamb and dried beans cooked in a pressure cooker. I don't have a pressure cooker, so I've adapted his recipe (in several ways). It's still fast, because I use canned beans. If you'd rather use dried beans, cook them separately according to package directions, and add them as indicated.

Among many other happy suggestions (some a little breathless) in Pépin's book is a short paragraph describing how to make cold black bean soup. In a food processor bowl, combine a can of black bean soup (Goya makes a good one), a little olive oil, a few drops of Tabasco, "a few" tablespoons of chopped onion, a crushed clove of garlic, salt, and enough chicken broth to make the mixture creamy. Pulse. He suggests topping each serving with sour cream, a few slices of banana, and some cilantro leaves. I like avocado, too. And that's a meal, with some tortilla chips or good bread, and a little cheese.

2 tablespoons extra virgin olive oil

4 shoulder lamb chops, trimmed of fat

1 cup diced onions (about ½ large Spanish onion)

2 cloves garlic, chopped

1 15-oz. can whole tomatoes, crushed with your fingers or a potato masher

1 can cannellini beans, rinsed and drained (or ½ cup dried beans, soaked and cooked)

1 teaspoon dried thyme

2 to 3 tablespoons chopped flat-leaf parsley

1 bay leaf

2 teaspoons Worcestershire sauce

Salt and freshly ground black pepper

1. Heat the olive oil in a large saucepan. Add the lamb chops and brown them on both sides. (Cook them in one layer; do two at a time if all four don't fit.) When the chops are browned, remove them to a plate. If there's more than a little fat left in the pan, drain it off.
2. Add the onions and cook several minutes until they're soft and translucent. Add the garlic and cook two minutes longer.
3. While the onion is cooking, cut the chops into sections. Return them to the pan, and add the remaining ingredients. Cover and cook over medium low heat for 1½ to 2 hours, stirring occasionally, and adding water, chicken broth, or tomato juice if the mixture becomes dry. Taste and add more salt and pepper if necessary.

SERVES 6

Note: This is one of those dishes that improves if it's made a day ahead—and while it's refrigerated the fat forms a layer at the top that can easily be lifted off before you reheat it the next day. (But it's fine served right away—if there seems to be too much fat, spoon off as much as you can, holding a large spoon just under the surface and letting the fat float in so you can discard it.) It can also be stretched to serve 8 or 10 by adding another can of beans.

Breaded Pork Chops

....

Pork chops, which should be lusciously soft and juicy, tend these days to be hard and dry. That's because they're marketed as "the other white meat," and to make that boast true, the fat has been bred out of the pigs they come from—sad, because it's the fat that makes them juicy. Brining is one solution, but it's not my favorite—it's time- and space-consuming, and it means pork chops for dinner can't be a last-minute decision. The solution is amazingly simple: Bread boneless pork chops well, sealing in tenderness and flavor, and bake them. (You can flavor the bread crumbs in other ways, if you like—with paprika and chopped garlic, for instance.)

3 tablespoons extra virgin olive oil

2 cups fresh bread crumbs

> *Don't use prepared bread crumbs. Pulse 3 slices of bread in the food processor to make fresh bread crumbs. If you save end pieces of bread in the freezer, you can process them when you have enough to make it worthwhile, and freeze the crumbs until you need them.*

1 teaspoon dried thyme

¼ cup freshly grated Parmigiano Reggiano cheese

1 teaspoon grated lemon peel

Salt and freshly ground black pepper

4 boneless pork chops, about ¾-inch thick

1. Preheat the oven to 350 degrees and film a baking dish with 2 tablespoons of the olive oil.
2. Mix the bread crumbs, thyme, cheese, lemon peel, salt, and pepper in a shallow bowl.
3. Place a chop in the bowl; pat it down lightly; turn it over, and pat again. Repeat until it is thickly coated with crumbs. Coat the sides with crumbs.

Carefully place it in the pan. Repeat with the other three chops. If there are any leftover crumbs, pile them on the top of the chops and pat them firmly in place. Dribble the remaining tablespoon of oil evenly over the chops.

4. Bake for 30 minutes, or until an instant-read thermometer registers 165 degrees when poked into the thickest piece of chop. Serve immediately.

SERVES 4

Austrian Goulash

Goulash didn't cause World War I, but it almost could have. It spread through the Austria-Hungarian Empire (Austria, Hungary, parts of Czechoslovakia and Poland, and the Balkan states) and reached to Germany and Italy—with recipes that vary from region to region and home to home. Each country, each family, of course, likes its own best and believes it to be the most genuine.

Goulash—from the Hungarian gulyás, cattle herdsman—most often is based on beef, though it can also be made with other meats, even beans. My old and sweet Austrian cookbook (Austrian Cooking for You, published in Vienna in 1960) says that the secret of a good goulash is to use equal quantities—by weight—of beef and onions, and I have never found any reason to doubt it.

The traditional accompaniments to goulash are wide egg noodles or boiled potatoes (or dumplings) and crusty bread or rolls to soak up the juices. This is another of those dishes that tastes even better the day after you've cooked it—though heaven knows, it's perfectly good on the same day.

2 tablespoons canola or other bland oil (original recipes used lard)

2 pounds beef chuck, in large (about 1-inch) cubes

2 pounds onions (1 to 2 large Spanish onions), sliced or chunked

2 tablespoons sweet paprika

Fresh cold water

2 tablespoons tomato purée

1 teaspoon vinegar

1 teaspoon marjoram

Salt and freshly ground black pepper

Optional: flat parsley leaves, chopped

1. Film the bottom of a large, heavy pot with the oil, and sauté the meat until it is nicely browned. Add the onions and continue to cook until they are soft and beginning to turn golden. Stir often to prevent burning, and add more oil if needed.

2. Add the paprika, stir well, and continue to cook for a minute or two. Cover, and cook over medium-high heat for 2 or 3 minutes longer.

3. Stir in ¼ cup of cold water, and add the remaining ingredients. Stir. Lower the heat and continue to cook, gently and slowly, over very low heat and with the cover on, checking from time to time to see if more water is needed, for 1½ to 2 hours, until the meat is soft and tender. If you like, before serving, sprinkle with chopped parsley.

SERVES 6 TO 8

Unstuffed Cabbage

. . . .

Stuffed cabbage is lovely. But preparing it is a tedious, time-consuming undertaking. Unstuffed cabbage is not for purists, perhaps, but it's fast and it's good enough to convince any purist who tastes it. The ingredients are the same for stuffed and unstuffed cabbage; it remains an authentic dish—just with cabbage chunks instead of neat rolls. And because it's easier and faster, you can make it much more often. (I also like unstuffed grape leaves, which you can find on page 182.)

For the meat:
   1 pound chopped beef
   1 egg, lightly beaten
   ½ cup fresh bread crumbs
   ¼ large onion, diced
   ½ lemon, juiced
   1½ tablespoons sugar
   2 to 3 tablespoons dried currants
   ½ teaspoon each salt and freshly ground black pepper

For the cabbage:
   1 head cabbage
   1 large onion, quartered and sliced
   3 tablespoons dried currants
   1 lemon, juiced
   3 tablespoons sugar
   1 28-ounce can whole tomatoes (I use Muir Glen or Redpack)
   Salt and freshly ground black pepper
   Fresh cold water

1. Using the pot you'll cook in (a large, heavy-bottomed pot), mix the
   ingredients for the meatballs. Shape into balls, choosing a size be-

tween a Ping-Pong ball and a tennis ball. Place the meatballs on a plate and reserve. Don't wash the pot.

2. Remove and discard any discolored or shriveled leaves from the cabbage. Quarter it, discard the solid white core, and chunk the remaining cabbage.

3. Place half the cabbage in the pot; add half the onion and half the currants. Place the meatballs evenly over. Add the remaining ingredients, crushing the tomatoes roughly (with your hands or a potato masher) before you add them. Add sufficient water to reach an inch below the surface of the cabbage.

4. Bring to a simmer over medium heat. Reduce the heat to medium-low and continue to cook, covered, for at least two hours, checking occasionally to see if more liquid is needed. After two hours, if the liquid is too thin and watery, remove the cover and cook over medium heat until it reduces, or, if you like, becomes slightly syrupy.

5. Spoon some of the liquid into a cup, let it cool slightly, and taste carefully. Adjust the seasonings—add more lemon juice or sugar, salt or pepper, as required. Mix very gently and serve.

SERVES 6

Note: Both the cabbage and the meat continue to improve as they are reheated. But leftover meatballs, cold, make wonderful sandwiches with deli mustard on good, solid rye bread.

Sausage, Vegetable, and Bean Stew

. . . .

With its carrots, beans, optional butternut squash, and sweet sausage, this is a hearty dish for when the weather changes—no more ripe peaches from the farmers' market or basil from the garden; those gifts are over, and new ones have arrived: pumpkin and pears, cabbage and squash. Seasonal good fortune is worth celebrating.

2 tablespoons extra virgin olive oil

6 links Italian pork or chicken sausage

1 stalk celery, chopped

1 to 4 carrots, chopped (use one carrot if you're including butternut squash; if not, use more)

1 medium onion, chopped

2 cloves garlic, minced

¼ cup flour

1 15-oz. can cannellini beans, rinsed and drained (see Note below about using other kinds of beans)

Optional: 1 butternut squash, peeled and cubed (see Note below about peeling)

1 15-oz. can whole tomatoes, crushed with your fingers

½ teaspoon dried sage

½ teaspoon dried rosemary or 1 teaspoon fresh, chopped

2 to 3 tablespoons chopped fresh flat-leaf parsley

2 to 3 cups homemade or low-sodium canned chicken broth

Salt and freshly ground pepper

¼ pound Parmigiano Reggiano rinds (doesn't have to be exact)

Garnish: freshly grated Parmigiano Reggiano cheese

1. Preheat oven to 350 degrees.
2. Film a large pot with olive oil; medium heat. Add the sausages and sauté until browned on all sides. Remove the sausages to a plate.

Drain excess fat (keeping about 2 or 3 tablespoons) from the pot and discard.

3. Add the celery, carrot, and onion to the pot and sauté until the onion becomes soft and translucent. Add the garlic and cook 2 minutes longer. Sprinkle with flour, and cook, stirring and scraping up the bottom, 3 minutes longer.

4. Add the beans, squash if using, tomatoes (with their juice), herbs, chicken broth, salt, pepper, and cheese rinds. Mix, and bring to a simmer.

5. Cover and bake at 350 degrees for 1 hour. (If using butternut squash, cook 15 minutes longer.) Slice the reserved sausage and add; cook until hot. Taste for seasoning and adjust if necessary. Remove and discard the cheese rinds or, if you like, slice into small cubes and add to the stew. Serve with additional grated cheese.

SERVES 6

Notes: Instead of cannellini beans, you can use butter beans, lima beans, chickpeas, or navy beans, if you wish. Beans can be canned or dried; if dried, use a generous ½ cup and cook according to package directions (soak overnight; simmer for an hour; drain) and add the beans to the pot before it goes into the oven. Cook until the beans are tender.

You can stretch the dish to serve 8 by adding additional beans.

Supermarkets often carry packages of peeled, cubed butternut squash. To do it yourself, cut the squash in half across its middle, just above where it swells out. Cut each section in half the long way. Discard the seeds. Use a swivel-bladed peeler to peel. Make large slices across, and cut into 1- to 2-inch chunks.

Fishmonger's Salmon

There aren't as many mongers as there used to be (except perhaps for rumormongers and warmongers). I asked a fishmonger once for a good way to cook salmon, and he told me to coat it with mayonnaise and bake or broil it. Odd? No, because mayonnaise is made of eggs and oil and a little vinegar, all of which go well with salmon. It's a very easy procedure, and he was a very nice fishmonger.

> Extra virgin olive oil
> Salmon fillets
> Hellmann's mayonnaise (regular or light, *not* low-fat)
> Optional garnish: parsley sprigs and lemon quarters

1. Preheat the oven to 350 degrees. Coat a baking dish lightly with olive oil.
2. Check to be sure the salmon is completely boned. If, when you run your fingers over the nonskin side, you find any bones, remove them with tweezers or by catching them between the side of your paring knife and your thumb. Place the salmon in the baking dish and coat all of it with a layer of mayonnaise about ⅛- to ¼-inch thick.
3. Bake for about 10 minutes for each inch of fish—measured at its thickest part, from top surface to bottom—or until the fish is done to your liking, either rare in the middle or well done throughout.
4. Serve immediately. Garnish with parsley and lemon, if you like.

Variation: Another way to cook salmon is to glaze a fillet with honey and mustard instead of mayonnaise. For a pound-sized fillet, mix 3 tablespoons of grainy Dijon mustard with 2 tablespoons of honey, a half-teaspoon of cider vinegar, and a little salt and pepper. Coat the salmon with this mixture and either broil it or bake as above.

9

SIDES TO THE CENTER

Supporting Cast

How luscious lies the pea within/The pod . . .
—*Emily Dickinson*

Animal, vegetable, or mineral? Or, more to the point, vegetable or fruit?

Well, in the kitchen, they overlap. Botanically speaking (you *were* speaking botanically, weren't you?), tomatoes, for example, are a fruit—technically, a berry—and also in the botanical category of fruit are eggplant, cucumbers, squash, pumpkins, green peas, and bell peppers. Can you see what they have in common? Seeds, especially on the inside. That's a large part of what makes them botanical fruits.

In the kitchen, there's only a little confusion. Pumpkin makes a lovely pie—aha! fruit!—as well as a nifty soup: oh! vegetable! Zucchini works in sweet bread as well as in a savory gratin; and potatoes roast very nicely with apples, onions, and garlic.

The United States Supreme Court has ruled—really!—on the tomato as fruit-or-vegetable issue. In 1883, American tariff laws included a tax on imported vegetables but not on fruits. In the case of *Nix. v. Hedden*, 149 U.S. 304 (1893), the court ruled that by popular definition and in common usage, tomatoes are vegetables, because they are usually served for dinner as a soup or side dish, but not as dessert, which is when one eats fruits. The court specified that it was not reclassifying tomatoes for botanical purposes—but only to decide whether or not a tax had to be paid on imported tomatoes. The plaintiff (Mr. Nix) had paid the tax (to Mr. Hedden, the tax collector) under protest—maintaining that tomatoes are fruits. After the Supreme Court ruling, poor Mr. Nix was given no refund. Thus, tomatoes are a fruit, unless—in the United States of America at least—you're having them for dinner or importing them, in which case they're a vegetable. Think of it this way: Tomatoes in the salad or the soup, stuffed, or in a sauce are a vegetable. Tomatoes in jam or green tomato pie (both of which are nicer than you'd think) are a fruit.

In the kitchen, the category of vegetables is pretty wide-ranging, from the flowers of broccoli to the stalks of celery to the roots that are carrots and parsnips. Here—in this chapter—because we are so broad-minded, we shall consider them all: the wonderfully common vegetables, and beans, and potatoes and rice, all including salad. These are the separate categories—vegetables, starches, beans, and salads—for the purposes of a cook, who might happily mix them all together with botanical, if not culinary, abandon.

The simplest statement is that vegetables are good for you. They hold vitamins, minerals, fiber, carbohydrates, antioxidants, flavonoids, carotenoids, and other good things. They are excellent fighters in the war against disease. Mother, once again, was right. (So is Michael Pollan, who wrote *In Defense of Food*. The book's cover says it all: "Eat food. Not too much. Mostly plants.")

But for all of that, vegetables have a bad reputation. Why? Is it just because the word has so many letters? Or is it that vegetables are so often badly cooked? I believe the latter, of course, and I faithfully insist that a well-cooked vegetable can be as delicious as—if not more delicious than—anything else. If you eat all your vegetables, in this chapter, you may have dessert, which is, given the nature of the meal, in a later chapter. My own opinion, to say it differently, is that well-cooked vegetables are just as wonderful as dessert. Well, maybe not quite as wonderful as ice cream, maybe. Or a good cookie. On the other hand, someday I'll try making butternut squash ice cream. (That seems very reasonable to me. Pumpkin ice cream is *good*.) I wouldn't put chocolate sauce on my broccoli, nor would I make cookies out of spinach—but there is a lot of latitude here; many vegetables are naturally sweet.

Hiding them—as spinach in the cookies—doesn't make much sense to me. In the first place, when vegetables are well cooked, they taste good. Hiding them implies they *need* to be hidden, and they don't. In the second place, generations of children have reached maturity without eating spinach left and right. In the third place, and perhaps most important, who can you trust?

If you aren't growing your own vegetables, the first step is buying them. Best choice, after your own garden, is a farmers' market; here you'll find local produce at its best. Second choice is a health food store. Third choice is making a good selection at a plain old market.

There are some things it helps to know about buying vegetables, and we'll get to them in chapter 13. For now, just remember that organic is always best, if it's not too expensive. Freshness, though, doesn't always matter as overwhelmingly as you think it might, no matter what we've been led to believe. My local supermarket puts together packages of endangered vegetables and fruits that sometimes are a rare bargain—tired red peppers, for instance, can be roasted and peeled, which gives them a whole new outlook on life; they're wonderful plain or with olive oil and garlic, and they add color and flavor to a great many dishes. On the other hand, mold and mush are not good things and they don't bode well for anything in the kitchen. Unless you're in fifth grade and as a science experiment you're supposed to put an orange in a dark place and forget about it for a while. But that, children know, is not cooking.

Storing, Peeling, Paring, and Scraping Vegetables

Once you have your vegetables in hand, however they arrived there, the best way to keep them as fresh as possible is, most of the time, to keep them in the refrigerator's vegetable drawer, just as the drawer itself says. You can keep many veggies (carrots and celery, for instance) in the fairly tight plastic bags they arrived in; others (broccoli and string beans, say) are best kept loosely in a plastic bag. Onions and garlic should be kept out in the air, at room temperature—already described in chapter 2. Things with a hard shell—like the various winter squashes—can be kept out at room temperature too (and they're lovely to look at); tomatoes should also be kept at room temperature—never in the refrigerator—and it works best to keep them with the stem end down, which helps prevent moisture and bacteria from entering. Beans can be kept in their package, or in a jar, on a shelf; potatoes should be kept at room temperature in a relatively dark spot. All of them, every last one, should be used with reasonable promptness. Vegetables lose nutrients while they stand around waiting for you to do something with them. Of course, if you have a root cellar, you can keep your turnips and beets and things underground for the winter. You have to be willing, then, to go down and get them. Otherwise, cook everything soon after you have bought it. Or picked it, depending on your good fortune. All vegetables need to be cleaned before they're cooked, and some need more than just a rinse in fresh water. Carrots need to be scraped (with a knife, running up and down the carrot's length) or peeled with a swivel-bladed peeler. Broccoli needs to have its stalks peeled. Spinach needs to be stemmed. (More about all this in chapter 13.)

Roasting

Cooking vegetables for their own sake (as opposed to using them as part of a soup or a stew) doesn't have to harken back to the meat-two-vegetables-and-a-starch days of yore. A vegetable can be a simple side dish or it can be front and center, a splashy display that is becomingly modest at one and the same time.

Roasting vegetables means cooking them in the oven, with olive oil and whatever flavorings you want, until they're lightly browned, and therefore intense and slightly sweet. You can do almost any vegetable this way. They can be mixed right in the baking pan—why bother with a bowl? And they should cook at relatively high heat (400 degrees or a little more) until they're done (tender and a little charred around the edges), usually between twenty and forty-five minutes, sometimes a bit longer. What goes along with vegetables to be roasted? Sliced garlic is lovely. An herb—thyme and rosemary are my own favorites, but there are many other possibilities. A touch of sugar sometimes, or a bit of honey. Salt and pepper, but we knew that. Another vegetable? What a good idea!

Boiling, Blanching, and Steaming

A way of cooking vegetables ahead—string beans and broccoli come to mind—is to plunge them into a large pot of boiling salted water. Keep a colander or a strainer handy in the sink. Let the veggies boil for about five minutes, and then start testing them for doneness. For me, a crisp vegetable is really just a variation on a raw vegetable; I like my cooked string beans (and all the other vegetables) on the softer side of crisp. When the vegetable has reached the consistency that pleases you most, quickly pour the contents of the pot—vegetable and water—into the colander or strainer. You can eat them immediately, with a little butter or olive oil, and salt and pepper, or you can cook with them—let's say you sautéed some onion or shallot until it was soft; you could then add the vegetables to the same pan, mix well, add salt and pepper and, if you like, an herb, and there you have a lovely dish. Or you can keep the vegetables to reheat later. In that case, as soon as the hot water has drained, turn on the cold water (there you are, in the sink, and it's right there with you), and let it run over the hot vegetables until they're reasonably cool. Refrigerate them if it's going to be more than two or three hours before you need them again.

Blanching a vegetable means first cooking it briefly in boiling water—not until it's completely done—and then plunging it into cold water to stop the cooking process. Some vegetables are blanched before they're frozen or canned.

Steaming is a lovely way to cook vegetables. A foldable steamer works with most pots, but all you need to do if you don't have one is keep the vegetables above the water level. Set a rack inside a pot, and place a bowl—holding the veggies—on the rack. If you have a steamer complete unto itself, count your blessings. Again, steam until the vegetables are done to your taste. Save the water when you drain the veggies; it's good for adding to soup or stews. You can partially cook most vegetables—boiling and blanching is the classic way, called parboiling. But some vegetables, like carrots or beets, can be roasted until they're almost done, and then finished later, or used as an ingredient in a more complicated dish.

Potatoes, Rice, and Beans

The most important thing to know about potatoes is that they come in extremes, like the right and the left and the independents. There are baking potatoes and boiling potatoes. And there's the middle. How can you tell which is which? It's easy. Potatoes are either brown, red, or white. (Or purple or blue, but that's another story.) Baking potatoes are always brown; they're elongated ovals; and when they're cooked, they have a soft, mealy sort of texture. Baking potatoes—like Russets and Idahos—have a high starch content. They're wonderful—

wonderful—simply baked and eaten with butter and sour cream or just plain. If you want good baked potatoes, don't rub them with oil; don't wrap them in tinfoil; don't put them in a microwave. Simply prick them gently with the point of a knife or the tines of a fork two or three times, put them on an oven shelf, and bake at 350 or 400 degrees until they're soft when you press them—usually about an hour. Making the holes with a knife or a fork is important; if you don't do that, steam will expand inside the potato and it might explode, leaving a great mess behind in your oven. If you're in a great rush, slice the potato in half or in quarters, and roast the pieces—mixed with a little melted butter or olive oil—in a baking dish. These are truly nice potatoes—they're just not the same as having a whole baked potato on your dish.

Red- and white-skinned potatoes are different. They're low-starch, called waxy, and hold their shape when they're in a soup, a stew, or a salad. They are usually boiled; they can be eaten just that way, sliced and cooked in a variety of ways, or they can be fried, grated, stewed, or used to make all the variations on potato salad.

And then there are Yukon Golds. They're brown-skinned, but round—not like the oval bakers—and their flesh is a buttery yellow. They're good baked or boiled or cooked in any number of ways. They're the independents. Or, if you prefer, they're in the middle, with some of the qualities of both baking and boiling potatoes, and good flavor of their own.

There are dozens—no, hundreds—of ways to cook potatoes, and they're cooked in countries around the world, from the fries that were probably born in Belgium rather than France, to the soups and stews of Peru—where potatoes originated. *Potato* is from the Spanish *patata*, which is from the South American *papa*. In many countries, potatoes are called *earth apples*—the fruit of the earth—*pommes de terre* in France, *Erdäpfel* in Austria. In Finland, *peruna*, the word for potato, means earth pear, in Persian, *seeb-i-zameen*, ground apple. In every language, potatoes are a blessing—they're delicious, go with almost everything, are easy to cook, good for you, and they're filling and sustaining. The fruit of the earth indeed.

Rice is less fanciful, less adaptable. Still—it has long been a nutritious and filling staple and it's the basis of many a wonderful dish. While potatoes are a tuber (they grow underground near the surface), rice is a grass. Potatoes grow in the dark, while rice reaches for the light. A large part of the world uses rice as the basis of its diet—pilaf, for instance, in the Middle East, is the center of a meal; in many parts of Asia, it's sustaining. Only those who are fortunate enough to have more than enough food think of rice as a side dish.

White rice doesn't have as much to offer, nutritionally, as brown. White rice is processed rice; the germ has been removed from the grains, and sometimes it has been polished and buffed as well. White rice can be enriched, but at heart, it has no heart. It's fairly close to empty calories, and it isn't good for blood sugar. Brown rice, on the other hand, is the whole grain, with only the chaff removed (you remember about telling the chaff from the wheat?). It contains a bevy of nutrients, including protein—though it needs certain other foods to become a complete protein. The rice and beans of Central and South America are a perfect example of a complete protein: Neither rice nor beans is a complete protein by itself, but they each have something the other lacks. Together, they have it all. There are many other food combinations like that—split pea soup with whole grain bread, tortillas with refried beans, hummus with pita. . . .

Cooking rice is not difficult, no matter what the myths may be. The way to cook both white or brown rice is to use twice as much water as rice—1 cup of rice, for instance, needs 2 cups of water. Add a half teaspoon of salt and a tablespoon of butter or olive oil; stir. Bring to the boil; reduce heat; cover; and cook white rice for fifteen minutes and brown rice for fifty minutes, unless the package directions are different. Test (eat some!) to be sure it's done, cover again, remove from the heat, and let stand for five minutes. (If it wasn't done when you tested, add a little more water if needed, cover, and cook five minutes longer. Test again.) Fluff with a fork before serving.

Beans are another kind of seed, and wonderful is what they are, whether cooked into soup or a kind of stew, or eaten as a vegetable or salad. They can stand on their own—like potatoes and rice—or they can offer a platform, a place on which to build, for the simplest or the most complicated compilations of food.

Cooking with beans usually means planning ahead—because most beans need to be presoaked and precooked (directions are on the package)—unless you buy a can of beans, and in that case all you need is a can opener (and a strainer in which to rinse them). Canned beans are good, never to be scorned, always to be admired as a convenience and a help. But dried beans, given the luxury of an overnight soak or the aid of a quicker drench in water that has been brought to the boil, have a quality of their own, a smoothness and richness that feels very good to the soul as well as the mouth. That's part of it, of course—it feels so good to make beans from scratch. They look so industrious, all by themselves, swelling in a pot of water; they make me feel virtuous. And they're much less expensive.

One thought: Once eaten, beans are famous for producing, in a word, gas. Nothing wrong with a little gas, but to avoid as much as possible without resorting to chemistry, soak your own beans, drain them before cooking them, cook them in a supply of fresh water, and drain them again before you embellish them further. You lose a certain amount of nutrition and flavor—just a little, really—but you gain a lot in terms of peace and quiet. And there's plenty of nutrition and flavor left.

Salad—Washing and Drying Salad Greens

You can make a salad out of almost anything—cold meat, chicken, seafood, pasta, eggs, cheese, fruit, vegetables—but the classic salad is simply greens in a vinaigrette dressing. Greens can be the varieties of lettuce, from crisp iceberg to buttery soft Bibb, with sturdy romaine and red and green leaf lettuce in the middle. The bitter greens include arugula, spinach, endive, escarole, and dandelion leaves, among others. Mesclun is a mixture (which is what *mesclun* means; it comes first from the French—it originated in Provence—*mescla*, to mix, related to the Latin for mixed, *miscellus,* whence, you can see, miscellaneous). The salad leaves in mesclun are young, and usually include leaf lettuce, arugula, frisée, radicchio, and a variety of other small leafy vegetables.

Unless they're in a package that says "prewashed"—and sometimes even then—all lettuces should be washed before using. In a perfect world, you'd wash them right after you brought them home, rinsing them in cold water until the water runs clear, not in a spinner, necessarily—a large bowl or pot will do—and then you'd scoop them out (not drain them, which would just redistribute the grit) and shake off as much water as you could and you'd put them on a flat terry-cloth or tea towel; you'd fold up the towel and you'd put it in the refrigerator inside a plastic bag. Then, when you needed greens, you'd open the towel and take what you needed, and you'd be amazed at how crisp and fresh and terrifically good your beautiful lettuce leaves would be. If you have a spinner—and room—you could wash and spin them, and store them in the refrigerator still in the spinner.

Making a Vinaigrette Dressing

A classic vinaigrette, to go with your beautiful greens, is a mixture of olive oil and vinegar, in proportions that suit your taste. Start with two tablespoons of vinegar to three of oil, and then try changing the ratio to find what you like best (some people like half and half; others like to just wave the vinegar bottle over the salad). Extra virgin first cold pressed is what olive oil means here. (See chapter 7.) Vinegar is usually red wine, but it can also be made from white wine, champagne, sherry, or a variety of other ingredients, including figs, pears, and berries. Buy the best vinegar you can find—you're going to mix it with the best olive oil, after all—except for balsamic vinegar. The best balsamic vinegar you can find has been aged for twenty-five years or longer and is priced accordingly. It's thick and deeply rich and complex in flavor. Even if you can afford to buy it at the rate of several hundred dollars for a small bottle, you probably can think of better things to do with it than mixing it with a bowl of lettuce. Commercial balsamics, the kind you find in the supermarket, have a nifty flavor even if all they are is wine vinegar with added coloring and sugar—though they may be a little more than that. A lovely thing to do with balsamic vinegar is to buy a bottle—organic is best—and pour it into a sauce-pan and boil it down until it's thick and syrupy. It's delicious with roasted red peppers, for instance, or sprinkled over the classic Caprese Salad—made with mozzarella, sliced fresh tomatoes, and fresh basil.

Once you have the kind of vinegar you want, and know the ratio of vinegar and oil you like best, it's time to consider all the other things that can be added to a vinaigrette dressing. Herbs, most obviously. A simple, classic dressing that goes with almost anything is made with one or two finely diced shallots and a tablespoon or two of Dijon mustard, both mixed into oil and vinegar and poured over well-washed and dried greens. (A good method of mixing the dressing is to measure everything into a small jar, put the lid on, and then shake it well.) Drying the greens, it must be said again, is very important, whether you use a salad spinner or a terry-cloth towel. Wet greens means the dressing can't adhere to the leaves (you remember about oil and water not mixing), and you end up with an unappetizing pool of liquid at the bottom of the salad bowl.

There are many other kinds of salad dressings—mayonnaise, most obviously, or mayonnaise mixed with many other things, from blue cheese to buttermilk, or both at once. Oscar Wilde summed up salads rather nicely. "To make a good salad," he said, "is to be a brilliant diplomatist—the problem is entirely the same in both cases. To know exactly how much oil one must put with one's vinegar."

General procedure for roasting vegetables (or cooking them on the stove-top) is on page 167, and directions for a green salad with vinaigrette dressing are on page 172.

Sweet and Sour Carrots

....

This way of cooking carrots is also excellent for string beans and, I'm sure, many other vegetables that I haven't yet tried.

2 tablespoons extra virgin olive oil or unsalted butter

12 carrots, cut into narrow sticks

2 small onions, quartered and sliced into crescents (see Note below about how to slice the onions)

1 apple, peeled, cored, quartered, and cubed

¼ to ½ cup apple juice

2 tablespoons dried currants or raisins

1 tablespoon dark brown sugar

2 tablespoons fresh lemon juice

Salt and freshly ground black pepper

Optional garnish: chopped fresh flat-leaf parsley

1. Heat oil in a sauté pan. Add carrots, onion, and apple, and cook, stirring occasionally, over medium heat for 25 minutes or until lightly golden.

2. Add ¼ cup apple juice and the remaining ingredients and continue to cook over medium-low heat, stirring occasionally, for 15 minutes, or until carrots are tender. (Add a little more juice if needed, but the liquid should be thick and syrupy.) Taste and adjust seasoning. Serve hot or at room temperature; sprinkle parsley over the top before serving, if using.

SERVES 4

Note: Slice each quarter-onion the long way, from top to bottom, rather than across, up to the root end. Remove the root to separate the crescent slices.

Variation: Another fine way to cook carrots (or butternut squash, parsnips, sweet potatoes, or rutabaga—one, some, or all together) is to glaze slices or chunks with cider and brown sugar: Use about ½ cup of apple cider and 2 tablespoons of brown sugar, mixed with a pound of carrots, sliced. Add salt and freshly ground black pepper, mix, spread in a lightly buttered pan, and roast at 400 degrees for 30 minutes to an hour, stirring from time to time, until the carrots are tender and glazed. (Add more cider if the pan is too dry, but you want a syrupy mixture—or just a glaze—at the end.) Mix in a little unsalted butter, and garnish, if you like, with chopped parsley leaves.

Roast Tomatoes Two Ways

. . . .

One way is savory and the other is sweet, but both are meant to be served with dinner, not after. (Thus they must be taxed as vegetables, as described on page 163.)

Slow Roasted Tomatoes

Extra virgin olive oil

Fresh tomatoes, peeled (see page 178)

Thyme, dried or fresh

Salt and freshly ground black pepper

Garlic, peeled and halved

1. Preheat oven to 250 degrees. Lightly film a baking dish with olive oil.
2. Halve the tomatoes and place them cut side down in the baking dish. Sprinkle with thyme, salt, and pepper, and dribble additional olive oil over each tomato. Tuck garlic halves among the tomatoes.
3. Bake for 3 to 4 hours, checking from time to time, basting the tomatoes with the oil in the pan and adding more oil if needed. The tomatoes will shrink to about half of their original size, and will be wrinkly and thin, but not dried on the inside. They'll still be bright red.
4. Store the tomatoes in a jar in the refrigerator for up to 2 weeks, or freeze them—either way, cover the tomatoes with olive oil.

Use the tomatoes as a pasta sauce, as a spread for bruschetta, or to add to soup or stew. They're also delicious just as is—intense and sweet, and full of flavor.

Sweet Roasted Tomatoes

2 tablespoons unsalted butter or extra virgin olive oil or a
combination
6 small garden-ripe tomatoes, peeled, or 1 28-oz. can whole
tomatoes (Muir Glen is excellent) in juice, drained
*To peel fresh tomatoes, cut a shallow X in the non-stem end; bring a
pot of water to the boil, drop the tomatoes in and cook them for 15
seconds. Immediately remove them and plunge them into cold water.
The peel should slip off.*
1 tablespoon sugar
½ teaspoon salt
½ teaspoon freshly ground black pepper

1. Preheat the oven to 350 degrees. Lightly film a baking dish with olive oil, or, if you're using it, butter.
2. Halve fresh tomatoes across their equator; leave canned tomatoes whole. Place tomatoes in the baking dish (cut side up, if halved) and sprinkle with sugar, salt, and pepper. Dot with butter cut into small pieces, or sprinkle with olive oil. Baste once or twice as the tomatoes cook.
3. Bake for 1½ to 2 hours, or until the tomatoes are soft and browned. Serve warm or at room temperature.

Venerable Vegetables: Potatoes, Apples, and Onions

Potatoes, apples and onions—the very stuff of life. Apples are sweet, onions are sharp, and potatoes are earthy. They have spirited conversations in a roasting pan, moderated and soothed by good olive oil and, if you like, a bit of butter. As easy as that.

Extra virgin olive oil
4 potatoes (Yukon Gold, or baking potatoes), peeled and chunked
1 tart, firm apple (Granny Smith works excellently), peeled, cored, chopped
1 onion, chopped
Optional: If you add one or two sweet potatoes, peeled and chunked, you'll serve more people. The addition works very well.
Salt and freshly ground black pepper
Optional: unsalted butter

1. Preheat the oven to 375 degrees. Film a baking dish with olive oil.
2. Add the potatoes, apple, and onion to the baking dish (and the sweet potatoes, if you're using them), and sprinkle with salt and pepper. Stir. Add additional olive oil—1 or 2 tablespoons, and stir again. If you also want to use butter, dot 1 or 2 tablespoons, in small pieces, over the top. Roast for 45 minutes to 1 hour, stirring occasionally, until the potatoes and onions have browned lightly, and the potatoes are tender.

SERVES 4 TO 6,
depending on the optional addition of sweet potatoes

Rice and Butternut Squash

. . . .

Essentially, this is a sort of deconstructed reconstructed risotto. Faux risotto, that is. My recipe takes off from one I found in a small cookbook my sister brought me from Venice, called The Gondolier's Cook Book, *a happy— but probably inaccurate—image.*

> 1 pound butternut squash, peeled, seeded, and cut into large cubes
>   (see Note below about how to prepare butternut squash for
>   cooking)
> 2 cups milk
> 1 teaspoon salt, divided
> 1 cup rice
> 2 tablespoons unsalted butter
> ¼ cup Parmigiano Reggiano cheese

1. Rinse a saucepan with cold water, and without drying it add the squash, milk, and ½ teaspoon salt. Bring to a simmer, lower the heat, and cook, covered, for 10 minutes.
2. Add the rice, the remaining salt, and the butter, stir, and continue to cook, covered, over low heat for 15 minutes or until the rice and squash are soft. Stir occasionally as it cooks.
3. Stir in the cheese—and additional butter, if you're in that mood— and serve.

SERVES 4 TO 6

Note: To prepare butternut squash, slice across above where it swells out. Cut each piece in half the long way. Remove the seeds. Peel with a swivel-bladed peeler.

Important: Keep in mind that if the heat the rice is cooked over is too high, the pan will scorch on the bottom. It won't affect the taste, but it'll be a major project to clean. This is the sad voice of experience.

Thoughts and variations on butternut squash: Butternut squash is so good—but even so, it seems underused, perhaps because peeling, seeding, and cutting it seems like a chore. As mentioned earlier, many supermarkets now sell it with the work already done, in a neat package. In any case, whether you peel it yourself or not, it makes a lovely vegetable—either roasted in the usual way (mixed with olive oil and baked at 400 degrees for 30 to 40 minutes, or until it's soft and lightly browned), or mixed with heavy cream (about a quarter-inch in the bottom of the pan), thyme, salt, and freshly ground black pepper and baked at 400 degrees for 30 minutes, until the squash is soft and lightly browned and the cream has thickened. (It'll thicken more if you let it stand for five minutes before serving.) Luscious by itself and extra-luscious with Parmigiano sprinkled over the top.

Unstuffed Grape Leaves

. . . .

Here is another vote for the easy way. Is this laziness? No. This isn't a lazy recipe. But it's easier than stuffing all those little leaves. Yes, they are delicious—but a lot of what's delicious is their stuffing, and using the stuffing this way means having it more often, and that makes delicious even better.

Boiling water

1 cup long-grained rice

3 or 4 tomatoes (2 peeled and chopped; 1 or 2 peeled and sliced)

1 large onion, chopped

2 tablespoons chopped flat-leaf parsley

¼ teaspoon ground cinnamon

¼ teaspoon ground allspice

3 tablespoons dried currants

¼ cup pine nuts

4 cloves garlic, peeled and halved

1 teaspoon salt

½ teaspoon freshly ground black pepper

¼ cup extra virgin olive oil

1 lemon, juiced

2 tablespoons sugar

1. Pour boiling water over the rice; mix well; drain. Rinse with cold water and drain again. In a bowl, mix the rice with the chopped tomatoes, onion, parsley, cinnamon, allspice, currants, pine nuts, garlic, salt, and pepper.

2. Line the bottom of a large saucepan with the sliced tomatoes. Add the rice. Mix the olive oil with 1½ cups fresh cold water, lemon juice, and sugar, and pour over the rice.

3. Bring to a boil, lower the heat, and cook, covered, for ½ hour or until the rice is soft, checking once or twice as it cooks to see if more water is needed. Taste and adjust the seasoning, adding more salt and pepper and more lemon juice or sugar, as necessary. Serve hot, warm, or cool.

SERVES 6 TO 8

Note: If you want to stuff grape leaves, buy a jar, pour boiling water over the leaves in a bowl, and let them soak for 20 minutes. Rinse well with cold water (or blanch fresh grape leaves for a few seconds in boiling water). To stuff, place a leaf flat on a board or plate; add a heaping teaspoon of filling near the stem, fold the stem over the filling, fold the sides in, and roll up. Squeeze lightly. Place the stuffed leaves over the sliced tomatoes, pour olive oil mixed with ⅔ cup of water, lemon juice, and sugar over, and top with a plate to hold the rolls down firmly. Cover and simmer for 1 hour, adding water frequently as the rice absorbs it. Allow to cool in the pan. Makes about 35 to 40 stuffed grape leaves.

Cucumber Salad

A Hungarian restaurant in New York City used to put a small dish of cucumber salad on every table, which made studying the menu much more enjoyable. The restaurant is gone, alas, but this is reasonably close to their salad.

1 English cucumber (the long kind, plastic-wrapped) or 3 kirby
     cucumbers, peeled and thinly sliced
2 teaspoons salt
¼ medium red onion, minced
1 clove garlic, crushed and finely minced (see page 24 for how to
     crush garlic)
2 tablespoons white vinegar
1 teaspoon sugar
2 tablespoons fresh cold water
Freshly ground black pepper
Optional: ½ cup sour cream, regular or low-fat, *not* no-fat
Optional garnish: sweet paprika and chopped flat-leaf parsley

1. Place the cucumber slices in a bowl; add the salt; stir well and let stand, chilled, for 20 to 30 minutes, until most of the liquid has drained off. Squeeze the cucumbers to eliminate more liquid; rinse well with cold water. Pat dry with paper towels.
2. Place the slices back in the (rinsed) bowl and add the remaining ingredients. Serve plain or mix in sour cream. Garnish with a sprinkling of paprika and some chopped parsley.

SERVES 4

Russian Potato Salad

A *classic Russian vegetable salad, called* Vinegret (*or sometimes* Salade Olivier, *though the original* Olivier *included cold meats*), *is a variety of cooked vegetables mixed with dill and either a vinaigrette dressing or mayonnaise and sour cream. This is a variation—I like the potatoes and beets best, so I've eliminated most of the other vegetables. You could add them back if you wanted—they're peas and carrots, mostly.*

4 medium potatoes (Yukon Gold or red boiling potatoes)
2 medium beets
2 tablespoons dill pickle, diced
¼ cup regular or low-fat sour cream (*not* no-fat)
¼ cup Hellmann's mayonnaise, regular or light (*not* low-fat)
1 tablespoon Dijon mustard
1 tablespoon horseradish (white or red)
1 tablespoon cider vinegar
2 teaspoons sugar
Salt and freshly ground black pepper

1. Boil the potatoes in lightly salted water for 20 minutes, or until tender when pierced with the tip of a paring knife. Let cool, peel, slice thickly or chunk, and place in a bowl.
2. Either boil the beets for 20 minutes, or roast them as described on page 186. Let cool, and peel. Dice the beets and add to the potatoes. Add the pickle cubes.
3. Mix the sour cream, mayonnaise, mustard, horseradish, vinegar, and sugar and add to the bowl; add the salt and pepper to taste. Mix gently. Cover and refrigerate for at least 30 minutes before serving.

SERVES 4 TO 6

Roasted Beet Salad

. . . .

Roasting the beets, rather than boiling them, gives them a deeper flavor and a beautiful color. They're also remarkably easy to peel once they're cooked, and you can roast them at least a day ahead; keep them wrapped in their own foil. In addition to this salad and Russian Potato Salad, you can also use them for soup (see Summer Borscht, Page 72), add lemon juice and sugar to make them sweet and sour, or heat them, sliced, with a little butter and serve them hot. Any which way you do it: yum.

4 to 8 beets, of a roughly uniform size

3 tablespoons extra virgin olive oil plus more for the roasting

¼ cup red onion, chopped, or 3 scallions, chopped (white and green parts)

1 tablespoon red wine vinegar

Salt and freshly ground black pepper

Optional: 1 or 2 tablespoons cooked beet greens (see Note)

Optional garnish: flat-leaf parsley, chopped

1. Place the beets on a large sheet of aluminum foil. Sprinkle lightly with a few drops of olive oil, and wrap tightly. Place directly on an oven rack and bake at 400 degrees for 1 to 1½ hours, or until the beets feel soft when pressed. Let cool before opening. (You can do this a day or two ahead.) Peel the beets over the foil, using your fingers—the peel will slip right off; scrape any stuck spots off with a knife. Slice the beets into a bowl. Discard the foil-wrapped peel.

2. Add the olive oil, onion, vinegar, salt and pepper. Taste to adjust seasoning; add more vinegar and the beet greens if you like. Garnish with parsley. Serve cold or at room temperature.

SERVES 4 TO 6

Note: If you have fresh beets, don't discard the greens. Wash them carefully and well, and slice them across in wide strips. Briefly sauté a chopped scallion or a little chopped red onion in olive oil; add the greens, salt and pepper, and a teaspoon or two of red wine vinegar. Stir, cover, and cook for 10 minutes, or until the greens are soft. They're lovely as is, but save a few tablespoons to chop roughly and add to the beet salad.

Black-eyed Pea Salad

....

According to tradition in the southern part of the United States, it's good luck to eat black-eyed peas on New Year's Day. What makes them lucky? One theory is that during the Civil War, when Union troops scoured the countryside for edibles, they ignored black-eyed peas, which they considered animal feed—and as a result, many Southern families survived who mightn't have made it otherwise. Another explanation is that traditional Jews, dating back to ancient Babylonia, considered black-eyed peas to be good-luck symbols; after the Spanish Inquisition, Sephardic Jews began arriving in Georgia early in the eighteenth century. Their practice of eating black-eyed peas for luck spread to other southern states from there. The New Year's dish of black-eyes is often served with cooked greens— good luck with folding money. I like this salad on any day of the year.

1 15-ounce can of black-eyed peas, drained and rinsed
¼ cup chopped red onions
4 tablespoons olive oil
3 tablespoons vinegar
¼ cup chopped Italian parsley leaves
Pinch of salt
¼ teaspoon of freshly ground black pepper, or to taste
Optional: 1 to 2 teaspoons chopped cilantro

1. Mix all ingredients. Let stand before serving for the flavors to meld.

SERVES 4

Blue Buttermilk Salad Dressing

The Romans, responsible for so much, liked salads. They sauced their raw vegetables with either oil and vinegar or a salty brine. Sal is Latin for salt; herba salata means salted herb. Salad comes in a straight line from salata. Feel free, historically, to salt your herbs. Or you could make this very simple, refreshing, and good salad dressing.

¼ cup Hellmann's mayonnaise (plain or reduced fat, *not* low-fat)
¼ cup sour cream (full or reduced fat, *not* low-fat)
2 to 4 tablespoons buttermilk
1 teaspoon wine vinegar
1 teaspoon Dijon mustard
Freshly ground black pepper
4 tablespoons blue cheese

1. Mix the mayonnaise, sour cream, 2 tablespoons of buttermilk, vinegar, mustard, and pepper. Add the blue cheese, crumbled right into the dressing, leaving large chunks. If the sauce is too thick, add the remaining buttermilk. The dressing can be mixed (ahead, if you like) in the empty salad bowl, and the greens added over it to be tossed. Serve immediately.

YIELD: ABOUT ¾ CUP, OR ENOUGH FOR ABOUT
4 SERVINGS OF SALAD, DEPENDING ON SIZE.
Increase amounts proportionately for additional servings.

10

THE DAIRY

From Milk to Cheese, with Stops Between

Poets have been mysteriously silent on the subject of cheese.
—*G. K. Chesterton*

Writer and critic Clifton Fadiman, longtime host of radio's *Information Please*, is remembered in food circles for having said that cheese is milk's leap toward immortality. For my money, since cheese can't live forever any more than milk can, I think milk, which is where it all starts, should get top billing. After all, milk, left to its own devices, gives us cream, and in its next metamorphosis, butter— neither of which is yet cheese. That doesn't even begin to mention cows, since none of us likes to remember where our food really comes from. We need to offer blessings on cows for giving us so much.

Today's dairy farms are highly mechanized from beginning to end, from how cows are fed to the machines that do the milking. It wasn't always so. The traditional, stereotypical image of a dairy maid is of a buxom, rosy-cheeked young woman, carrying pails of milk from the barn to the kitchen, perhaps flirting with the stable boy along the way, and trying her best to keep the lord of the manor at a distance. Somewhat along those lines, France's Louis XVI gave Marie Antoinette a dairy farm of her very own before they both lost their heads. She had what was called an ornamental farm at Versailles—a very fashionable thing to have then, and, at about the same time that the farm was built, Louis had the dairy farm (the *laiterie d'agrement*, or the pleasure dairy) made for her near his hunting lodge in Rambouillet. She didn't like the lodge—too gloomy—and he hoped she'd be more willing to visit there if she had the dairy to play with. It was a pretty setting, a place to have a light meal, or some sort of dessert. One Louis generation earlier, Louis XV's daughters were rowed to *their* pleasure dairy in gondolas, followed by a sloop carrying musicians, who performed as the princesses and their guests ate.

Jean-Jacques Rousseau recommended pleasure dairies in his 1762 book *Émile*. He believed in simple, seasonal, and natural food—so far, so good—and specifically suggested keeping a cow as a source of fresh dairy products.

Now, I'm not recommending that you keep your own cow. In fact, I have to quibble with Rousseau, since he also believed that a woman's primary function is to nurse her children. (But how did the children get there? How primary is *that* function?) Apparently, Rousseau believed that because they are capable of producing them, women must love dairy products. Does this mean that men don't love dairy products? Or because they aren't capable of producing dairy products, they love them—and the necessary equipment—all the more? Male or female, you may not have a pleasure dairy, but you do have a refrigerator, and therefore you can have long-lasting supplies of your favorite forms of milk, cream, butter, buttermilk, yogurt, sour cream, cheese, and even ice cream. And there is so much you can do with those things— beginning with the pure pleasure of drinking a glass of milk when you're thirsty, or eating a chunk of cheese when you're hungry, or just spreading a hunk of good bread with some equally good butter at any time of day or night. (Yes! There are definite differences in the quality of butter. More on this soon.)

Milk and Cream

Milk at the market means understanding a few basics. Whole milk, for instance, is not quite what it says: The cream has been removed; it's that much less whole. In a perfect world, it would be called partial milk.

What can be removed next is the remaining milk fat, in varying degrees: there's 2% milk, 1% milk, and skim milk, each with less fat than the one before. Skim milk has no fat at all—it has all, yes, been skimmed away. Does it matter which kind of milk you use in a recipe? Not usually, not unless you're baking, sometimes not even then. (Baking is more complicated because fat content matters in cakes, cookies, pies, and puddings.) And this is important: Very often you can get away with using canned evaporated skim milk, even when cream is called for. It works in sauces; it works in cream soups. Keep a can of evaporated skim milk in your pantry. When the hurricane comes, you'll still have milk, and in the meantime, you'll have healthier soup and sauce because you've saved all those grams of fat from falling into your dinner.

Cream, of course, is full of fat—that's why it tastes so good. Among the things you can do with cream that you can't do with milk: When you've ladled cream soups into mugs or bowls, you can float a little bit of cream on the top by carefully and gently pouring it into a spoon that you hold just under the surface. That's a pretty effect, and it adds a rich taste to the soup.

Whipping Cream

Best of all, you can whip cream. The way to whip is to use a cold bowl (either put it briefly in the freezer, if you have room, or in the refrigerator until it feels cold to your fingers) and cold beaters. If you whip it by hand—I doubt that you will—use wide strokes and your wrist more than your arm. Whether by hand or in an electric mixer, vary your speed—moderate until it begins to form clouds of cream, then faster until it's nearly firm, and then more slowly toward the end. Whipping cream in the food processor is remarkably easy, but the end result doesn't have the cloudlike loft of cream that has been whipped in a mixer or by hand. If you have a mixer, and the time (just a few minutes, really) and the energy, use it. If not—and if puffy billows of cream don't matter—by all means use the processor. It works. It's fast. It's easy.

You can happily add things to whipped cream—a bit of booze or a liqueur, a dash of cinnamon, a bit of cocoa—but the basics are simply cream and air. A spoonful of sugar, if you like. A drop or two of vanilla, perhaps. But it all comes down to cream and air; they make magic together and everything else is more wonder added to what already *is* a wonder.

Butter and Buttermilk

If you whip cream long enough, it turns into butter. It's fun—at least once—to do that on purpose, though it's hardly economical. You need a lot of cream to make a little butter, because what you leave behind is a kind of skimmed cream: buttermilk. Light and creamy and low in fat, buttermilk adds a nifty tang to a variety of foods—like pancakes and muffins, salad dressings and desserts. (A buttermilk salad dressing is on page 189, and buttermilk blueberry muffins on page 254.)

Making your own butter isn't anything like the way it used to be done on the farm (with a churn, by hand) but it's easy and fast, and it's fun to do just to see how it happens—and to taste. Start with one or two cups of heavy (or whipping) cream—not ultrapasteurized, if you can find it. Put it in the food processor and turn the processor on; that's all you have to do other than watch. The cream will go through its stages: frothy and bubbly; softly whipped; firmly whipped, and then sort of a crumbly-looking mess, and then it turns out that the mess is the beginning of butter. There will be bits of butter at first, and after a second or two, a glob of butter will separate from the remaining liquid (that liquid is the buttermilk). Strain the butter over a bowl, saving the extraordinarily delicious fresh buttermilk, and then pat and push the butter (with your hands, a potato masher, a wooden spoon, or two forks) to get as much liquid out of it as possible. Add a bit of plain cold water to the butter, and continue working it until it's firm and water stops oozing from it. Presto! Chango! Butter.

If you like salted butter, add a bit of salt and work it in. If you like European-style butter (if you've never tasted it, try it!), add one or two tablespoons of yogurt or sour cream to the cream before you start whipping it and let it sit unwhipped at room temperature for about twelve hours; then put it in the processor and let it go to work. Cream was always slightly soured back on the farm, where it had to sit and wait until enough had been skimmed off the milk to make the work of churning worthwhile. In Europe, butter is still made from cultured cream; in the United States, it isn't.

Sour Cream and Crème Fraîche

A friend of mine says that a spoonful of sour cream makes anything taste better except a dry martini. I don't disagree; I add only that the same thing is true of whipped cream. But what, you ask, is *sour* cream? If it has gone bad, why eat it?

It isn't sour in that sense; it's what is called "cultured"—which doesn't mean that it goes to the ballet. It means that lactic acid bacteria have been added to milk under controlled conditions. The bacteria—those devils—produce lactic acid by fermenting lactose, a sugar naturally present in milk and cream. This is why lactose-intolerant people can often drink buttermilk (or eat yogurt, sour cream, and cheese) without any ill effects—the bacteria have forged ahead first, and gotten rid of a lot of the lactose. When milk had to sit to allow the cream to separate, and then the cream had to sit until there was enough to churn, the bacteria were at work, making the milk and cream sufficiently acid to keep other, nastier bacteria away, but without affecting the taste of the milk and cream so much that people would also be kept away. The end result of all this is sour cream, yogurt, and buttermilk, and they're all fine. And you thought all bacteria were bad!

Milk, to sum up so far, gives us cream, which can be churned to make butter, and what's left from that process is buttermilk. All of that is like Chinese boxes or Russian dolls, but much more magical. And nicer to eat. Sour cream and cheese come along in their own turns, equally magical—kitchen science aside.

Making Crème Fraîche

Another good thing to know about sour cream: Mix it (in almost any proportion, as long as there's more sour cream) with sweet cream and the result is an immediate sort of crème fraîche. French for fresh cream, crème fraîche is slightly tangy, slightly nutty, slightly sour, slightly sweet. Did I say wonderful? It is. It can be used in a variety of ways—dolloped over a bowl of soup, to make a fast sauce, with fruit, by itself with a bit of sugar . . . and lots more. In France, crème fraîche is made from naturally cultured cream (or it used to be); in other places—and it's more and more available throughout Europe and some of the United States—it's processed.

A slower version of crème fraîche is also fun to make. It's done by adding a little buttermilk to a lot of cream—about 1 tablespoon of buttermilk to each cup of cream, heating it very gently to no more than 110 degrees Fahrenheit (just above body temperature), mixing it, and letting it stand until it thickens, usually at least twelve hours, sometimes longer—up to about twenty-four hours. Mix it several times, tasting it each time, as you go along. When it's done, keep it refrigerated.

Crème fraîche has two advantages over sour cream: It can be whipped, and it can be brought to the boiling point without curdling. It's lovely to have a little around to adorn just about anything. Except that dull martini that plain sour cream didn't help either.

Both sour cream and crème fraîche are consistently lovely eaten with berries or sliced fruit. Mash some strawberries with a few spoonfuls of sour cream (or crème fraîche) and a little sugar. Or sprinkle a little brown sugar over either cream and eat with white grapes. Float a spoonful of sour cream or crème fraîche on the top of a bowl of soup—with or without chopped dill, parsley, or chives. Mix sour cream with mayonnaise to make lovely salad dressings for potato or chicken salad or cole slaw. Add a little blue cheese and use the mixture as a dressing for salad greens.

The possibilities go on and on—sometimes you need a recipe, and sometimes you don't. The spirit of adventure counts for a great deal.

Yogurt, How to Make It, and Yogurt Cheese

Which leads us to yogurt. Yogurt has a long and honorable history, probably beginning with milk being stored in animal skins (thus giving wild bacteria a chance to go to work) as far back as 4,500 years ago, if not longer. Two highlights along the way: Suleiman the Magnificent (tenth sultan of the Ottoman Empire) sent a doctor to the ailing French king Francis I, who was suffering from severe diarrhea. (Odd how word gets around!) The Turkish doctor cured the poor king by feeding him yogurt.

Some time later, in 1919, Isaac Carasso, a Sephardic Jew who had lived in the Balkans, where yogurt was an everyday food (Sephardic Jews, you know, are descended from the Jews expelled from Spain during the Inquisition), started a small yogurt business in 1919. He named his company after his son, Danone (little Daniel), who went on to establish their company in France in 1929. Danone Carasso came to the United States during World War II and started making yogurt again, this time Americanizing the company's name to Dannon. Earlier, in Prague, fruit jam had been added to yogurt to prevent it from spoiling. Dannon brought sugared fruit to yogurt in the United States in 1947, and yogurt became big business on both sides of the Atlantic.

You can make your own yogurt almost as easily as you can make your own butter and crème fraîche. You need live bacteria—which sounds awful, but is simply a matter of either buying dried bacteria at a health food store, or using a few tablespoons of a yogurt you know has live bacteria in it (it will say on the label)—and adding milk, gentle heat, and patience. Directions for making yogurt can be complicated (with words like sterile and incubation and much worse— pathogenic bacteria, for instance), and they can be very simple. I aim for the simple.

Heat one quart of milk (whole, low-fat, or skim) very gently (in a double boiler, if you have one) to about 185 degrees Fahrenheit. Don't let it boil. (If you like your yogurt to be quite firm, stir two tablespoons of powdered milk into the milk.) Let the milk pan stand, covered, in a larger pan of cold water until it has cooled to slightly above body temperature. Stir in one-quarter cup of live-bacteria plain yogurt, and pour into clean bottles. Cover the bottles, wrap them nicely with a baby blanket or a towel, and keep them in a warm, draftless place—like an oven with a pilot light, or one that has been heated gently and very briefly at its lowest temperature, with the heat now turned off. Partway through the yogurt-making process, turn the oven on again, *briefly*, at the lowest temperature and then off again. You should have yogurt in about three or four hours—open a bottle, check its consistency, and taste a bit. If it needs longer, rewrap it, and let it stand again. Once it's finished, keep it in the refrigerator. Save some of each batch to use as a starter for the next batch.

Considerably simpler is straining yogurt to make yogurt cheese, or a thick yogurt. Simply place a strainer over a bowl (you can buy a yogurt strainer, which does the same thing—it usually comes in the shape of a box, and has a removable strainer at the top), pour the yogurt into the strainer, and refrigerate for several hours. Please do remember to empty the bowl from time to time, so that the liquid doesn't spill all over your fridge. (If you can find an old Chemex coffeemaker at a flea market, it makes an ideal strainer—just spoon the yogurt into two drip filters in the top section. A Chemex also makes good coffee, but that's another story.) Then simply wait until the yogurt is as thick as you'd like it to be. Eat it flavored with cinnamon and sugar or chopped scallions, spread it on toast, with jam or sugar, or plain on crackers, make tzatziki out of it (recipe follows), cover it with a fruit purée, make a smoothie out of it with some fruit and sugar, or do as the Greeks do— eat it for dessert with honey and walnuts. (And, with great good fortune, thick Greek yogurt is now available at many supermarkets. Saves the straining. And it tastes wonderful.) Few things are better. Even whipped cream with honey and walnuts isn't as good—the tang is what does it, and the thickness on your tongue. And this from a whipped cream nut (me).

Cheese

And now we come to cheese. Cheese, we've already established, is made from milk—from cows, sheep, or goats, for the most part. Something is added to it, usually rennet (natural enzymes that coagulate milk), to separate the milk into the quivery solid of curds and liquid whey—you remember Miss Muffet? Sitting there so prettily on her tuffet, eating a bowl of curds and whey—that was milk being turned into cheese. The curds are what becomes cheese; the whey is drained away and sometimes it's fed to the pigs. There aren't enough Miss Muffets in the world.

What happens to the curds is what determines what the cheese will be like—how long they're allowed to stand, how hard they're pressed, how long they're kept after they've been pressed, and what's added to them (think mold and bacteria—or don't, if you'd rather not). Other factors are which animal the milk came from (goat cheese, no matter how it's made, doesn't taste like cheese made from cow's milk, for instance), how rich and creamy the milk was to begin with, and whether or not any flavorings—like herbs, garlic, or wood smoke—have been added to it.

What a simple way of describing cheese! There are hundreds of different kinds of cheese—fresh cheeses like cream cheese and cottage cheese, firm cheeses like Cheddar and Gouda, moldy cheese like Roquefort, Stilton, and Gorgonzola, creamy cheeses like Brie and St. André, aged cheeses like Parmigiano Reggiano . . . and dozens of others. (It was Charles de Gaulle who asked how it's possible to govern a country that has 246 varieties of cheese.) They're all beautiful. Cheese travels well, it's everything from a great picnic food to a complete meal to a marvelous dessert, it's full of nutrition, and it's an investment in the future, because the future is its very nature.

Let's hear it for cheese! Or, to be fair, it's milk that we should cheer. From milk come cream and butter and cheese, which doesn't even say anything about ice cream, cheesecake, custard: oh, a host of things, cream soups, sauces, and a glass of cold milk with a cookie—no, several cookies—next to it on a flowered dish. Heaven after school, and heaven in old age. Like cheese, heaven forever. Will there be cheese in heaven? Yes, and bread and butter as well. Would it be heaven otherwise?

Russian Cream

....

I've had this dessert recipe for years, and have only recently begun to see a few like it—none as good, I believe. With only five ingredients (plus a little water) it's wonderfully simple. There's no need to dwell on fat; if you aren't having fruit for dessert, you're having something with fat in it. Look at it this way: It's divided among several people, and it makes all of them happy.

The recipe is reprinted from my book The Sex Life of Food.

1 tablespoon gelatin
½ cup cold water
½ cup sugar
1 cup heavy cream
2 cups sour cream (regular or low-fat; *not* no-fat)
1 teaspoon pure vanilla extract

1. Sprinkle the gelatin over the water and let sit for 5 minutes, until the gelatin softens.
2. Add the sugar to the cream and heat gently (in the top of a double boiler or over low heat, stirring often and watching carefully) until the mixture is warm.
3. Still over low heat, add the gelatin mixture to the cream and stir until it and the sugar are completely dissolved.
4. Chill until it begins to thicken, and at that point, add the sour cream and the vanilla, folding them in well.
5. Pour into a serving bowl or individual dessert cups.

SERVES 6

This is lovely served with fresh fruit and a little sauce—a coulis of raspberries, strawberries, or blueberries, for instance. A coulis is a thick sauce, made from puréed and strained fruit or vegetables. To make one to go with the Russian Cream, cook fresh or frozen berries quickly—just until softened—with 1 or 2 spoonfuls of water and a spoonful or two of sugar. Use as is or push through a strainer, pressing hard on the solids to extract as much juice as possible; discard the solids. Taste either the strained juice or the whole berry sauce and add more sugar if needed. A dash of lemon juice and a tiny pinch of salt perk up berry flavor. Coulis keeps for 3 or 4 days, covered and chilled. The Russian Cream can be made a day ahead.

Sweet Potato Cheesecake

. . . .

Here we have a variation on a recipe from the Vardaman Sweet Potato Festival, held every year in Mississippi. If you want a T-shirt with a picture of a sweet potato on it, Vardaman is the place to get one. Sweet potatoes deserve a T-shirt; they're not only marvelous, they're also good for you; they're full of vitamins and other goodies. That's all it takes to make cheesecake healthy.

Crust:

    1½ cups crushed ginger cookies

    ¼ cup sugar

    ⅓ cup unsalted butter, melted

Cake:

    3 8-oz. packages cream cheese at room temperature

    1 cup sugar

    ¼ cup light brown sugar

    1¾ cups sweet potatoes, cooked and mashed

    2 eggs

    ⅔ cup evaporated milk (undiluted)

    1 tablespoon cornstarch

    Pinch of freshly ground nutmeg

Topping:

    2 cups sour cream (regular or low-fat, *not* no-fat) at room temperature

    ⅓ cup sugar

    1 teaspoon pure vanilla extract

1. Preheat the oven to 350 degrees.

2. Make the crust: Combine the crumbs, sugar, and butter in a 9-inch springform pan, mixing well. Press onto the bottom and 1 inch up the sides. Place the pan either on a large sheet of foil or in a larger baking pan to catch drips. Bake at 350 degrees for 6 to 8 minutes; don't brown. Remove from the oven and cool.

3. To make the filling, combine the cream cheese and the sugars in a large bowl. Whisk in the sweet potatoes, eggs, and milk. Add cornstarch and nutmeg, mixing well. Pour into crust. Bake at 350 degrees for 1 hour, or until the edge is set. (Cake will continue to cook and set as it cools.)

4. Prepare the topping by combining the sour cream, sugar, and vanilla. Spread over the warm cheesecake. Return to the oven, still at 350 degrees, and bake 5 minutes. Cook on a wire rack. Chill several hours or overnight.

Remove sides of pan and serve.

SERVES 8

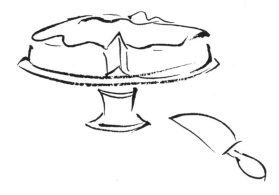

Fromage Fort; or, What to do with Leftover Cheese

Fromage fort *(strong cheese) is a traditional recipe in France, varying slightly from region to region and household to household. Jacques Pépin has written that he learned his* Fromage Fort *recipe from his father. I've seen several versions (from other people's fathers, no doubt), including one that uses cream instead of wine. His recipe uses raisins; I often leave them out. When I want that extra taste, I use a tablespoon or two of dried currants instead—because they're smaller.*

> About ½ pound leftover cheese pieces (see Note below about what kinds of cheese to use)
> 2 cloves garlic, peeled and chopped
> ¼ cup dry white wine (or heavy cream or a mixture)
> 1 to 2 tablespoons honey
> Freshly ground black pepper

1. Place cheese in food processor bowl. Add garlic and wine, and pulse several times. The goal is not a purée, but a smooth mixture with some chunks in it.
2. Add 1 tablespoon of honey; pulse; taste. Add more honey if you like, and the black pepper, and pulse again.
3. Scrape into a jar or serving bowl. Let stand, if possible, for a few hours before serving so that the flavors can meld.

YIELD: ABOUT 1 CUP

Note: Use whatever cheese you have, mixing soft and hard cheeses, trimming off any crusts or mold. I like to have at least a little blue cheese and Parmigiano Reggiano or Gruyère; goat cheese works well, and so does Brie. Be brave! Use as a spread for crackers or good bread. It's also good toasted, on bread, heated under the broiler, and makes lovely bruschetta that way. The spread keeps for one week in a refrigerated covered jar.

It's dangerous to keep mixtures with uncooked fresh garlic for longer than ten days because botulism can develop. I stop at a week.

Tzatziki

A friend gave me this recipe after she had returned from a trip to Greece. I've seen other recipes for tzatziki since then, but I like this one best. Is it seasoned with friendship?

1 pound plain yogurt, drained (see page 198), or use Greek yogurt, which is already drained

¼ cup grated or very finely diced onion

1 clove garlic, pressed or finely minced

1 English cucumber peeled, seeded, and grated or very finely chopped (seed cucumbers by cutting them in half the long way and using a teaspoon to scrape out the seeds)

2 tablespoons extra virgin olive oil

2 teaspoons wine vinegar

½ teaspoon sugar

¼ cup chopped dill (or flat-leaf parsley leaves or mint, or a combination)

Salt and freshly ground black pepper

1. Place the drained yogurt in a bowl and add the remaining ingredients. Mix; taste for seasoning and adjust if necessary. If you like, garnish the serving bowl with a sprig of dill. Serve with pita and raw vegetables.

YIELD: 2 TO 3 CUPS

Blue Cheese Spread

....

In no way is this good for you. It's a retro recipe, from the time before fat phobia became a national preoccupation—the opposite of an infatuation. Disfatuation? Having said all that, admitted to the unprincipled fat and attendant calories, I can only add that this is delicious. Brandy is the secret ingredient. But if you choose to keep the whole thing secret, you may find that your guests enjoy it just that much more.

Roughly equal quantities of:
Cream cheese, at room temperature
Unsalted butter, at room temperature
Blue cheese, at room temperature

1. Blend all smoothly together with a spoon or in the processor.
2. Add a splash of Cognac or brandy, and mix in.
3. Serve in a small bowl, with crackers or bread. A light sprinkle of paprika on the top of the cheese mixture looks fetching.

11

DESSERT 101

At Last, the Sweetness

Ice-cream is exquisite. What a pity it isn't illegal.
—*Voltaire*

Butter, eggs, flour, milk or cream, sugar, and perhaps a bit of fruit:
This is the short alphabet of dessert. (Plus chocolate, of course.)
The variations on those few simple ingredients are almost endless—
from brownies to ice cream (together or separately), from s'mores
around the campfire to an English trifle, with its layers of cake, sherry,
jam, custard, fruit, and whipped cream. Divine. All of them.

What is dessert, after all? Yes, just a trifle, perhaps—no matter how
complicated, how baroque. It's from the Old French, *desservir*, to clear
the table—and that's what it is, essentially: an afterthought, a play-
thing, a puff . . . pure pleasure. Don't trust a man who doesn't like
dessert. A woman who doesn't eat dessert in public might very well eat
pie with her fingers when she's home alone in the middle of the night.
Dessert is meant to make us happy—and it's a comfort at the end of a
meal just as it is in the middle of the night.

At heart, dessert has an aristocratic history. Sugar was once expensive, and only those who could afford it were able to use it in desserts. With the mechanization of sugar production and more sources for sugar, sweet desserts found their way down the social scale and made more people happy, aristocrats and plain folk alike. Sugar is the single universal ingredient of dessert—aside from desserts that are a presentation of nuts, a plate of cheeses, or just fresh fruit. Everything else means sugar, and thus sugar is almost the sine qua non of dessert.

Since nothing is simple, you know that there are several different kinds of sugar. Brown and white sugars are the beginning, but even brown sugar can be either light or dark. Then there are demerara, muscovado, and turbinado sugars, with varying degrees of molasses, which is also what makes the difference between light and dark brown sugar. The more molasses there is, the darker the sugar is. In baking, it matters which sugar you use, so follow your recipe's instructions. And don't substitute brown sugar for white; there will be changes in the recipe's taste and texture that may not be quite what you're hoping for.

But what, you may ask with your eyebrows raised, is molasses? It's a product of the sugar-making process—cane juice that has been boiled and thus concentrated. The resulting thick syrup is boiled again and the syrup darkens. By the third boiling we have the strongest-tasting molasses, blackstrap. Sulphured molasses has sulfur dioxide added to it as a preservative.

There is plenty of evidence to say that sugar isn't good for you. There's tooth decay, and diabetes, and obesity, and the plain old sugar blues. Add to the list, in its way, the Boston Molasses Disaster, an unhealthy event of a completely different character. On a midwinter day in 1919, a large molasses tank, holding well over two million gallons of molasses, burst. The escaping molasses formed a wave that some survivors said was fifteen feet high; the surprisingly swift tide of molasses flowed through the streets at about thirty-five miles an hour. A hundred and fifty people were injured, and twenty-one died. Too much sugar is not good for you.

But dessert does not have to be immoderate. A little sweetness goes a long way. Even shoofly pie—a Pennsylvania Dutch dessert made with brown sugar and molasses and sometimes white sugar as well—is sliced before being served. It's possible to have just one small piece. Moderation is the key, as in all things. But yes, I know that it's hard to be moderate about a dessert you love.

Cake and cookies probably rank at the top of everybody's favorite dessert list (especially with a scoop of ice cream on the side), and we've been making both for a long time. Once we—the historical we—knew how to make bread, we weren't far from making cake.

The Romans made cheesecake and a kind of fruitcake. They made wedding cakes, too, but early wedding cakes were nothing like the towering extravaganzas we know today—they were more like a matzo than a cake, flat, and made of just flour, salt, and water. But then, as now, they were fertility wishes—flour is made from grain, and grain is a seed; seeds, after all, have almost always been a symbol of fertility.

By medieval times, flat wheat cakes were crumbled over the heads of brides—still for the sake of fertility. Eventually, there was less crumbling and more eating; spices, sweeteners, and flavorings like honey and bitter almonds were added, symbols of the pleasures and pains that follow every wedding. In France, by the time of Louis XIV, cakes were being soaked in alcohol (whence the rum cake) to perk up the night ahead. English bakers, more sedate, added dried fruits. Eventually, sugar arrived as an ingredient, and one of the first cakes to follow was the Banbury cake, a dark English fruitcake, and a wedding cake before it became a Christmas cake. The first icings were French, a combination of sugar and egg whites—rock hard when dry. Later, ground nuts were added; Banbury cakes were covered with this new recipe for white sugar icing—as virginal as the white wedding dress and, it was to be hoped, the bride.

Fortune, fertility, and virginity don't matter so much in cakes these days. There are dozens of after-dinner and tea cakes, from Angel Food to Devil's Food, from German Black Forest to Latino Tres Leches, from Boston Cream Pie (actually a cake) to Lady Baltimore Cake.

There are gateaus and sponges, tortes and tartes, tiramisu, trifle, and zuppa inglese—cakes of a sort, every one.

And there are cookies, which may have been the result of professional bakers testing bits of cake batter to check their seasoning and to be sure that the oven temperature was on target.

Measuring

When you're baking, you need to measure everything carefully. Usually, cooking is relatively carefree; it's simply a matter of chopping, mixing, cooking, and serving. There *are* things you need to know— that's what this book is about—but in general there's room for play. If the onions aren't perfect cubes, they'll still taste good; if you use too many carrots, you'll just have created a new version of what you were aiming for. But baking is different. Baking is a chemical process in many ways, and it matters what the balance of ingredients is. You don't need to go to graduate school to make a cake; you just need to be careful and do what you're told. If you find that hard—if you're given to questioning authority—buy some ice cream for dessert.

Otherwise, get out those little spoons and separate measuring cups (for dry ingredients; liquid ingredients can go into one- or two-cup measures) and a knife. Why the knife? The best way to measure flour (aside from by weight) is to spoon it into a measuring cup. Don't scoop the measuring cup into the flour; you get a more accurate measure by spooning. Then sweep the flat side of a knife across the top of the cup, thus removing the excess (do this over a plate or a piece of waxed paper so that you can pour the excess back into whatever it came from). The knife-sweep makes it possible for you to know that when you need a quarter of a cup of something, you *have* a quarter of a cup of something, not more and not less. Use the same method for teaspoons and tablespoons of dry ingredients, like baking powder and baking soda. A pinch, should you need one, is the amount you can hold between your

first and second fingertips. It's not a crowd, just a bit. If it were supposed to be a crowd, you could measure it with a small measuring
spoon. A pinch is just tiny. And it has nothing to do with pressing the
flesh.

It is a great help here to have all the measurements done before you
begin mixing, so that you can add whatever comes next when it's due.
Batter shouldn't stand around and wait for you—the bubbles get dis-
couraged, baking powder loses its oomph, the butter gets too soft—
you need to encourage the batter, and give it what it needs when it
needs it.

Oven Temperature

One of the things you need to measure—too often overlooked—is
your oven's temperature. Some ovens work hotter than others; you
need to know what yours does. Buy an oven thermometer and put it inside the oven. Choose a setting on your oven's dial; close the door and
let it heat for fifteen minutes; then open the door and check the thermometer. Has it reached the setting you chose? Then you have no
problem. You're good to go. If it doesn't match, check your oven's instructions if you have them; they should tell you what to do. If you
don't have them (somebody moved away and took them along) but the
difference isn't huge, simply adjust your thinking accordingly. Set the
dial a little lower or higher when you use the oven and rest secure
knowing that you're where you should be. But check the oven thermometer to be sure you've adapted correctly. If you have a convection
oven (convection ovens have a fan to keep the heat constant and even),
bake at a slightly lower temperature than recipe directions tell you,
and start checking for doneness a little earlier than you're told to. In
any case, convection or not, start checking cakes and cookies just a
few minutes before they're supposed to be done. Cookies especially
burn quickly; you want to be ahead of that curve.

Using Unsalted Butter

It's time to talk about unsalted butter. Always use it for baking. I use it for everything—for two reasons: one, it tastes better, and two, it's fresher. Originally, the purpose of adding salt to butter was to mask any unpleasant flavors the butter might develop and to help it last a little longer—to prolong its shelf life. Phooey on that. And beyond *that* phooey, salt in butter affects recipes; it's hard to know exactly how much salt is in the butter—it varies from company to company. Using unsalted butter (also called sweet butter—now what does that tell you?) allows you to know exactly what you're putting in your cake and cookies. I buy a pound of butter at a time, and put it in the freezer in its box, just as it comes from the shopping bag. I take out a quarter-pound at a time to keep in the refrigerator.

I don't feel as strongly about higher-fat (European-style) butters like Plugrá, which have more butterfat solids than American-style butters. They taste good, but it's possible that the extra fat will affect baking results, so if you're using an American recipe, it makes sense to stay with an American butter. I use Land O'Lakes, or, when I can find it, Cabot, which is my first choice.

Creaming Butter and Sugar for Cookies and Cakes

Many baking recipes begin with this phrase: "Cream the butter and sugar together until light." This means beating *room-temperature* butter with an electric mixer and gradually adding sugar until the mixture is fluffy. The purpose is to beat in air bubbles, which results in a lighter, moister cake; the process also makes it possible to completely dissolve the sugar. Start mixing slowly and increase the speed after you've begun to add the sugar; stop and scrape down the sides of the bowl from time to time to be sure the mixing is complete. The first key to this process is to start with room-temperature butter—the consistency of cold butter is too hard to work with; it won't become fluffy or blend well with the sugar. Second key is not to rush it—patience in the kitchen is our maxim. If you have an electric mixer, it's perfect for creaming. If you don't, use a wooden spoon, beat hard and long, and think of all the calories you're using that you can replace later with a nice piece of cake.

In your enthusiasm, don't get carried away—don't overmix. When the butter seems to have expanded, when its color becomes lighter (from yellow to creamy ivory), when the mixture becomes fluffy but still holds its shape—when all that happens, stop. Too much mixing affects all those bubbles you worked so hard to create. Admire what you've done—you did so well!—and move on.

Adding Eggs, Flour, and Milk

The next step in cookie and cake making is to add eggs, almost always one at a time. The eggs emulsify the butter-sugar mixture and hold in moisture. Crack the eggs (see chapter 6) in a separate little bowl one at a time, then add each to the larger bowl, so that if a piece of shell somehow—no matter how adept you are—falls into the egg, you won't have to spend hours trying to find it in the mixing bowl, before giving up and treating it like a prize in an Epiphany cake.

After the eggs come the flour, liquid (usually added alternately and gradually, about a third of each at a time), and flavorings. Those are the basics; there are nearly endless variations.

Folding

Sometimes ingredients have to be folded into a batter, especially when beaten eggs whites are involved. It's best to proceed in sections—add about a quarter of the lighter matter (the egg whites or whipped cream, usually) into the heavier batter. Hold the edge of the mixing bowl with one hand. Use a spatula with a wide end and, holding it in the other hand, plunge it into the middle of the batter. Drag the spatula to the

side of the bowl, and bring it back to the top with the flat side of the
spatula doing the folding work. Almost at the same time, move the bowl
in a circular motion, a bit at a time, with your other hand. That's the
motion you need: dip, drag, up, turn; dip, drag, up, turn, until the first
portion is mixed into the batter. Then add the rest, and continue folding it in until everything is together in one big happy blend. Folding
something into a batter is one of those things that feels like pure fun—
it's easy, it does what you want it to, and it looks so very grown up.
Don't get carried away—you want to fold the lightness in until you can't
see it anymore, but you don't want it to get bogged down. Too much
folding will eliminate the air bubbles you worked to achieve. That's the
whole purpose of folding, to add a measure of lightness. Enjoy doing
it, and know when to stop. The secret of life? Well, one of them, at
least.

Using Vanilla Extract

Plain old vanilla is kitchen heaven. But it has to be the real thing. Pure
vanilla extract is made from vanilla beans and alcohol; imitation vanilla
extract involves alcohol and wood. Yes, wood. Imitation vanilla doesn't
taste very good. Stick to pure vanilla extract. It's expensive, but you
only use a little bit at a time.

Vanilla is harvested from a species of orchid, and it's a difficult and
demanding process, which is why vanilla is so expensive. You can
make your own extract, if you're so inclined—it's expensive too, but it's
fun to do. You need three vanilla beans, and one cup of either plain
vodka or brandy. Cut the beans in half the long way. Put them in a
glass bottle, cover them with the alcohol (pushing them down until
they're completely covered), close the bottle, put it in a dark place—
like the back of a closet—and wait. And wait. Wait about two months,
remembering all the time that the longer you wait, the stronger your
extract will be. If you used vodka, you'll see it begin to get darker and
stronger as it goes along. When it has a lovely amber color and you feel

it's done, pour the liquid into smaller bottles, adding a half or whole bean to each bottle. As you use the extract, replenish the bottle with more vodka or brandy—at first, the remaining extract will be weaker because it has been diluted, but it will soon regain its strength (up to a point, of course).

Using Baking Powder and Making Your Own

Baking powder is the magical—and chemical—substance that changed cake baking from a tedious and time-consuming chore, what with all the mixing, to something fairly easy to do and relatively dependable. What baking powder does is give off carbon dioxide when it's added to a batter, thus making the cake lighter. Double-acting baking powders affect the rise of the batter at two points: first, when the baking powder is added and comes into contact with the batter's moisture, and again, when the batter encounters the oven's heat. Single-acting baking powders affect only the immediate reaction, the one caused by meeting up with the batter. In either case, because the reaction begins immediately, you need to move your batter along—take too long and the cake falls flat.

There are people who find the aftertaste of commercial baking powder to be unpleasant—it's slightly metallic, even bitter, a bit chemical. It's very easy to mix your own and avoid that possibility. Use two parts of cream of tartar to each one part of baking soda. (I find that easy to remember, because cream of tartar is much more expensive than baking soda, so inevitably you need more of it.) If your recipe calls for a teaspoon of baking powder, use a little more than a quarter of a teaspoon of baking soda to a little more than a half-teaspoon of cream of tartar—or mix a larger amount and use a teaspoon of that. Just don't let it stand too long; it won't be effective if it's old. Acidic batters—those that include buttermilk or sour cream, for instance—need additional plain baking soda; recipes for batters like these will include both baking powder and baking soda.

Preparing a Cake Pan; Baking Time
and Temperature; Removing Cake from the Pan

There are three more things to know: how do you prepare the cake pan, how do you know for sure when the cake is done, and finally how do you get it out of the pan?

Butter is the key to preparing a pan—use your fingers, a piece of waxed paper, or a pastry brush (or the wrapper the stick of butter came in), and cover the sides and bottom of the pan all over with a thin layer of butter; usually, you need about a tablespoon of butter for one pan. Follow the butter up with a thin layer of flour or bread or cake crumbs. That's done by adding the flour (or crumbs), and then tilting and rotating the pan to cover the whole bottom and sides; turn the pan upside down over a piece of paper—or the sink—and tap it gently; the excess flour or crumbs will spill out, and your pan is ready to go.

One of the great secrets of cake baking is to keep the oven temperature just a bit lower than the recipe probably tells you to. Ideal temperature is no higher than 325 degrees; most recipes call for 350. The lower temperature bakes more evenly—the outer edges of the cake tend to cook faster at higher temperatures than the inside does, which causes the cake to rise more in the middle—that homemade hump you've seen on so many cakes. Cakes look better when their tops are even, and if you're icing the cake, that homey hump is a problem that has to be eliminated. If you do have a bump, you can cut it off—carefully, with a serrated knife, with one hand on the top of the cake to hold it steady. You can consider it your own personal, and very large, cookie; you can save it for making a wee trifle; you can put it in the food processor to make cake crumbs—to sprinkle over pudding or ice cream. I'm sure you'll think of something. You could freeze the crumbs and use them for preparing the pan for your next cake.

About five minutes before your cake is supposed to be done is when you should start checking to see if it is, in fact, finished. Use a toothpick, a thin wood skewer, a clean straw from a broom—even, in a pinch, a short piece of spaghetti or, worst case, the tip of a knife—and poke it quickly into the middle of the cake. If when you pull it out moist bits of batter are stuck to it, the cake isn't quite finished; give it four or five minutes longer and try again. If it's clean and dry, your cake is done. There are exceptions—if you like fudgy brownies, for instance, it's all right if there are bits of batter stuck to the toothpick when you withdraw it. Take the cake out of the oven and let it sit for a minute—the residual heat will be more than enough to finish the baking.

Okay, now it's done. Put a cake rack over the top of the pan; invert the pan; and tap it lightly. The cake—given how well you buttered and floured the pan—should slide out easily. If it doesn't, insert a narrow sharp knife along the edge and slide it around the cake; then try the rack again. In a dire emergency, alas, let the cake cool in the pan and try once more. If all else fails, you can always slice it in the pan—but that won't happen, really it won't.

From here on, things get more complicated—with icing and such. Icing can be tricky or easy, but the best cakes to start with are cakes that don't need to be iced. There are lots of these: cakes with streusel tops, cakes that are glazed, cakes that are gorgeous just the way they are. Icing is Dessert 102. For advanced students, a quick chocolate icing can be made by melting 6 ounces of premium dark chocolate, in pieces or chunks, in the top of a double boiler, letting it cool for a minute, and whisking in a generous ½ cup of sour cream (*not* low-fat), about a teaspoon of grated orange peel, and, if you want a more intensely chocolate flavor, a tablespoon of cocoa powder; let it cool—it will thicken as it cools—but use it before it becomes too thick to spread. If it does, reheat it in a double boiler and let it cool again—but this time, don't wait too long. There's another icing recipe, for cream cheese icing, on page 239. Don't lose the knowledge, though, that it's perfectly lovely to cover a cake with whipped cream.

Making and Baking Cookies

Some cookie batters have to be refrigerated before they're baked; others are ready to use as soon as they're mixed. If you're not working with a cookie roll that just gets sliced, you use two spoons (usually teaspoons) to form the cookies. Scoop up the batter with one spoon and use the other to push it onto the baking pan. There are also spring-loaded batter scoops in various sizes; using them means that each cookie will be almost exactly the same size as all the others. The problem with scoops is where to keep them—that gadget drawer near the stove tends to get crowded.

The easiest way to bake any kind of cookie is on a Silpat silicone baking mat—the cookies lift right off when they're done. Cookie recipes tell you whether or not you need to butter the baking pan. (Silpat doesn't need to be buttered.) Otherwise use a sturdy, relatively heavy sheet pan, and turn it around halfway through the baking to make sure all the cookies are evenly exposed to the heat. Have a rack ready, and lift the cookies with a spatula onto the rack to cool. That way, air reaches them on both sides and they cool without cooking further, or without steaming, as they would if one hot cookie were simply piled on top of another. It helps to work quickly—cookies tend to crisp as they cool, and they're easier to remove from the baking pan when they're hot.

I don't worry much about storing cookies—they're always gone within a day or two—but if you need to think about it (while munching on a cookie), know that they should be kept in an air-tight package or jar. (Yes, that's why we have cookie jars.) Most cookies can be frozen—but somehow that seems to me to be a bit oxymoronic; a cookie is a small thing, by its nature somewhat ephemeral. It comes, it brings joy, and it's gone. You can't freeze joy. You, however, may be more sensible than I am; in that case, wrap your cookies (after they've cooled) carefully in plastic wrap or tin foil—individually if you are so given; freeze them; and bring them back to room temperature, by all means, before you eat them. You could also microwave them briefly, or let them heat in the oven on its lowest setting.

Pie, Pudding, and Ice Cream

The first pies were probably savory, not sweet, and the first piecrusts were probably dense and hard, meant as containers for filling, rather than to be eaten for their own sake. Possibly the most unusual pies were the kind that sprang to life when they were opened, like the four and twenty blackbirds of the children's rhyme. I've read that sometimes small animals—frogs, turtles, rabbits—were set into pies (obviously, after the pies had been baked) to appear when the crust was cut. Oddest of all, dwarfs might spring from the pie and walk down the table, reciting poetry or otherwise amusing the startled guests. I'd rather have blueberries.

Piecrusts can be tricky until you get used to them, and in addition to the knacks of mixing, rolling out, and transferring to the pie plate, you also need the space to do all that, and to store the rolling pin. I tend to stay with cookie crusts—they're simple and very good; combining the cookie flavor with the filling is fun, too. There's no need to stick to the tried-and-true graham cracker crust. Ginger cookies go beautifully with pumpkin filling, for instance; chocolate wafer cookies are lovely with pecan pie. The general rule is to crush the cookies (in the food processor; failing that, put them in a sealable plastic bag and crush them with a rolling pin or something heavy, like a wine bottle), add melted butter, and a little extra sugar. Proportions are roughly a third to a half cup of melted butter to a cup and a half of crumbs and two to four tablespoons of sugar plus a tiny pinch of salt. You'll have to taste—add the sugar slowly—and you need enough melted butter so that the crumbs stick together and look like wet sand. Mix them right in the pie pan or a baking dish (an eight-inch square dish usually works well if you don't have a pie pan) and then pat them down in an even layer, with a little going up the sides; bake five minutes at 350 degrees if you're going to bake the pie after a filling has been added. If you want a crunchier crust, or you aren't baking the filling, bake the crust for a total of ten minutes.

For all of that, the best of all for me is a dessert that can be eaten with a spoon. Ice cream. Whipped cream. And pudding. All sorts of puddings. The comfort! The joy! The fleeting moment! The sweetness! The lightness! Crisp or smooth, fluffy or sturdy, creamy or chunky—pudding has it all. Crème brûlée, for instance, is perfection. You don't need to tart it up with pumpkin or raspberries—not that there's anything wrong with that. But how can anything be more perfect than perfection?

Most puddings aren't hard to make; it's usually just a question of mixing a few ingredients and then boiling or baking. Rice pudding (recipe below) is an easy example. But custards and custard sauces, on the other hand, can be tricky, because the line between scrambled eggs (which now you don't want) and custard (which now you do) is so thin. Custard on its own (crème brûlée is the ultimate example, all rich and creamy) is easier than custard sauce, which decorates other desserts. (There's a recipe for custard on page 234.)

The trick with a custard pudding baked in the oven is to use a bain-marie—a water bath: You set the custard pan (or the custard cups) inside a larger pan that has been filled with hot water (not any higher than the top of the inner pan, just about halfway up its sides). The water bath maintains a constant temperature and helps the custard cook evenly. The second trick is not to overcook the custard. Check it a bit before the recipe tells you it should be done. It needn't be totally set—the center should have a bit of wiggle to it; residual heat will finish it quite nicely.

You can make almost any cream- or milk-based pudding before you've mastered custard. Why wait? Rice pudding, bread pudding—each is a marvel in its own right, and neither is difficult to deal with. An easy and classic rice pudding can be made by simmering a cup of rice in two and a half cups of water, with half a teaspoon of salt added, for fifteen or twenty minutes over low heat in a covered pan, until the water has been absorbed. Then add two cups of milk and half a cup of sugar, and simmer for another fifteen minutes, stirring well every few minutes. Taste, and add more sugar if you'd like it to be sweeter. Stir in a handful of raisins or dried currants if you want, and cook for another fifteen minutes, again stirring every few minutes and watching to see that it doesn't dry out and scorch. At the end, the milk should be absorbed and the rice very soft. Add a teaspoon of vanilla; if you like, sprinkle a bit of cinnamon (or nutmeg) over the top; and—go for it!—stir in a little cream. Next time you're having rice for dinner, make some extra rice at the same time (with butter, not olive oil), and later you can add milk and sugar to the remaining rice and make rice pudding—just serve it warm, so the butter isn't firm and obvious. (A recipe for bread pudding is on page 237.)

Ice cream isn't hard to make, either, especially if you have an electric ice cream maker. They're not hugely expensive (the lowest price I've seen is just over twenty-five dollars; they can reach into the thousands, but that's not at all necessary). We need the same old ingredients to make ice cream: cream (or milk), sugar, and flavoring, and sometimes eggs—but oh! how different they are when they're frozen.

Ice cream, of course, used to be "iced cream"—and there you have, in a word, the history of ice cream. How far back do you want to go? Ancient Greece, China, Persia, Egypt? As long as there was snow—and ice—there was ice(d) cream. And sometimes, if there was no snow just here, it was imported from there.

There are lots of ice cream myths. Marco Polo, for instance, is said to have brought not only a recipe for pasta but also one for ice cream with him on his return from points east. Well, no. Nero, for one, in the first century A.D., ordered ice to be brought from the mountains so that it could be mixed with fruit, and there was iced cream in one place or another way before that—as far back as the fourth century B.C.

Making iced cream isn't complicated. In midwinter, if you have clean snow, you can mix it with a little sugar and vanilla, pour a little cream over it (work fast), and what you have, historically, is iced cream. (Boiling maple sap into syrup sometimes involves a dish of well-packed snow on the side, over which the hot syrup is poured. The result is a cross between ice cream and candy, achingly sweet, but very much worth trying if you feel like heating up some real maple syrup. The caramel-colored maple-flavored stuff won't do.) You can make less snow-dependent ice cream in your freezer in a shallow bowl or pan; you have to stir it frequently so that large ice crystals don't form, but you'll end up with a tasty dish. And, at the other end of the possibilities, if you have an ice cream maker, be it electric or hand churned, you can make wonderfully smooth ice cream in what could be called a trice.

Ice cream is officially defined by the amount of butterfat—cream—it contains. But there are variations without any butterfat at all. Sherbet is made with milk and fruit; sorbet is fruit puréed and frozen without either milk or cream. Ice milk is the bridge between ice cream and sherbet. And frozen yogurt is made with—can you guess?

There's more. There's ice cream made with a custard base, which involves eggs, and ice cream made with just cream. There are ices made with shaved ice and fruit or a fruit syrup. There's semifreddo, literally half-cold, like an almost-frozen pudding, and there are frozen creams of a nearly infinite range.

There was even ice cream in outer space. Freeze-dried ice cream was more or less dehydrated through a magical process that ranks right up there with space travel. Someone put ice cream in a vacuum chamber—oh, never mind the process. The resultant package of not-quite ice cream flew with *Apollo* 7 in 1968, but it's available now in the Kennedy Space Center gift shop, among other museum stores. It tastes amazingly like warm ice cream.

It would be a sadder world—even out in space—with no dessert in it. Dessert, like love, may not last. Enjoy it while you have it, and when you don't, make more. As long as you have a spoon and a dish of ice cream, all can never be lost. All is always found once again.

A recipe for Sweet Potato Cheesecake is on page 202.

Four Ways to Have Berries and Cream

1. Berries with Faux Crème Fraîche

There are three kinds of crème fraîche: the real thing, and two good imitations, one involving several hours of waiting, and the other ready instantly (see chapter 10). You know which one I use. It goes admirably well with a great many things, especially fruit, and especially berries. Any berries will work, but strawberries are quite fine.

1 quart fresh whole strawberries
½ cup heavy sweet cream
½ cup sour cream (regular or low fat; *not* no-fat)
2 tablespoons sugar
Optional: 4 shortbread cookies (Walker's, in the plaid box, are excellent)

1. Rinse the berries quickly and gently pat dry with paper towels. Remove the hulls, either with your fingers or, using your thumb as a pivot, with the tip of a paring knife. Slice the berries into a bowl.
2. Add the sweet and sour creams and the sugar and mix well. Refrigerate and let stand for an hour or two to let the flavors meld. Add a cookie to each serving, if you like.

SERVES 4

2. Berry Fool

Is this a fool as in silly? Not really. It's quite serious. But like the king's jester, as well as being full of light spirits it's also smart. It probably got its name from the French fouler, *to mash. Even so, it's a classic English dessert, and with very good reason.*

2 cups fresh berries—raspberries or strawberries or a combination
2 tablespoons sugar
2 cups heavy cream, whipped

1. Rinse and dry all the berries. Reserving 6 berries for a garnish, remove the hulls from the remaining strawberries. Using a potato masher or a fork, mash the berries and the sugar together. The mixture should be chunky. Taste to see if additional sugar is needed—it will depend on the sweetness of the berries.
2. Fold the berries gently into the whipped cream, leaving streaks of white. Chill, and serve cold with a whole berry on top of each serving.

SERVES 6

Note: Gooseberries also make a classic fool; they need to be topped and tailed and briefly cooked with a little sugar. Quickly cooked (with a little sugar, a tiny bit of lemon juice, and a small pinch of salt) blueberries are nice, too.

3. Berries with Chocolate Whipped Cream

Chocolate whipped cream is sensationally good. Don't tell anybody how easy it is to make.

1 quart strawberries
2 tablespoons sugar

For the whipped cream:

¼ cup unsweetened Dutch-process cocoa powder
3 tablespoons sugar
1 cup heavy cream
½ teaspoon pure vanilla extract

1. Rinse and dry the strawberries and remove their hulls. Slice them into a bowl; add the sugar; mix. Chill for at least one hour, or up to three hours.
2. Mix the cocoa and sugar in a small bowl. In a chilled bowl, combine the cream and vanilla and whip until soft peaks form. Gradually add, still whisking or beating, the cocoa mixture, and beat until stiff and well blended (can be done in a food processor).
3. Spoon the berries into individual serving dishes and top with the whipped cream.

SERVES 6

4. Blueberries and Maple Cream

Use real maple syrup for this (Grade B is better for cooking than Grade A; it's darker and deeper, but it's much harder to find), not imitation— which is sugar water that has been artificially colored and flavored. Stick to the real thing for this very simple and quite delicious dessert.

Blueberries, rinsed and well drained
Real maple syrup
Heavy cream

1. Serve the blueberries, and pass the syrup and cream, each in its own pitcher.

And one more, for luck: What's called Eton Mess (truly, that's its name) is strawberries, hulled, sliced, slightly sweetened, and mixed lightly, just before serving, with whipped cream and crushed meringues (egg white cookies slowly baked until they're meltingly crisp—you can buy them in good bakeries if you don't want to make your own). You could also use raspberries or sliced peaches, and name it after another school.

Blueberry Ginger Roll

Descended in a straight line from the classically simple Chocolate Wafer Whipped Cream Roll that teenagers used to love to make, this isn't retro. It's much more grown up, but it's still simple—and surprising, in the way the chocolate roll was the first time you ate it. If you've never eaten it, rush out and buy some thin chocolate wafers (Nabisco makes them); slather each with whipped cream; make little stacks of them; put the stacks together; cover all with more whipped cream and refrigerate at least 5 hours; overnight is even better. (You can also add raspberries or sliced strawberries between the cookies, but that's not how the original was made.) How can anything so simple be so good?

2 cups heavy cream, whipped (see page 193 about whipping cream
   in a food processor)

2 tablespoons sugar

1 teaspoon pure vanilla extract

2 tablespoons crystallized ginger, chopped

1 to 2 boxes very thin ginger crisps (English crisps are thinner and
   they have a purer flavor than American [Nabisco] ginger snaps,
   but they both work)

1 pint blueberries

1. Whip the cream, sugar, and vanilla together until firm peaks form. Add all but 1 teaspoon of the ginger and mix well.

2. One by one, using a knife as a spreader, cover one side of each cookie with whipped cream; top with the next cookie and then more whipped cream. Make stacks of six cookies, embedding a few blueberries in the cream between several cookies; put 2 or 3 stacks together the long way, on a serving dish, to form a long roll. (If you'd rather have a cake-shaped cake, place the cookie stacks in a circle, surrounding a stack in the middle.) Continue until you've used all

or most of the cookies, making 2 adjacent rolls if that's what's needed for your serving dish. (If you don't use all the cookies, the leftovers go nicely with tea.)

3. Frost the cookie roll with the remaining whipped cream. Cover lightly with plastic wrap (stick a few toothpicks in the top of the roll to keep the wrap from touching the cream) and refrigerate for at least 5 hours or overnight.

4. Just before serving, sprinkle the top of the roll with the reserved ginger and add the remaining blueberries on the plate as a garnish. Slice the roll diagonally to serve, with blueberries accompanying each serving.

SERVES 8

Mint Ice Cream

Minthe was a nymph, according to Greek mythology, who was almost seduced by Hades; Persephone, in the nick of time, changed her into a plant. (Would you rather be seduced by Hades or spend eternity growing green?) Mint has gladdened millions of people since then, and that's a rather nice heritage. One more way to be gladdened is this relatively light mint ice cream, with or without chocolate chips.

1 cup mint leaves, packed
2 cups milk
2 cups heavy cream
¾ cup sugar
Pinch of salt
1 teaspoon pure vanilla extract
Optional: ½ cup miniature semisweet chocolate chips

1. Place the mint leaves, milk, and cream in a medium saucepan and bring to a simmer. Add the sugar and salt and stir until the sugar is dissolved, cooking for a minute or two. Remove from the heat and let steep until cool. Strain, pressing on the leaves to extract as much liquid as possible. Add vanilla.

3. Pour the mixture into an ice cream maker and freeze according to the machine's directions. If using the chocolate chips, add them about 10 minutes into the churning process. Spoon ice cream into a container and place in your freezer for 1 or 2 hours before serving.

YIELD: ABOUT I QUART

Cinnamon Ice Cream

Cinnamon ice cream goes with all the things that cinnamon goes with—pecan pie, pumpkin pie, apple pie, a variety of crumbles and crisps . . . the list isn't endless, but it's very large. VERY. I think the word is huge. Unless it's enormous. It's also hugely and enormously good all by itself.

2 cups cream
²⁄₃ cup sugar
½ teaspoon pure vanilla extract
1 heaping tablespoon ground cinnamon
1 cup milk (regular or low-fat)

1. Mix cream with half the sugar, and whip (use a food processor or an electric mixer) until firm peaks form. Add the remaining sugar, pulsing or beating. Add the vanilla and cinnamon, and finally fold in the milk.

2. Pour into the container of an ice cream maker and mix according to machine directions. Transfer ice cream to a freezer until ready to serve.

YIELD: ABOUT 3 CUPS

Berry Yogurt Ice Cream

. . . .

I love ice cream, its coldness, sweetness, and creaminess. As a cook, the idea of mixing cream or, in this case, yogurt, with flavoring and putting it straight into the freezer appeals to me. This recipe offers a way to make ice cream if you don't have an ice cream machine. The results—light and not overly sweet—also appeal to me, but that's another story.

1 cup raspberries or strawberries
1 cup plain yogurt (full-fat or low-fat, *not* no-fat)
¼ cup honey or extra-fine sugar
1 cup heavy cream, whipped, plus 1 tablespoon extra unwhipped cream

1. Place berries, yogurt, and honey in a food processor bowl and process until smooth.
2. Fold into the whipped cream.
3. Pour into ice cube trays and freeze until solid. You'll need more than one ice cream tray—if you have two to spare, fine. Otherwise, pour the remainder into a container you can freeze, allowing an inch or so at the top for expansion. Remove from the freezer, allow to thaw slightly, place into processor bowl, and process until smooth. (Cubes work best in the processor; if you've used anything else, chop into large chunks.) If the mixture seems too dry and icy, add a tablespoon of heavy cream and mix again; that should make it smooth and creamy. If you still need more, add another tablespoon. Store in freezer containers.

SERVES 4 TO 6

Other possible fruits: peaches, apricots, bananas . . .

Dinah Shore's Cheesecake Cookies

Dinah Shore was a band singer first and then a star in her own right, as a recording artist and a television personality. She also wrote three cookbooks; her recipe for cheesecake cookies was in the first, Someone's in the Kitchen with Dinah, *published in 1971. Like Dinah Shore herself, cheesecake cookies combine the best of several worlds—cookies, cheesecake, and nut crusts. I've adapted her recipe. These are wonderful cookies, and everybody always loves them.*

Crust:
   ⅓ cup brown sugar, packed
   ½ cup chopped pecans
   1 cup flour
   ⅓ cup butter, melted

Filling:
   1 8-oz. package cream cheese (regular or reduced-fat)
   ¼ cup granulated (white) sugar
   1 egg
   1 tablespoon lemon juice
   2 tablespoons milk
   1 teaspoon pure vanilla extract

1. Preheat oven to 350 degrees.
2. Mix brown sugar, nuts, and flour together; add the melted butter and stir until crumbly (can be done in the baking pan). Reserve 3 tablespoons of the mixture to use as a topping, and press the remainder evenly into an 8-inch square pan. Bake at 350 degrees for 12 to 15 minutes.
3. Combine cream cheese, sugar, egg, lemon juice, milk, and vanilla in

a bowl or pulse in a food processor until smooth. Pour into the crust, and sprinkle with the reserved crumb mixture.

4. Bake at 350 degrees for 25 minutes; cool. Chill well, at least 4 hours (or a day ahead), covered with plastic wrap. Cut into squares; leave as is or cut each square diagonally.

YIELD: 12 SQUARE OR 24 TRIANGULAR COOKIES

Katharine Hepburn's Brownies

Katharine Hepburn's brownies have been around a long time. I first saw the recipe years ago in a magazine; I can't remember whether the article was about her or about food, because the only thing I clipped is the recipe. I've seen it in a great many places since then, one of which explains that the brownies are a Hepburn family recipe. That makes sense; they couldn't be easier to make (and only need one pan before they go into the oven), but somehow I could never quite imagine Katharine Hepburn herself, cheekbones and all, stirring up a batch of brownies.

I must also say that these brownies are crisp on the outside and soft and fudgy on the inside, and that's what makes them so good, not their heritage, not even their single pan—though the pan is a big plus.

Unsalted butter for the baking dish plus ¼ pound (1 stick) unsalted butter

2 squares unsweetened chocolate

1 cup sugar

2 eggs

½ teaspoon vanilla

¼ cup flour

¼ teaspoon salt

1 cup chopped walnuts

1. Preheat the oven to 325 degrees. Generously butter an 8-inch square baking dish.
2. Over low heat, melt the chocolate with the butter in a heavy saucepan. Remove from the heat.
3. Stir in the sugar. Add the eggs and vanilla and, says Ms. Hepburn, "beat like mad." Stir in the flour, salt, and walnuts and mix well.
4. Pour and scrape the batter into the baking dish and bake at 325 degrees for 40 minutes. Take the pan out of the oven and let it cool. Cut into 12 squares.

MAKES 12

Joan's Comforting Custard

Custard is a little confusing: It can be a sauce—in France, a crème anglaise, or English cream, thin enough to pour; a pastry cream, or crème pâtissière, thick enough to fill éclairs or Napoleons or fruit tarts; or a dessert unto itself—cup custard, flan, caramel custard, or the divinely rich crème brûlée. And there's more. Custard can be the foundation of a wide variety of other desserts or, for that matter, a savory like a quiche. Almost no matter how you spin the globe, you can find a form of custard, wherever there are eggs, milk, and sugar. All the forms are lovely, and that's almost a definition.

Are they hard to make? Well, the pourable ones are a little tricky. Cup custard is easier and it is a great comfort food. As with all custards, the cooking trick is all about controlling heat. For dessert custard, a water bath does this—the custard dish or dishes are set in a larger pan that is filled with hot water to keep the heat constant and even. Then be sure not to overcook it, and you're home free.

Water
2 cups milk
2 eggs
½ cup sugar
Dash of salt
½ teaspoon white vinegar
Garnish: freshly grated nutmeg

1. Heat a kettle of water on the stove.
2. Scald the milk by heating it in a small saucepan over moderate heat until tiny bubbles form around the edges of the pan.
3. In a bowl, mix the eggs, sugar, and salt together with a fork or a whisk; mix in the vinegar. Don't overmix; you don't want foamy bubbles to form.

4. Slowly add a stream of hot milk to the eggs, mixing constantly, until all the milk has been added. Pour the mixture into six 4- to 6-ounce custard cups or a heat-proof bowl. Grate nutmeg over the top.

5. Place a large baking pan on an oven rack, and set the cups or bowl in it. Pour the hot (but *not* boiling) water into the large pan so that it comes up about halfway to the top of the inner cups or the bowl. Bake at 325 degrees until the outer edges of the custard are set and the middle still has a wobble—about 25 to 30 minutes for the cups, or about 35 to 40 minutes for the bowl. Don't wait until the whole thing is set—that's overcooked, and it will be watery; if you take it out of the oven while the middle still wobbles, residual heat will finish the cooking.

SERVES 6 (WARM, COLD, OR AT ROOM TEMPERATURE)

Joan's Apple Bread Pudding with Sauce

....

Bread pudding was originally another good way of using leftover bread. It was good partly because the bread was good. It still needs to be made with good bread, even if you buy it in the morning to make pudding with in the afternoon. You don't get to eat this recipe until the next day—the very definition of a make-ahead dessert. It is also lovely for breakfast or brunch (without the whiskey sauce), having been prepared the night before.

At least 12 hours ahead:

　　3 Granny Smith apples, peeled and cubed

　　1 tablespoon sugar

　　8 cups cubed bread (use French or Italian bread, challah, biscuits, croissants, or a mixture)

　　½ cup raisins or dried currants

　　5 cups milk

That evening or the next day:

　　Unsalted butter for the baking dish

　　4 eggs

　　1 tablespoon pure vanilla extract

　　1 cup sugar

　　½ teaspoon freshly ground nutmeg

Optional: whiskey, rum or brandy sauce (see Note below for alternative vanilla sauce):

　　6 tablespoons unsalted butter

　　1 cup powdered sugar

　　1 egg, beaten

　　2 to 3 tablespoons whiskey, bourbon, rum, or brandy

　　Optional: 2 cups heavy cream, whipped

1. The night before, mix the apples and sugar together in a large bowl. Add the bread, raisins, and milk, and mix well. Cover with plastic wrap and refrigerate for at least 12 hours.

2. The next day: Preheat the oven to 350 degrees. Generously butter a 9×13-inch baking dish.

3. Whisk together, in a small bowl, the eggs, vanilla, sugar, and nutmeg. Pour this mixture over the bread cubes and mix well. Pour all into the baking dish.

4. Bake at 350 degrees for 60 minutes, or until the top of the pudding is lightly browned. Remove from the oven and immediately pour either the whiskey or the vanilla sauce over the top. (The pudding can also be served without any sauce.) Let cool briefly before serving.

5. Whiskey sauce: In a double boiler or in a saucepan over very low heat, cook butter and sugar together, whisking, until the mixture is thick and the sugar is dissolved. Add a little of this hot mixture to the egg in a small bowl, and whisk together. Add the egg back into the melted butter and sugar, whisking continuously. Cool slightly, and add the whiskey, bourbon, rum, or brandy, and mix well. Pour over the hot pudding, as above. Whipped cream, served separately (or instead of the whiskey sauce), makes everybody happy.

SERVES 10

Note: Instead of an alcohol sauce, you can make a quick vanilla sauce. Mix together in a small saucepan ¼ cup each white and brown sugar and add ½ cup milk and ½ cup butter. Bring almost to a boil, remove from the heat, and stir in 1 teaspoon vanilla. Pour over the pudding.

Variation: A simpler bread pudding can be made by buttering an 8-inch square baking pan and filling it with good bread, cubed or torn into large pieces. (The bread should be a day or so old—on the dry side. If you're very refined, remove the crusts, but it's fine to leave them.) Mix 2 cups of milk, 2 eggs, 2 tablespoons sugar, a pinch of salt, and 1 teaspoon vanilla, and pour this mixture over the bread. (If you like raisins or dried currants, add a handful—soaking them ahead in warm water until they're soft and plump, and then draining them. Mix with the bread.) Let stand a few minutes, pressing the bread into the milk with the back of a spoon. Bake at 350 degrees for 40 to 50 minutes, until the top is browned and crisp. To complicate things, if you want an effect reminiscent of crème brûlée, sprinkle 3 tablespoons of brown sugar over the top and dot with 2 tablespoons of butter. Put it under the broiler for a few seconds, watching super-carefully to be sure it doesn't burn, until the butter and sugar melt and begin to bubble. Serve warm or at room temperature.

SERVES 6

Cream Cheese Frosting

....

Cream cheese. Butter. Tangy, but sweet. Cream cheese frosting has always seemed a bit magical to me—and I keep meaning to try it on toast. That seems a little decadent, but I bet it's good.

8 ounces cream cheese, at room temperature (see Note about
     reduced-fat cream cheese)
8 ounces unsalted butter, at room temperature
1 pound confectioners' sugar (the whole pound may not be
     necessary)
1 teaspoon pure vanilla extract
¼ teaspoon coarse sea salt (see Note)
1 teaspoon grated orange rind
1 tablespoon fresh orange juice

1. In an electric mixer (standing or hand-held), mix the cream cheese
   and butter until the mixture is light and fluffy.
2. Slowly beat in the sugar, tasting as you go to check the sweetness—
   if you'd rather have it less sweet, don't add the whole pound.
3. Beat in the remaining ingredients.

YIELD: ENOUGH ICING AND FILLING FOR A TWO-LAYER CAKE

Note: Coarse sea salt doesn't completely dissolve in the icing—it leaves lovely specks of salt that accent the taste of the frosting. If you don't have it, just add a pinch of regular or kosher salt. You can use full- or reduced-fat cream cheese (*not* no-fat)—but why bother, given all that butter? And then there's the cake . . . One can always be more sensible tomorrow. Assuming the cake is gone.

Orange Processor Cake

In Classic Cakes and Other Great Cuisinart Desserts, *by Carl Son-theimer (who developed the Cuisinart food processor) and Cecily Brown-stone (food writer and author of a long-running newspaper column about food), there is a recipe for a cake that has apparently been around for a very long time. One version was included in* The Williamsburg Art of Cookery; or, Accomplish'd Gentlewoman's Companion *(a collection of recipes used in eighteenth- and nineteenth-century Virginia homes, gath-ered together and published by the Colonial Williamsburg Foundation in 1985); another won the 1950 Pillsbury Bake-Off Contest. It's apparently a timeless recipe—it still works. And it's all done, now, in the processor.*

Cake:

   Unsalted butter for the baking pan plus ¼ pound (1 stick), cut into 8
      pieces

   1 orange

   1 cup sugar

   1 teaspoon pure vanilla extract

   1 cup buttermilk

   2 large eggs

   2 cups flour

   1 teaspoon baking soda

   ½ teaspoon salt

   ½ cup walnuts

   1 cup raisins

Glaze:

   ½ cup sugar

   3 tablespoons orange juice

1. Preheat the oven to 325 degrees. Butter a 9-inch square baking pan.

2. Using a swivel-bladed peeler, remove the orange peel without taking any of the white pith, beneath the peel, with it. Place the peel pieces in the bowl of the food processor with the sugar and pulse until the peel is finely chopped, scraping the work bowl as needed.

3. Add the vanilla, buttermilk, eggs, and butter and process until combined, about 15 seconds. Add the flour, baking soda, salt, walnuts, and raisins, and pulse 3 to 5 times, until the flour is no longer visible. Pour into the baking pan.

4. Bake at 325 degrees for 30 to 40 minutes, or until a toothpick inserted into the cake's center comes out clean.

5. While the cake is baking, prepare the glaze: Stir together the sugar and juice. As soon as the cake comes out of the oven, spoon the glaze evenly over the hot cake. Return to the oven for 5 minutes. Cool in the pan on a rack. Cut into 16 squares before removing from the pan.

16 SERVINGS

12

THE ANT AND THE GRASSHOPPER

For Now and for Later

If more of us valued food and cheer and song above hoarded gold, it
would be a merrier world. —*J. R. R. Tolkien*

It's nice to know some dishes that can be prepared in a trice—when
all you have is a trice—but there are also many recipes for foods that
need time to mellow. There are, for instance, drop biscuits, on the one
hand, and preserved sweet lemons, on the other (on pages 252 and
257). It's partly that some people like to prepare for snow days and
others would rather revel in the seasons while they're here; some worry
about the future, and others take pleasure in the continuing now. It
seems to me that, in food terms, the best thing to do is to know how to
hurry when you need to, and equally to know how to enjoy waiting
when you have the time—and the shelf space—to do so.

Aesop told the story, dividing things up, with planning ahead on
this side, and pleasure on that. This is how it went, on the off chance

you don't already know: The ant worked hard all through the summer, dragging bits of things back home to stockpile for the winter. On his way to and fro, he passed the grasshopper, who was just sitting around making music. The hardworking ant took the time to warn the grasshopper—it won't always be summer, you know—but the grasshopper politely continued to enjoy his song. Inevitably, the days grew shorter and colder, and the ant retreated to his snuggery to contemplate breakfast, lunch, and dinner for the long winter ahead. Equally inevitably, the grasshopper grew hungry, and in the spirit of friendship asked the ant to help him out with a bite or two. No way, said the ant. You laughed and sang while I worked; you would have bought a Cadillac while I walked if you could have. Learn from this, you lazy bum, and if you live through the winter, you'll know to do better when summer comes around again. But I doubt if you'll still be here to benefit from what you've learned.

I'm not overly fond of the ant. He strikes me as the kind of fellow who wins attendance awards—a prize I've never understood. All you have to do is show up, and eventually, you win. The grasshopper can be annoying, too, of course. All play and no work; that sort of thing. Beach bum, ski bum, loving and leaving, and letting somebody else do the dishes, make the beds, and pay the rent. Yes, he sings beautifully, but he's doesn't really work at it—he doesn't practice, he doesn't study; if he can't get it right the first time, he moves along to another song. But if we allow them both their necessities, they make a lovely combination. The ant would be a lot better off with a little music in his life, and the grasshopper does need to provide for his personal winter. How fortunate the life that includes both!

How on earth is all of this related to cooking? Is it a question of a long-simmered stew versus takeout Chinese or a slice of pizza? Well, sometimes you want one and sometimes you want the other, as simple as that. Sometimes you're hungry and you want to eat right away and make glorious music of your food, and other times, you're able to plan ahead, and you want to contemplate—and make—jams and chutneys to put in jars and save. Here today and still here tomorrow—we shall consider that near-perfect state.

Jams

Making jam is a way of preserving summer—it appeals to the planner in our souls. It feels so well cared for, not to say providential, to imagine rows of jars of preserves on our shelves. That raises a question: What's the difference between jam and jelly? Preserves and conserves? Fruit butter and fruit curd? Where does marmalade go in all of those names? Simple. Really. Jam is fruit (whole, crushed, or puréed, as you like) that has been heated with sugar until it thickens and sets (or gels); it can also be made from vegetables, like peppers, carrots, and rhubarb, or vegetable-fruits, like tomatoes. Jelly is jam that has been strained. Preserves are basically jam, but if you want to quibble, they're made from whole fruits instead of crushed or puréed. Conserves often have other things—like raisins or nuts—mixed in. Fruit butters are jam that has been sieved; then spices are added and it cooks again. Fruit curds are different; they're fruit juice (most often, lemon juice) and sugar that have been cooked with eggs and butter until thickened.

Marmalade is made from citrus fruits—most often oranges—and sugar, and includes the rind, either thin or thick cut; it also usually has a bitter tang to its sweetness. Marmalade comes from the Portuguese *marmelada*, which, in its turn, comes from *marmelo*, quince. *Marmelo* derives from the Latin *melimelum*, honey apple; the ancient Romans cooked quinces with honey. The Greeks, too, had a word for it— *melimelon*, or honey fruit; they also cooked quinces with honey—but the Greek *melon* meant any round fruit. Until the European Union decreed that only jams made from citrus fruits could be called marmalade, many countries in Europe used words related to *marmalade* to mean any kind of conserve.

Whatever they are, marmalades, jams, or preserves, they're all part of that lovely vision of the bounty of summer, preserved for winter. The actual preserving—an enormous amount of work: slicing, measuring, mixing, cooking, stirring, and sterilizing, all to be done in the heat of summer—isn't quite as appealing as the vision of the happy results. It's a nice fantasy, even if few of us want to spend summer days that way (see the grasshopper about this), or have enough room on our shelves for the resultant jars of jam and jelly—and a place to keep the canning equipment during the winter. That doesn't have to mean abandoning the dream. There is a way to preserve the fruits of summer without consigning ourselves to the kitchen on a hot day in August, without filling our closets and sock drawers with jars of jam to get us through a snowy day in January, and without buying our jam at the corner store.

Think quick jam (either using it at once or freezing it for later), and how it appeals to the grasshopper in our souls. I'd just as soon not have an ant in my soul, when I stop and think about it.

Most jams can be made in small quantities without sterilizing the jars and lids at the beginning or ending with paraffin or a hot water bath processing of the filled jars. Pectin (a fruit extract) helps jams to set, but if you don't mind jam that's less thick (perhaps sometimes even a little syrupy), you can plunge ahead without adding pectin. Making a few small jars means that you can keep one in the refrigerator and give the others away. Your friends will be very happy with you (but only if you're sure to tell them to keep their jars in the refrigerator or the freezer). Your small jars may not last until February, but when the strawberries are all gone, at the end of June, it may be time to make blueberry, and that still leaves the weeks when the peaches are ripe and then the golden days when the pears first come to the farmers' market. If you're desperate in February, you can always make jam with frozen fruit—it'll still be perfectly good. Last summer, I made some very good green tomato jam at the end of the summer and enjoyed it in January, and I've also made some lovely fig preserve when there were no fresh berries anywhere.

Making jam for the freezer (a recipe for quick blueberry jam is on page 249) means making small quantities that can be kept in the freezer for several months. A jar of frozen berry jam, your own jam, on a bitterly cold morning when the sun is low in the south and the dark comes early, is a thing full of sunshine, memories of what was and hope for what is yet to come. A jar of jam in the freezer is poetry in the hand.

Chutneys, Relishes, Salsa, and Sauce

The consistency of chutney is chunky, but the word chutney isn't related to the word chunky, appealing as that would be. It's from the Hindi word *chatni*, to crush—and that's how chutney is made: fruits are crushed, and then cooked with sugar and other ingredients (often vinegar, onions, garlic, spices, and mangoes—though there is a wide variety of other possibilities). The prevailing taste is a spicy sweetness, with a tang of sour.

Today, chutney is mass-produced, and it's available almost everywhere. But originally, chutney was an exotic condiment, made to accompany Indian curries and other main dishes. It was shipped to European countries in the seventeenth century as a luxury; by the nineteenth century brands like Major Grey's were popular, and soon Western manufacturers were making their own versions—often called "mangoed," because they so often included mangoes. In India, chutneys might contain spinach, guava, coconut, or shrimp. Obviously, the west is just beginning to know what chutney might be.

Relish isn't a kind of chutney—though you could make a case for chutney as a kind of relish. A relish is usually made from vegetables, and chutney is made mostly from fruit, but both are meant to do the same things: complement a main course—not as a side dish, but as a condiment—while they perk up the appetite for more. A relish can contain all sorts of things—everything from avocados to peppers; they're not crushed, as the *chatni*-based chutneys are, but rather are chopped or sliced into small pieces.

Then there's salsa—another kind of relish, from another part of the world. Salsa is the Spanish word for sauce, and it was so named eons ago, when the Spanish came to Mexico and discovered, among a great many other things, the tomato, and the sauces made from it. (The Spanish word *salsa* descends from the Latin word for salt—*sal*.) Salsa was around way before the Spanish noticed it—it goes back to the Aztecs, Mayans, and Incas. A long time later, and a little to the north, the sales of salsa in the United States surpassed that of ketchup in 1991 for the first time in our history. *Vaya con dios.*

Salsas are frequently not cooked; relishes usually are. But salsa, too, is a condiment meant to accompany a primary dish, and it, too, spices the appetite. We think of salsa as Mexican or Tex-Mex, there it is in the little bowl in the Mexican restaurant, next to the basket of tortilla chips. We're just touching the surface with that little bowl—salsa can be a simple combination of tomato, onion, garlic, and chili peppers, or it can be more complicated and more unusual, and both ways are delicious. It can also be—as the label says—mild, medium, or hot, and when you make your own, you get to choose.

White sauce is neither chutney nor relish, but, in its way, it is definitely part of that which enhances the main dish. White sauce is exactly the same thing as French béchamel and Italian balsamella. It's one of French cooking's five mother sauces—called mother because each has so many offspring. The other mother sauces are velouté, which is made the same way as béchamel, with a roux of butter and flour, but using meat, poultry, or fish stock instead of milk; brown or espagnole; hollandaise; and tomato sauce; some would add mayonnaise and vinaigrette. Béchamel's descendants include Mornay sauce (with cheese), soubise (with finely diced onions), and Nantua (shrimp).

White sauce was once the height of food fashion, flowing from coast to coast in the United States during the nineteenth century, covering a host of sins beneath its blanket of white. Before refrigerators, sauce disguised the taste of food that was often a bit off—or even more than a bit. Our fortunate food revolution involves revealing food tastes, not hiding them—and white sauce, with its high fat content, is not in favor. Still, there are moments when a little sauce goes a long way, and it's much better to use your own sauce than to make do with a can of cream of chicken soup. White sauce is also the basis of other recipes—soufflés, for instance, begin with béchamel. It's not hard to make white sauce (the recipe is on page 250), and when you make it, you not only have a host of choices about how to flavor it, should you wish to, but you also take your place in a history of sauce that goes back to the Roman Empire. Kind of neat, that.

There are a host of dishes that fit under the same umbrella of sweet, smooth, or spicy accompaniments to a meal—kimchi in Korea, raita in India, harissa in Morocco, sambals in Asia, pesto in Italy— some tailored for the reliable ant, needing to be prepared ahead, and others last-minute food for the musical grasshopper, ready at a moment's notice. So many things, so close together! So much to eat, so much to cook—how lucky we are, grasshoppers and ants alike! What joy a little chopping can bring! Quickly done, as a salsa or a white sauce, for the grasshoppers, or if you cook the condiment—as a chutney or a relish—I think you rank, for a moment at least, with the ant: You're planning ahead, admit it. Be proud. Just share a little, please, with your less provident friends. The grasshopper would gladly give you some of the salsa that was made just a minute ago. This is a world that needs both grasshoppers and ants.

For the Grasshopper

Quick Blueberry Jam

Blueberries are one of the world's few blue foods. How many others can you think of? And they are incredibly healthy, helping you avoid all the bad things you might catch and underlining all the good. There are two ways in which they are especially delicious, aside from straight from the bush: The first is standing over the sink, washing the first batch of the season and eating them by the handful, and the second is concentrating their essence in a few moments of time and space and making jam.

3 cups blueberries (about 2 full pints)
½ cup sugar plus 2 to 4 tablespoons, depending on sweetness of the berries
½ teaspoon grated lemon rind
1 teaspoon fresh lemon juice
Small dash of salt

1. Wash the berries in a strainer, and place them in a wide skillet with no additional water, just the moisture left from the washing. (A wide skillet encourages evaporation.) Over medium heat, add the ½ cup of sugar. Stir, adding the lemon rind and juice and the salt.
2. Bring to a boil, reduce the heat slightly, and cook, with the juices bubbling, stirring often, for 15 minutes. Taste to see if more sugar is needed. The jam may look syrupy—it thickens when it cools. (If it stays syrupy, it's still delicious—drippy on toast, perhaps, but lovely on ice cream or yogurt.)
3. Pour into clean jars. Refrigerate for up to a week; it can also be frozen.

YIELD: ABOUT 2 CUPS

White Sauce = Cream Sauce = Béchamel = Balsamella

To make white sauce, you need butter, flour, milk, a saucepan, and a whisk. You don't get to eat the whisk, but making the sauce is infinitely harder without it—and very easy with it. And once you've learned how to make white sauce, you can make all sorts of other dishes and sauces, and you'll never need to make do with a can of cream of chicken or mushroom soup again, as long as you live.

2 tablespoons butter
2 tablespoons flour
1 cup of milk
Salt and freshly ground pepper
Optional: a pinch of freshly ground nutmeg

1. Melt the butter in a saucepan over moderate heat. When it's melted, whisk in the flour. Let it cook and keep whisking for 2 to 3 minutes, to remove the raw flour taste. (If you whisk too long, your butter and flour mixture—which is a roux—will turn brown; a brown roux is the basis of a great many other things, including much of Cajun cooking, but it isn't what you want for a white sauce.)

2. Whisk in a little milk, stirring all around the pan—including the edges—until it thickens, and then whisk the rest of the milk in gradually. (Some cooks add the milk all at once, whisking madly, but I like doing it this way better.) Keep stirring until the sauce has thickened; it can be used right away, but will be a little better if it cooks for 5 to 10 minutes longer; whisking frequently. (If the sauce is too thick, whisk in a little more milk.)

4. Season the sauce with salt and freshly ground pepper to taste and, if you like, a pinch of freshly ground nutmeg, or use one of the variations below.

YIELD: ABOUT 1 CUP

Variations:

Mornay (cheese) sauce—Off-heat, stir in 1 cup of grated cheese (Gruyère, Cheddar, etc.), about ¼ teaspoon of freshly grated nutmeg, a dash of cayenne, and a teaspoon of Worcestershire sauce, in addition to a pinch of salt and freshly ground pepper to taste.

Soubise (onion) sauce—Sauté two tablespoons of minced onion with the butter before adding the flour at the beginning of the recipe; then proceed.

Mustard sauce—Whisk in a tablespoon of Dijonnaise mustard after the sauce has thickened.

Brown sauce—Stir the roux until it begins to brown; add chicken, beef, or fish stock instead of milk.

Curry sauce—Add a tablespoon of curry powder (or to taste) to the butter at the beginning of the recipe. Simmer for a minute or two before adding the flour and proceeding with the milk.

Note: 2 tablespoons each of butter and flour to a cup of milk makes a sauce of a medium consistency; for a thin sauce, use 1 tablespoon each of butter and flour to a cup of milk. For a very thick sauce, use 3 tablespoons each of butter and flour to a cup of milk.

Drop Biscuits

....

What you call a biscuit depends on where you live. For the British, a biscuit is what Americans call a cookie (though the National Biscuit Company—Nabisco—tends to confuse things, when you stop and think about it).

   On the west side of the pond, a biscuit is a whole different thing. It's a tiny bread, needing no yeast to make it rise, and therefore in the category of "Quick Breads," and closely related to scones. Biscuits can be rolled and cut into rounds, but given a little extra liquid, they can be pushed out of spoons and are then known as drop biscuits—much easier and faster.

2 cups flour

2½ teaspoons baking powder

½ teaspoon salt

⅓ cup cold unsalted butter, cut into pieces

1 cup milk

1. Preheat the oven to 425 degrees.

2. *In a food processor:* Place the dry ingredients in the bowl; pulse briefly to mix. Add the butter, and pulse briefly to mix; the batter should resemble coarse meal. Add the milk and pulse briefly again. *By hand:* Mix the dry ingredients together in a bowl. Cut in the butter, using a pastry blender or two knives (start the knives from opposite sides of the bowl, and cut toward the other side; repeat), until the batter resembles coarse meal. Add the milk, and stir briefly.
   Either way: If the batter is too thick and doesn't stick together in a spoon, mix in additional milk, a little bit at a time, until it is the right consistency.

3. Using two teaspoons, scoop up batter in one spoon, and use the other to push the batter off the spoon onto a baking sheet. Bake at

425 degrees for 12 to 15 minutes, until the biscuits are golden brown and a toothpick inserted in the center of one comes out clean. Cool on a rack.

MAKES ABOUT 12 BISCUITS

Variations:

For strawberry shortcake—Add 1 tablespoon of sugar to the dry ingredients. After baking, while the biscuits are still warm, cut them in half horizontally; if you like, butter them lightly with unsalted butter. In serving dishes, add several spoons of strawberries (hulled, sliced, and sugared about an hour before the biscuits are baked) over the bottom half of each biscuit; place the top half over, tilted slightly, and add more strawberries and a generous dollop of whipped cream. *Other fruit shortcake possibilities:* sliced and sugared ripe peaches, sugared raspberries, blueberries that have been briefly cooked with sugar and a little water, etc.

For buttermilk biscuits—Add ½ teaspoon baking soda to the dry ingredients and substitute buttermilk for the regular milk.

For herb biscuits—Add 2 tablespoons of herbs (rosemary, thyme, parsley, etc.) to the dry ingredients.

For cheese biscuits—Add ½ teaspoon dry mustard to the dry ingredients and add ⅔ cup shredded sharp Cheddar cheese with the milk.

Joan's Blueberry Buttermilk Muffins

July is National Blueberry Month in the United States—I suppose because blueberries are fresh and ripe in July almost everywhere in the country—but we are fortunate enough to be able to have frozen blueberries available all year, bringing July to January, and filling the month of the Cold Moon with the memory of summer sunshine. Let it be noted, on chilly mornings as well as warm, that blueberries are outstandingly good for you, filled with multisyllable nutrients. The North American Blueberry Council tells us that of 40 different fruits, juices, and vegetables, blueberries have the highest antioxidant level and that just 3½ ounces of blueberries are equivalent to over 1,700 International Units of Vitamin E. Have another muffin!

Unsalted butter for muffin tins plus additional 6 tablespoons (¾ stick), cut into pieces

1¾ cups flour

⅔ cup sugar

1 tablespoon baking powder

¼ teaspoon salt

1 large egg, beaten

1 cup buttermilk

1 teaspoon grated lemon zest

½ teaspoon pure vanilla extract

2 cups fresh or frozen blueberries

1. Preheat oven to 400 degrees. Butter two 6-muffin pans.
2. *In a food processor:* Place the flour, sugar, baking powder, and salt in the bowl. Add butter pieces and pulse briefly. Separately, blend the egg, buttermilk, lemon zest, and vanilla, and add all to the batter. Pulse very briefly—batter should be lumpy. Using a spoon, fold blueberries into the batter.

By hand: Mix the dry ingredients in a bowl. Using a pastry blender or two knives, cut in the butter. Separately, mix the egg, buttermilk, zest, and vanilla, and add all to the batter. Stir very briefly—batter should be lumpy. Fold in blueberries.

3. Spoon batter into muffin cups and bake at 400 degrees for 20 to 25 minutes, until golden brown. Remove from oven, but leave the muffins in the pan for a few minutes before removing them. Serve warm.

YIELD: 12 MUFFINS

Note: this recipe can also be baked in an 8-inch square baking pan; the pan still needs to be buttered; the baking time should be about 5 or 10 minutes longer than that for muffins. Test with a toothpick (as described on page 216) after 5 minutes, and cook a few minutes longer, if needed.

Raita

Raita is part salad, part sauce, part remedy—it balances spicy food and is a balm to a palate in need of succor. (When you're eating spicy food, water spreads the pain; milk, yogurt, or cream soothes it.) It's fast and easy to make, and goes with all sorts of food—curry is just the beginning. It's lovely with raw vegetables, as a dip for bread, good with chicken or fish, and even very nice eaten with a spoon.

1 English cucumber, peeled, seeded, and grated (slice it in half the long way and use the point of a teaspoon to scrape out the seeds)
1 cup plain yogurt—regular or low-fat, *not* no-fat—Greek yogurt works well
½ lime, juiced
½ teaspoon sugar
Pinch of salt
2 tablespoons chopped cilantro
Optional: 1 clove garlic, crushed; 1 teaspoon fresh mint, chopped
Garnish: ground cumin

1. Place all the ingredients in a bowl and mix well. Store, covered, in the refrigerator until ready to serve. Sprinkle a bit of ground cumin over the top.

YIELD: ABOUT 1½ CUPS

For the Ant

Preserved SWEET Lemons

These lemons are like the positive to the salty negative of Moroccan lemons—they're preserved in sugar, not salt. Salty lemons add the same zesty tang to food as do olives or capers. Sweet lemons are as beautiful to look at in a jar, but to me, they seem a lot handier—they go with so many things: they can be diced and added to a vinaigrette dressing over a salad; they can be minced and added, with a little of their syrup, to fruit desserts; or they can be diced (or sliced) and added to poultry, meat, fish, or vegetable recipes. They are surprising and they are good.

2 whole lemons, organic if possible, washed
Water to cover plus 1½ cups fresh cold water
1½ cups sugar

1. Place the lemons in a small saucepan, cover with water, and bring to a boil. Reduce the heat and simmer until the lemons can be easily pierced by a toothpick. Drain and let cool.
2. Bring the water and sugar to a boil and cook until the sugar has completely dissolved.
3. Halve the lemons and add them to the syrup; reduce the heat and simmer for 30 minutes. Turn them at least once as they cook.
4. Place the lemons in a hot, clean jar; cover them with the syrup. Cool and refrigerate.

YIELD: 4 LEMON HALVES

This recipe is from my book *The Old-Time Brand-Name Cookbook.*

Cathy's Utah Apple Chili Sauce

Here we have a recipe that spans the seasons, combining late summer and early fall, with its ripe tomatoes and early apples. The recipe was given to me in double the quantity that follows. I prefer to make a smaller amount (in a somewhat less huge pot), and refrigerate what I don't give away. It has a marvelous, happy aroma while it's cooking down. It's very good with meat, poultry, or seafood—even with cheese—or spread on bread to augment a sandwich.

4 firm, crisp apples, peeled, cored, and
    chopped
1 cup sugar
8 ripe tomatoes, peeled and chopped
8 medium onions, chopped
1 sweet red pepper, chopped
1 cup cider vinegar
1 teaspoon celery seed
1 teaspoon salt
$\frac{1}{2}$ teaspoon cinnamon
$\frac{1}{4}$ teaspoon cloves
$\frac{1}{4}$ teaspoon dry mustard
Large pinch of crushed pepper
Pinch of chili powder, or to taste
Optional: 3 jalapeño peppers, chopped

1. Use a large pot—this cooks down, but starts big. Cook the apples and sugar together over low heat until they are well blended and the mixture is slightly syrupy.
2. Add all the remaining ingredients and continue to cook over low heat. Stir frequently to be sure the mixture is not scalding or stick-

ing on the bottom. Continue to cook until the sauce is thick—
between 2 and 3 hours, usually.

3. Use sterile jars and refrigerate, or preserve in jars according to recommended canning procedures.

YIELD: 2 QUARTS

Chocolate Truffles

At the heart of chocolate truffles is ganache—a tender and velvety smooth combination of chocolate and cream that melts like a dream in your mouth. It can hardly be improved upon, though there are nearly endless possibilities for decoration and flavoring.

Truffles are named for the fungus they supposedly look like—the bumpy lumps Brillat-Savarin called "the diamond of the kitchen." Chocolate truffles are the real thing—just chocolate, not fungus. All the better, when you think of it that way.

¾ cup plus 2 tablespoons heavy cream

8 ounces best quality bittersweet chocolate, chopped

Optional flavoring—2 tablespoons of raspberry jam, orange marmalade, Cognac, rum, or a liqueur

Optional coating—Dutch-processed cocoa powder, confectioners' sugar, toasted and chopped nuts (see Note below for how to toast nuts), toasted coconut, sugar mixed with cinnamon

1. Scald the cream in a saucepan by heating it until tiny bubbles form around its edges. Take off the heat and add the chocolate.

2. Let the mixture sit for a minute and then whisk until the chocolate is melted and the mixture is dark, glossy, and smooth. Let stand for 5 minutes. If you're using a flavoring, add 2 tablespoons of your choice now; mix well. Pour into a bowl or jar; cover and refrigerate for several hours or overnight, until the ganache is firm.

3. If you're using a coating (cocoa powder is traditional), place it on a plate. Line a tray or baking pan with parchment or waxed paper. Use a melon-baller or a small spoon to scoop up small balls of chocolate, a second spoon to push them out, and your fingers to finish shaping the chocolate into roughly round balls. Roll the truffles

in the coating and place them on the tray. If the ganache becomes too soft to work with, place it in the refrigerator or freezer for a few minutes. The truffles can be served immediately or stored, covered in plastic, in the refrigerator for up to a week or frozen for up to two months. Bring to room temperature before serving.

YIELD: ABOUT 24 TRUFFLES

Note: To toast nuts, preheat the oven to 350 degrees. Spread the nuts (pecans, walnuts, or almonds) on a baking dish and bake for 8 to 10 minutes, or until light brown and fragrant. Hazelnuts should toast for about 15 minutes, or until the skins start to blister. Remove from the oven and roll in a clean dishtowel; let them sit for 5 minutes and then rub them in the towel and remove any remaining skins. Once the nuts are cool, they can be chopped.

Eau-de-Vie and Limoncello

....

In France, eau-de-vie, the water of life, is distilled from fruit—raspberries, plums, cherries, pears . . . This recipe is simpler, but it requires patience. It is to be begun now, and it won't be finished for six weeks. Once you have it, though, it keeps for a long, long time, if you want it to, and through all that time, it remains beautiful and you remain proud.

First:

    Fruit—organic is best

    Alcohol—Cognac or brandy, rum, or vodka

Six weeks later:

    1 cup sugar

    1 cup fresh cold water

1. Use one kind of fruit, or fruit peel (raspberries, plums, cherries, apples, pears, quince, orange rind, etc.). Cut large fruit into halves or quarters; place in a clean bottle or jar, and cover with whichever alcohol you think matches best. Close the bottle and place it in a closet or pantry for six weeks.
2. At the end of the six weeks, make a simple syrup by placing the sugar and water in a saucepan; cook without stirring over medium-low heat until the sugar is completely dissolved and the syrup is clear. Cool.
3. Pour the fruit and alcohol into a large bowl. Add simple syrup, a little at a time, tasting, until it reaches a taste you like. It shouldn't be sweet; use just enough syrup to take the alcohol edge off. Remove the fruit; pour the eau-de-vie into a clean bottle; cover.

Note: Leftover simple syrup can be used to sweeten iced tea, mixed with lemon, lime, or orange juice to make lemonade, limeade, or orangeade, used to sweeten cut-up fresh fruit, or for many other purposes. Keep it in a jar in the refrigerator; it, too, lasts a long, long time.

Variation: When life hands you lemons, make limoncello. This is how: Use the best lemons you can find—unblemished, and with a nice lemony scent; organic is best. (Ten lemons to one bottle of vodka is a good ratio. Use a reasonably good vodka.) Wash the lemons with hot water; dry. Use a swivel-bladed peeler or a sharp paring knife to remove thin strips of peel, carefully avoiding the bitter white pith beneath the skin. (If any pith remains on peel you've removed, scrape it off. It's much better to avoid it in the first place.) Put the peels, as you remove them, into a large, clean glass jar and cover them generously with vodka; seal, and leave the jar in a closet for at least six weeks; every two weeks, swirl the bottle to mix the peels. At the end of the closet time (the longer the better, up to two or three months), make simple syrup as above, and proceed in the same way to mix with the lemon vodka, but add a little more syrup at the beginning than you would with a sweeter fruit. Rebottle, and put the bottle back in the closet for at least two more weeks. Over a bowl, strain out the lemon peels, pressing down to remove as much of the oils as possible; put the liqueur into a clean bottle, and leave for one week before using. After that, keep the bottle in the freezer—it won't freeze because of the alcohol content, and it should be served ice cold. Drink it straight up, serve it over ice cream, add it to fresh fruit, or spike a glass of lemonade. You'll think of more things to do with it once you have it.

The recipe for eau-de-vie is reprinted from my book *The Sex Life of Food*.

13

AND...

Final Thoughts on Things It Helps to Know—

*On fruits and vegetables; advice on
buying and storing; a few relevant recipes;
and general thoughts on leftovers.*

Always eat grapes downwards—that is, always eat the best grape first;
in this way there will be none better left on the bunch, and each grape
will seem good down to the last. If you eat the other way, you will not
have a good grape in the lot. —*Samuel Butler*

Some Fruits and Vegetables

*I*ndividual *foods may already have been discussed in an earlier chapter.
Don't despair; check the index. Garlic, for instance is on page 24,
leeks on page 23, and potatoes on page 168.*

A is for **apple** ... Macintosh apples are probably what we think of
when we think of biting into an apple on a bright day in September,
but they aren't necessarily the best apples for cooking or for eating. My

all-around favorite for cooking is the Granny Smith, because it's hard and crisp and tart, is available in markets all year, and bakes beautifully in a variety of dishes. There are many other good apples, for most purposes, but in terms of availability, Granny Smith is it. (Granny Smith was Maria Ann Sherwood Smith, who propagated her apples in Australia in 1868.) If you'd like to read about apples, Michael Pollan's *The Botany of Desire* is excellent.

Asparagus belong to springtime, as do rhubarb and fresh peas. Look for fat spears—they're usually healthier and juicier, despite the mythological elegance of thin asparagus. You can snap off their bases, but you lose a lot of good asparagus that way. If you have time, cut off the bottom inch and a half, and peel up from there for another two inches—with a swivel-bladed peeler or a sharp paring knife. Save the cuttings and parings; rinse them; cook them in broth with a little sautéed onion, purée if you like, or strain, add a little milk or cream, salt and pepper, and you have a creamy asparagus soup.

Avocados should feel heavy for their size. If they're rock hard at the store, just leave them out and expect them to feed you in a few days—they'll ripen at room temperature; once there's a tiny bit of give when you apply pressure, refrigerate them to keep them fresh as long as possible. To use, cut in half the long way; twist the halves apart. Hold the pit half in your hand and stick the blade of your knife into the pit; twist and pull the pit out. Either scoop the flesh out with a spoon or make crisscross cuts (making diamonds) in the flesh with your knife without going through the skin; use a spoon to scoop out the flesh, which will fall in cubes. To make guacamole, mash (with a fork) the flesh with minced garlic, a bit of minced red onion, chili powder, cumin, salt, a little lime juice, and chopped cilantro, if you like. To keep—strange as it sounds—smooth the guacamole in a small bowl and cover the top with mayonnaise. You won't taste the mayo, but it'll keep the avocado from turning brown. To make avocado soup, pulse in the processor with milk or buttermilk, a bit of onion, and a jolt of lime juice. To make a great sandwich, layer with a little red onion and use mayonnaise on the bread. For bruschetta, toast Italian bread, sprinkle with olive oil, and spread with avocado, mashed or sliced. Add a dash of salt and freshly ground black pepper.

Basil doesn't keep fresh long, but can easily be preserved to last for weeks, if not months. See page 137.

Berries shouldn't be washed until you're ready to use them; rinse them quickly, and gently pat them dry with paper towels. To hull strawberries, use your thumb as a pivot and scoop around the hull with a paring knife held with your other four fingers. Buy berries fresh all summer; in the winter, use frozen.

Broccoli is at its best when it's dark green; there should be no yellow. Its stalks are just as good as the flowery heads. Cut off the stems below the florets; peel the stems with a paring knife. Their insides are a paler green; you can slice them any way you like. When I'm steaming broccoli, I use the sliced stems on the bottom of the pan as a rack for the florets—the stems need more heat than the flowers do.

Cantaloupes ripen after they're picked; if the only kind you can find is hard as a bowling ball, keep it on your counter and let it ripen. It's ready when there's a little give when you press on the end opposite the stem and when it has a slight floral scent. See honeydew and watermelon, below.

Carrots are nicest when they're smallish—not babies. The packaged baby carrots are cut from larger carrots, but they just don't have the same taste as whole carrots. They shouldn't be sylphlike, but reasonably slim and long (as we all wish we were). Carrots can be scraped with a knife rather than a peeler—fast, simple, easy, and you lose less of the carrot that's just under the skin that way.

Corn is best bought at a farmers' market or a farm stand—and in those cases, don't pull the husks down to check on the kernels; that's not nice. You can tell freshness without doing that—the husk should be green and not dry; the silk tassels should be golden and, again, not dry. If you trust the farmer, buy the corn. You'll very rarely have a problem. Should you encounter anything alive, cut those kernels away and consider it proof that all nature loves sweet corn. Refrigerate corn in the husk, and use it as quickly as possible. You can roast it in the oven, with the husk and silk on, and peel it easily (though carefully) while it's hot. It's delicious this way, part steamed, part roasted. Use potholders or paper towels to hold the hot ears.

Eggplant suffers under its legends. It isn't usually bitter; salting removes a lot of its water content, but not the bitterness that isn't there if it's reasonably fresh. If you want to salt it anyway, cut it in slices or cubes, sprinkle generously with salt, and let it drain in a colander with a bowl underneath for an hour or longer. Rinse and pat dry with paper towels. The worst thing you can do to an eggplant is undercook it. Undercooked eggplant *is* bitter. And unpleasant.

   Eggplant is like a sponge—it soaks up oil when you fry it; that's the bad news, and the good is that it soaks up flavor when you cook it with other foods. To avoid the oil problem, there are two good possibilities: heat olive oil in your pan until it is VERY hot—you can see ripples on its surface; at that point add the eggplant, and stir it quickly and often with a pancake turner so that it doesn't have a chance to stick. Or place slices (sliced thick, the long way or simply halves) on a Silpat pad and roast them; brush the pad first with olive oil if you like. Cut it into chunks after it softens. If you haven't yet bought a baking mat, use a lightly oiled flat baking dish and bake for ten minutes; lightly brush the top of each slice with oil and turn it over for another five or ten minutes. To buy a good eggplant, pick one heavy for its size, with shiny skin and no blemishes or dents.

Fennel is a beautiful-looking thing. It's also crunchy when it's raw in a salad or as part of a crudité platter. Raw or cooked, it offers a sweet anise flavor, milder when it's cooked. Buy a bulb with long stalks and feathery leaves; the bulb should be creamy white and not blemished. Cut the stalks off (they can be added to soup; the leaves can be used as an herb or as a garnish). Remove the outer layer of the bulb if there's any discoloration or splitting. Cut a slice off the bottom and top of the bulb; halve it from top to bottom and remove the core. Section, slice, or quarter the remaining bulb, according to your recipe or your desire.

Honeydew melons don't ripen after they're picked, so you have to be careful about choosing them in the store. Most helpful: A ripe honeydew melon will feel slightly tacky (good tacky, not bad). Rub the tips of two fingers on your forehead; that's how the outside of a ripe honeydew should feel. It should also have a creamy color, and a slight give at the end opposite the stem.

Lemons should feel heavy for their size (also true for grapefruit, limes, and oranges), and their skin shouldn't look thick and bubbly. Heaviness equals juice for citrus fruit, the opposite of red and green peppers, which should feel light—otherwise I believe you're paying for seeds.

Lettuce comes in several varieties, some of which aren't officially lettuce but are still great in a salad bowl. While the glory days of iceberg
lettuce are in its past (it's still good with blue cheese dressing, though),
we now have romaine (the classic for Caesar salad), oak leaf, and buttery lettuces like Bibb, as well as radicchio, endive, arugula, baby
spinach, mâche, mesclun, and, as they say, more. Bagged greens often
note that they're washed and ready to eat; some people wash the leaves
at home even so. Be sure to check the "use by" date—nothing lasts forever, especially lettuce.

Mushrooms are treasures. Even little white button mushrooms,
which we tend to take for granted because they're so easily available
and relatively inexpensive. (You'd think that would be a plus and not a
minus!) Crimini mushrooms are a brown variant of white button
mushrooms, and portobellos (a word made up by marketers because it
sounded Italian and pretty) are simply crimini grown large. (And, to
complete the circle, we now have baby bellos.) Store mushrooms in a
topless container; drape a lightly dampened paper towel over the top,
without letting it touch any of the mushrooms. Use them as soon as
possible after buying; don't wash them until you're ready to use them,
but don't be afraid of getting them wet. You don't need a special brush;
hold them under running water, and brush off any dirt with your fingers. Still have mushrooms left after you've finished your recipe? Sauté
finely chopped onions and one or two chopped shallots in butter; add
finely chopped mushrooms, salt and pepper and chopped parsley; cook
until mushrooms give off their liquid and it evaporates; cool, and
freeze for up to two months. This is *duxelles*, which tastes like
what it is: concentrated mushrooms, all buttery and
delicious. It can be added to a wide variety of
dishes, from sauces to stuffings, and it makes
a fine garnish for chicken, beef, or mashed
potatoes.

Olives are either black or green. Just like everything else, try various kinds until you know which ones you like best. Only a few words, then, about pitting olives when you need to do so: Place an olive under the flat side of the broad end of a knife; make a fist and hit the blade. The pit should come out; if it doesn't, make a small slit, punch again, and pull it out—it isn't hard to do and goes fairly quickly.

Peaches are often unripe when they're sold. Choose peaches that are golden with a touch of orange (a peachy color, that is). Avoid any that are green. Apply light pressure—don't squeeze; if they're ripe, they'll give slightly under your fingers. If they're hard, keep them together in a paper bag; close it, and put a rubber band around it—they ripen fastest that way, and best. Once ripe, eat them as soon as possible (over the sink is one delicious way); store in the refrigerator. To remove the skin: Plunge them into boiling water for fifteen seconds; immediately put them in a cold water bath. The skin should slide off. (You can sometimes peel with a knife or peeler, but that can be difficult.) Sliced and lightly sugared, with or without sweet or sour cream—there's nothing better.

Pears are autumn's way of hoping to be forgiven for the end of summer. Best of all is a Comice: buttery, winey, and sweet. Next best: Bartletts. For my money, avoid Anjou; I find they have less flavor. Pears, like peaches, yield to soft pressure. Unripe pears do well at room temperature or inside a closed paper bag—but don't forget to check them daily; their time is brief. When they're ripe, there's a little give near the stem; if the body of the pear feels soft, they're overripe—and beware, it happens fast. To peel or not is your choice. If all your pears are ripe on the same day, consider making pear sauce—just as you would apple sauce. Peel, core, chunk, and cook the pears briefly with just a bit of sugar (or even none) and a tablespoon or two of water in a covered saucepan.

Peas are available fresh for a very brief time, just a few weeks at the end of springtime and the very beginning of summer. And they require shelling, tedious work with little reward—a pound of pods gives about a cup of peas. Frozen peas—especially the small ones, *petits pois*—are frozen so quickly after harvesting that they're almost as good. And some canned peas—Le Sueur, in the silver can—are a thing unto themselves, quite delicious if you're not expecting fresh peas. Try them roasted with small chunks of potatoes, chopped onion, and garlic. Surprisingly good. Sugar snaps and snow peas are lovely—pods eaten with the peas—and do nicely raw or braised, with their strings removed, cooked with a bit of water and butter.

Red peppers are what happens to green peppers when they're allowed to ripen. They turn red. And because they stay on the plant longer, they cost more to grow and thus cost more at the market. But they're sweeter, less unpleasantly assertive, and easier to digest than green peppers. Some people say they're fresher when they're heavy—because of retained moisture; I like them better when they're lighter. They certainly cost less that way. It's very nice to peel them and it's not difficult: cut them along their natural indentations; use a swivel-bladed peeler. You don't have to get every scrap of skin off, but it isn't hard to remove most of it.

Roasting peppers brings out another taste. You can do that directly over the flame of a gas stove until they char, but it's easier and cleaner to place them on a large sheet of foil under the broiler; turn them as they blister and bubble and blacken; when all sides are done, wrap the foil around them and put them in a lidded container—a pot works well—and let them steam (without peeking!) until they're cool. (If you have enough foil, simply wrap them in the foil and let them steam that way.) Open or unwrap, and peel over a bowl (to save the juices), discarding the seeds, stems, and skin. Without washing, slice the peppers into strips and place them in a jar with any accumulated juices.

If you're not going to use them right away, cover them with olive oil, adding, if you like, garlic slivers. Use within a week.

Potatoes are hard workers. They can be as plain as a baked potato, or as elegant as a decoration of duchesse potatoes (mashed potatoes that have grown up and gone to a fancy dress ball—they're mixed with lots of melted butter, milk or cream, and egg yolks and then baked until browned, or piped around something else to be baked as a decoration); they can be unpretentious home fries, or ubiquitous French fries. No matter what we do with them, they're almost always wonderful. There are baking potatoes (Russets and Idahos) and boiling potatoes (red and white) and everything potatoes (Yukon Golds), not to mention blues and fingerlings and more different kinds every year. Whether or not they're peeled is up to you—sometimes the peel is bitter and must be removed; you don't lose too many nutrients by peeling, but you do lose some. Potatoes that have been hanging around too long have a green layer under the skin; definitely pare that away. Store them in a cool, dark place, and it'll take longer for that green to develop. No sunlight; no refrigerator. Mashed potatoes to die for, almost: mixed with sour cream (or cream cheese) and onions that have been fried in tons of butter; piled into a baking dish, topped with more butter, and baked.

Tomatoes are like bananas—they do not want to be refrigerated. (Though bananas have their own song, courtesy of Chiquita Banana; tomatoes have poetry, but no music.) Green tomatoes, left out, will ripen slowly—they won't be as amazing as a ripe tomato from the garden (yours or the farmer's), but they'll still be good. Store tomatoes at room temperature, stem down (because leaving the stem up makes it easier for moisture and bacteria to get inside). Peel them the same way as peaches—plunge into boiling water for fifteen seconds, then immediately into ice cold water. If you first make a large shallow X with your knife on the end opposite the stem, peeling will be easier. (Cooked peach and tomato skins are tough and unpleasant to chew.) It's also possible to peel both peaches and tomatoes (without the hot water bath) with a serrated swivel-knife peeler. Or, try a plain peeler or paring knife; use a zigzag sawing kind of motion over a small bowl, to catch any juices.

To remove a tomato's seeds, cut each tomato in half horizontally (across its equator). Hold the half over a bowl and squeeze—the seeds will fall out; if they don't, use your finger to pry them loose. (The seeds make a lovely cook's treat, mixed with a little oil, vinegar, salt, and pepper. If you don't want them, save them in a jar to add to soup or stew or to a glass of tomato or V8 juice.)

Buy tomatoes that smell good—sharply tomatoey. First tomatoes of summer, sliced, and sandwiched between slices of white bread with lots of Hellmann's mayonnaise: a celebration. Gazpacho, the classic Spanish tomato soup, is remarkably easy to make if you don't fuss: quarter several tomatoes (peeled or not; that's up to you) and place them in the food processor bowl with peeled cucumber, red bell pepper, garlic, red onion (not too much of any of those; the emphasis is on tomatoes here), a little olive oil and vinegar (vinaigrette ratio), salt and pepper, a dash of Tabasco, and—to help things move along—a little tomato juice. (I add one miniature can.) Pulse several times. Taste to correct the balance and refrigerate. Serve cold.

Canned tomatoes: After the first frost in autumn, you're left with canned tomatoes. My favorite is Muir Glen whole tomatoes—not because they're organic, but because they're sweet and thick *and* organic. Second choice: Redpack whole tomatoes with tomato purée.

Watermelon, the baby, seedless kind, tends to look like a bowling ball. In theory, if you knock on it, it should sound and feel hollow. The little ones are usually good. As for the big ones—the classic picnic kind—choosing a good one is a bit of a gamble. Best way to go is to choose a precut section, and judge it by its color. It should be a happy, uncomplicated red.

Leftovers

Some things get better every day after they're cooked—soup and stew are easy examples. Other things blend into the next thing you're going to cook—leftover ham, for example, makes for a fine jambalaya. I save leftover pork sausages in the freezer to add to the mix, and a few frozen shrimp go in, too. Ham also points toward quiche, croque-monsieur, eggs Benedict, and a lovely salad, cubed and mixed with julienned Gruyère, finely chopped celery, and mayonnaise. Some kinds of meatloaf do very nicely crumbled into marinara sauce to make a fast meat sauce—that is, if somebody hasn't made sandwiches when you weren't looking and used it up. Leftover turkey makes (in addition to soup made from the carcass) a classic leftover dish—in a baking dish: layers of turkey, stuffing, sweet potato, and anything else that seems to match, with a mixture of two beaten eggs to one cup of milk, mixed, poured over and the whole thing baked. Leftover chicken points toward broth, enchiladas, quesadillas, chicken (or turkey) Tetrazzini (made with pasta and mushrooms in a creamy cheese sauce), and salad, among many other possibilities. Leftover vegetables can be turned into soup or salad. Leftover pork can be shredded and mixed with leftover rice, bean sprouts if you have them, and chopped scallions, to make Chinese fried rice, with a little soy sauce mixed in and an egg (either scrambled separately and cut into strips as a garnish, or mixed into the hot rice). Other ingredients can be added—for example, a little sesame oil and other vegetables. Another way with leftover rice: It can be cooked with milk and sugar to make rice pudding. Leftover bread is just what you want for bread pudding, cheese strata, croutons, or bread crumbs. Leftover meat is the definition of hash, and can also be the basis of a curry or shepherd's pie. Fishcakes can evolve from leftover fish; fish also makes a fine salad. Leftover vegetables can be stuffed—or used in stuffing. Gratins can hold all sorts of surprising leftovers under a blanket of bread crumbs mixed with Parmigiano and olive oil or butter. In short: Don't dread leftovers; they're valuable.

FURTHER READING—

Some Favorite Books

I love asking people what their favorite (book, poem, movie, play, musical, opera . . .) is, but I don't like answering that question when it's asked of me. Nevertheless, this is an abbreviated list of some of my favorite books about food and cooking. They are kitchen-table books, as opposed to coffee-table books.

Cookbooks, Alphabetical by Author

Mark Bittman

How to Cook Everything: Simple Recipes for Great Food (paperback, Wiley, 2006; hardcover, Wiley, 1998)
A comprehensive, and thus invaluable, resource—simple and clear throughout. There's a revised, tenth anniversary edition (Wiley, 2008).

Julia Child

The Way to Cook (Knopf, 1989)
Julia Child was a great teacher and a fine cook. This book is lavishly illustrated (not quite coffee-table) and very thorough. I also value both Mastering the Art of French Cooking *books, and* The French Chef, *her first book, which taught a whole generation about their own possibilities in the kitchen.*

Laurie Colwin

Home Cooking: A Writer in the Kitchen (paperback, Harper Perennial, 2000; originally published in 1988)
More Home Cooking: A Writer Returns to the Kitchen (paperback, Harper Perennial, 2000; originally published in 1993)
Both these books are good reading—they're friendly—and have many good recipes.

Elizabeth David

Elizabeth David Classics: Mediterranean Food, French Country Cooking, Italian Cooking (Grub Street, 1999)

Three of the best, combined in one book, but also available separately. All of her books are wonderful—springboards for the imagination—to dream over, and to cook from.

Michael Field

Culinary Classics and Improvisations (paperback, Norton, 1989)

What to do with leftovers. A bit on the fussy side, but good ideas nonetheless.

Jane Grigson

Jane Grigson's Vegetable Book (Atheneum, 1979; paperback, Bison Books, 2007)

Jane Grigson's Fruit Book (Atheneum, 1982; paperback, Bison Books, 2007)

All of Jane Grigson's books are impeccably researched; she's literate and witty, and there is much to learn in her pages, including often fascinating recipes.

Marcella Hazan

Essentials of Classic Italian Cooking (Knopf, 1992; paperback, Macmillan, 1995)

A combination, updated and expanded, of Hazan's two earlier Italian cookbooks, The Classic Italian Cook Book *and* More Classic Italian Cooking, *making it definitive. Her recipes are careful and clear; the flavors of her food are equally clear, and also delicious. Everything one needs to know about Italian cooking may be right here.*

Edna Lewis

The Taste of Country Cooking (Knopf, 1976; thirtieth anniversary edition, Knopf, 2006)

In Pursuit of Flavor (Knopf, 1988)

The Edna Lewis Cookbook (Ecco, 1972)

From southern country cooking to chocolate soufflé—many, many favorites.

Deborah Madison

Vegetarian Cooking for Everyone (Broadway, tenth anniversary edition, 2007)
Just as the title says. Comprehensive, wide-ranging, clear recipes.

Richard Olney

Simple French Food (paperback, Wiley, 1992; original hardcover, Atheneum,
   1974)
*A classic, pure and simple, and a book that has inspired many of today's finest
cooks. All of his books are estimable.*

Jacques Pépin

Julia and Jacques Cooking at Home (Knopf, 1999)
Fast Food My Way (Houghton Mifflin, 2004)
Cooking at Home *(another book that verges on coffee-table) compares the way
the two master cooks approach the same dishes (point: there's more than one
route to good food); it's fun and instructive. The fast food book is about simple,
easy, attractive food; there are many excellent ideas here. There's a follow-up
book, but of the two, I choose the first. His method and technique books are helpful guides.*

Claudia Roden

The New Book of Middle Eastern Food (Knopf, 2000)
*A classic, first published in 1972, now updated and revised, still wonderful. As
are all her books, especially* Mediterranean Cookery, The Good Food of Italy,
and Everything Tastes Better Outdoors.

John Thorne

Simple Cooking (paperback, North Point Press, 1996)
Mouth Wide Open: A Cook and His Appetite, with Matt Lewis Thorne (paperback, North Point Press, 2008)
Essays about food (many first published in Thorne's excellent food newsletter,
Simple Cooking. *There are several books between the two listed above (the first
and the most recent); they're all both personal and academic, discussions about
recipes and recipes themselves.*

There are many books to add to this list of favorites among favorites. Just a few, then, more informally, beginning with three of my own: *The Old-Time Brand-Name Cook Book, Old-Time Brand-Name Desserts*, and *The Sex Life of Food*. The first two are a look at American cooking from 1875 to 1950, through the medium of recipe pamphlets, with original illustrations, quotations, and updated recipes. *The Sex Life of Food* is about those places where psychology meets the food we eat and the way we eat it—serious fun, wide-ranging, from sex and food to Adolf Hitler's vegetarianism. It includes a few recipes, two of which are included in this book.

A few others I can't resist listing: Nigel Slater's books; *Love, Time & Butter* by Joe Hyde; *The Splendid Table's How to Eat Supper*, by Lynne Rossetto Kasper and Sally Swift; Arthur Schwartz's *What to Cook When You Think There's Nothing in the House to Eat* and his *Soup Suppers* and *Jewish Home Cooking*; Mimi Sheraton's *The German Cookbook*; *The Foods and Wines of Spain* by Penelope Casas; *Bistro Cooking* by Patricia Wells; and almost any early edition (mine is 1964, but I believe 1975 is considered the classic) of *Joy of Cooking*.

If you like reading about food, there are many excellent books from which to choose, by such writers as A. J. Liebling (*Between Meals*) and, years later, Calvin Trillin (the wonderful Alice trilogy). About professional cooking and what it's like behind the scenes in big kitchens, there's Bill Buford's *Heat*, and—from earlier days, but still very much worth reading—George Orwell's *Down and Out in Paris and London*, and mystery writer Nicolas Freeling's *The Kitchen*.

Out-of-print books can almost always be found at reasonable prices (if you're not looking for first editions) at used bookstores and online through AbeBooks, Powell's Books, Amazon, and Barnes & Noble.

A BRIEF GLOSSARY OF COOKING TERMS

Bain-marie—a pot of hot water over (or in) which another pot is placed for cooking

Bake—to cook by dry heat in an oven

Bard—to cover (or layer inside) lean meat with strips of fat meat to keep it moist

Baste—to spoon hot liquid over food while it cooks

Bisque—a creamy, rich soup, usually seafood

Boil—to cook a liquid over high heat so that bubbles rise

Bouquet garni—a small bunch of herbs, tied together or in a muslin bag, to be removed before serving; usually parsley, thyme, and bay leaf

Braise—to cook in a lidded pot with a liquid; especially good for tenderizing inexpensive cuts of meat

Caramelize—to create melted and glazed sugar, or to brown meat or vegetables until natural sugars are released

Casserole—an ovenproof container with a lid, or the dish cooked in it

Chiffonade—vegetables or herbs cut into fine strips

Chowder—a thick, chunky soup, usually seafood but not always

Deglaze—heating a liquid in a cooking pan to remove the browned bits and to make a sauce

Dredge—to cover a food with flour or sugar

Fillet—to debone a cut of meat, fish, or poultry; the cut of fish itself

Fold—a way of mixing ingredients if one is lighter than the other

Fond—the browned and caramelized bits stuck to the bottom of a pan after initial cooking; can be melted into a sauce by deglazing

Gratin—a crust atop a dish, made with bread crumbs or cheese that are baked until browned or the dish itself

Knead—to work dough to make it smoother and more elastic

Leavening—substance that raises and lightens a batter

Marinate—to soak in a liquid, in order to flavor or tenderize or both

Poach—to cook in a simmering liquid

Purée—to make a smooth mixture

Reduce—to thicken a liquid by boiling it over high heat

Render—to extract fat by slow cooking

Roast—to cook in an oven, usually hotter and faster than baking

Sauté—to fry in a small amount of oil or butter

Scald—to bring a liquid to just below the boiling point, until tiny bubbles form around its edges

Simmer—to keep a liquid just below the boiling point

Sweat—to sauté vegetables in a little fat, to soften but not brown them

BASIC MEASUREMENTS

1 tablespoon	=	3 teaspoons
¼ cup	=	4 tablespoons
⅓ cup	=	5⅓ tablespoons
½ cup	=	8 tablespoons
1 cup	=	16 tablespoons
½ pint	=	1 cup
1 pint	=	2 cups
1 quart	=	4 cups

1 stick butter	=	¼ pound or ½ cup or 8 tablespoons
4 sticks butter	=	1 pound or 2 cups

½ pound cheese	=	2 cups grated
1 slice fresh white bread	=	about ½ cup fresh bread crumbs

2 large eggs	=	about ½ cup
4 cups flour	=	about 1 pound
2 cups sugar	=	about 1 pound
3½ cups powdered sugar	=	about 1 pound
2⅔ cups brown sugar	=	about 1 pound

RECIPE LIST

Starters and Salads

Starters

Avocado Bruschetta	Page 266
Blue Cheese Spread	Page 206
Bruschetta with Fromage Fort	Page 204
Classic Chopped Chicken Liver	Page 102
Crustless Quiche	Page 118
Fromage Fort: or What to do with Leftover Cheese	Page 204
Guacamole	Page 265
Pesto, Tomato, and Goat Cheese Tarts	Page 138
Stuffed Grape Leaves	Page 183
Tzatziki	Page 205

Salads

Black-eyed Pea Salad	Page 188
Blue Buttermilk Salad Dressing	Page 189
Caprese Salad with Balsamic Syrup	Page 173
Cucumber Salad	Page 184
Ham Salad	Page 274
Mayonnaise and Sour Cream Salad Dressing with Blue Cheese	Page 196
Roasted Beet Salad	Page 186
Russian Potato Salad	Page 185
Tomato Salad with Pesto	Page 138
Shallot and Mustard Vinaigrette Salad Dressing	Page 173
Vinaigrette Salad Dressing	Page 172

Soup

Asparagus Paring Soup	Page 265
Avocado Soup	Page 266
Bean Soup	Page 71
Carrot Soup	Page 75
Carrot Vichyssoise	Page 75
Chicken Broth	Page 86
Cold Black Bean Soup	Page 153
Corn Chowder	Page 76
Garlic Soup	Page 69
Gazpacho	Page 273
Onion Soup	Page 70
Pink Vichyssoise	Page 75
Potato and Leek Soup	Page 74
Quick Soup	Page 68
Summer Borscht	Page 72
Vichyssoise	Page 74
Yellow Pea Soup (Split or whole)	Page 78

Main Courses—Meat, Poultry, Fish, Cheese, and Eggs

Meat

Austrian Goulash	Page 156
Breaded Pork Chops	Page 155
Hamburgers	Page 151
Lamb and Beans Provençal	Page 153
Lamburgers	Page 151
Sausage, Vegetable, and Bean Stew	Page 160
Unstuffed Cabbage	Page 158

Chicken

Chicken and Peppers	Page 99
Chicken in Peanut Butter Barbecue Sauce	Page 98
Chicken Breasts with Spiced Yogurt	Page 95
Classic Bread Stuffing for Roast Chicken	Page 87

Honey Orange Chicken with Rosemary | Page 100
Jil's Honey-Mustard Chicken Breasts | Page 97
Pan Gravy | Page 92
Roast Chicken | Page 86
Sautéed Chicken Breast with Thai Sauce | Page 96

Fish
Fishmonger's Salmon | Page 162
Glazed Honey Mustard Salmon | Page 162

Cheese
Cheese Strata | Page 122
Fromage Fort | Page 204

Eggs
Crustless Quiche | Page 118
Fried Eggs | Page 110
Hard-Cooked Eggs | Page 106
June's Shakshouka | Page 116
Poached Eggs | Page 110
Scrambled Eggs | Page 109
Soft-Cooked Eggs | Page 106
Stuffed Eggs | Page 108
Swiss Baked Eggs | Page 115

Vegetables, Potatoes, Rice, and Beans

Vegetables
Baked Onions | Page 31
Baked Potatoes | Page 169
Baked Red Onions | Page 31
Beet Greens | Page 187
Cider-Glazed Carrots or Other Vegetables | Page 176
Duxelles (Cooked Chopped Mushrooms) | Page 269
Roast Corn on the Cob | Page 267

Roast Onions with Thyme and Honey   Page 32
Roast Vegetables—General Procedure   Page 167
Roasted Butternut Squash with Cream   Page 181
Roasted Butternut Squash with Olive Oil   Page 181
Roasted Red Peppers   Page 271
Sautéed Onions with Butter or Brown Sugar   Page 33
Slow Roasted Tomatoes   Page 177
Steaming Vegetables, General Method   Page 168
Sugar Snap or Snow Peas   Page 271
Sweet Roasted Tomatoes   Page 178
Sweet and Sour Carrots   Page 175
Turkish Leeks   Page 37

Potatoes

Baked Potatoes   Page 169
Mashed Potatoes with Sour Cream and Fried Onions   Page 272
Roast Potatoes with Peas   Page 271
Venerable Vegetables: Potatoes, Apples, and Onions   Page 179

Rice

Fried Rice   Page 274
Rice—Basic Recipe   Page 170
Rice and Butternut Squash   Page 180
Unstuffed Grape Leaves   Page 182

Beans

Basic Recipe for Cooking Dry Beans   Page 171
Black-eyed Pea Salad   Page 188

Pasta

Anchovy Sauce for Pasta   Page 131
Basic Recipe for Cooking Pasta   Page 126
Broccoli Anchovy Sauce for Pasta   Page 132
Broccoli and Penne   Page 135
David's Pasta with Celery and Tomato Sauce   Page 140

Marinara Sauce   Page 132
Oil and Garlic Sauce for Pasta   Page 132
Pesto   Page 137
Pesto with pasta, potatoes, and string beans   Page 138
Preserved Basil   Page 153
Summer Sauce for Pasta   Page 139
Uncooked Summer Sauce for Pasta   Page 139

Desserts

Apple Sauce   Page 258
Berries with Faux Crème Fraîche   Page 223
Berry Fool   Page 224
Berry Yogurt Ice Cream   Page 230
Berries with Chocolate Whipped Cream   Page 225
Blueberries and Maple Cream   Page 226
Blueberry Ginger Roll   Page 227
Bread Pudding   Page 237
Chocolate Wafer Roll   Page 227
Chocolate Truffles   Page 260
Cinnamon Ice Cream   Page 229
Cookie Crust for Pie   Page 219
Cream Cheese Frosting   Page 239
Dinah Shore's Cheesecake Cookies   Page 231
Eton Mess   Page 226
Grapes with Sugar and Cream   Page 196
Joan's Apple Bread Pudding with Sauce   Page 236
Joan's Comforting Custard   Page 234–235
Katharine Hepburn's Brownies   Page 232
Mint Ice Cream   Page 228
Orange Processor Cake   Page 240
Pear Sauce   Page 270
Quick Chocolate Icing   Page 217
Rice Pudding   Page 220
Russian Cream   Page 200
Salzburger Nockerl   Page 120

Snow Ice Cream   Page 221
Strawberries with Crème Fraîche   Page 196
Strawberry Shortcake   Page 253
Sweet Potato Cheesecake   Page 202

Beverages

Almost Herbal Iced Tea   Page 51
Banana Anna   Page 55
Black Cow Ice Cream Soda   Page 59
Black and White Ice Cream Soda   Page 59
Brown Cow Ice Cream Soda   Page 59
Chocolate-Strawberry Ice Cream Soda   Page 59
Cocoa   Page 57
Coffee   Page 45
Eau-de-Vie   Page 262
Iced Tea   Page 51
Limoncello   Page 263
Mango Lassi   Page 58
Mocha Ice Cream Soda   Page 59
Rhubarb Juice   Page 53
Russian Coffee—Hot, Cold, and Frozen   Page 56
Strawberry Lassi   Page 58
Tea   Page 50
Tomato Juice   Page 54

Relishes, Sauces, and Spreads

Béchamel (or White Sauce)   Page 250
   Brown Sauce   Page 251
   Curry Sauce   Page 251
   Mornay Sauce   Page 251
   Mustard Sauce   Page 251
Cathy's Utah Apple Chili Sauce   Page 258
Coulis   Page 200–201
Garlic Butter   Page 36

Homemade Butter   Page 193
Homemade Crème Fraîche   Page 195
Homemade Yogurt   Page 197
Mediterranean Onion Relish   Page 34
Preserved Sweet Lemons   Page 257
Quick Blueberry Jam   Page 249
Raita   Page 256
Shallot Butter   Page 36
Toasted Nuts   Page 261

Quick Breads

Biscuits for Shortcake   Page 253
Buttermilk Biscuits   Page 253
Cheese Biscuits   Page 253
Drop Biscuits   Page 252
Herb Biscuits   Page 253
Italian Bread with Garlic, Oil, and Tomato   Page 36
Joan's Blueberry Buttermilk Muffins   Page 254

Miscellaneous

Avocado Sandwich   Page 266
Chocolate Sandwich   Page 62
Classic Chopped Chicken Liver   Page 102
Garlic Bread   Page 36
Homemade Baking Powder   Page 215
Homemade Vanilla Extract   Page 214
Rendering Chicken Fat   Page 103
Shallot Bread   Page 36
Tomato Sandwich—First of the Year   Page 273

INDEX

Aesop, 242–43
afternoon tea, 50
allergies, 2
almonds, 261
Anchovy Sauce for Pasta, 131
    with broccoli, 132
Anjou pears, 270
antibacterial quality, of onions, 28
antioxidants, 135, 254
apples, 264–65
    Apple Sauce, 265
    Cathy's Utah Apple Chili Sauce,
        258–59
    Joan's Apple Bread Pudding with
        Sauce, 236–37
    Granny Smith apples, 265
    Macintosh apples, 264
    Venerable Vegetables, 179
art, of cooking, 1
*The Art of Cooking Sicilian Macaroni and
    Vermicelli* (Martino Corno), 125
asparagus, 265
    soup, 265
Austrian Cooking for You, 156
Austrian Goulash, 156–57
avocado, 265–66
    Avocado Bruschetta, 266
    Avocado Sandwich, 266
    Avocado Soup, 266

bacteria, 40, 83
Baked Onions, 31
Baked Potatoes, 169
Baked Red Onions, 31–32

baking pans, 14–15
baking powder, homemade, 215
Balsamella, 250
balsamic syrup, 173
Banana Anna, 55
Bartlett pears, 270
basil, 137, 266
beans. *See Recipe List on p. 288*
    basic recipe for cooking dry beans,
        171
    Bean Soup, 71
    Black-eyed Pea Salad, 188
    cold black bean soup, 153
    Lamb and Beans Provençal,
        153–54
    pesto with pasta, potatoes, and string
        beans, 138
    Sausage, Vegetable, and Bean Stew,
        160
Béchamel, 250
beets
    beet greens, 187
    Roasted Beet Salad, 186
    Russian Potato Salad, 185
Bemelmans, Ludwig, *The Street Where
    My Heart Lies*, 60–61
berries, 266
    Berries with Chocolate Whipped
        Cream, 225
    Berries with Faux Crème Fraîche,
        223
    Berry Fool, 224
    Berry Yogurt Ice Cream, 230
beverages. *See Recipe List on p. 290*

biscuits
    buttermilk biscuits, 253
    cheese biscuits, 253
    Drop Biscuits, 252
    herb biscuits, 253
    for shortcake, 253
bisque, 62
Bittman, Mark, "The Minimalist," 19
Black and White Ice Cream Soda, 59
black bean soup, cold, 153
black cow ice cream soda, 59
Black-eyed Pea Salad, 188
blanching, 167–68
blenders, 17–18, 79
Blue Buttermilk Salad Dressing, 189
blue cheese
    Blue Cheese Spread, 206
    Mayonnaise and Sour Cream Salad
        Dressing with Blue Cheese, 196
blueberries, 2
    Blueberries and Maple Cream, 226
    Blueberry Ginger Roll, 227
    Joan's Blueberry Buttermilk Muffins,
        254
    North American Blueberry Council,
        254
    Quick Blueberry Jam, 249
Bodhidharma, 47
boiling, 29, 167–68
boiling water, 40
Bon Appétit magazine, 7–8
Borscht, Summer, 72–73
The Botany of Desire (Pollan), 265
bowls, mixing, 13
braising, 42–43, 148–50
bread pudding
    Joan's Apple Bread Pudding with
        Sauce, 236–37
    plain, 220, 237–38
Breaded Pork Chops, 155–56
Brillat-Savarin, Jean, 80, 260
broccoli, 266
    Anchovy Sauce for Pasta, with broccoli,
        132
    Broccoli and Penne, 135–36

broth, 62, 66, 82
brown cow ice cream soda, 59
brown sauce, 251
Brownies, Katharine Hepburn's, 232
browning meat, 144–45
Brownstone, Cecily, Classic Cakes and
        Other Great Cuisinart Desserts,
        240
bruschetta
    Avocado Bruschetta, 266
    Bruschetta with Fromage Fort, 204
    onion spread for, 33
Bush, George H. W., 135
butter
    creaming butter and sugar, 212–13
    Garlic Butter, 36
    homemade, 193
    Love, Time & Butter (Hyde), 90
    Shallot Butter, 36
    unsalted, 212
buttermilk, 193–94
    Blue Buttermilk Salad Dressing, 189
    buttermilk biscuits, 253
    Joan's Blueberry Buttermilk Muffins,
        254
butternut squash, 3, 160–61
    Rice and Butternut Squash, 180
    roasted butternut squash with cream,
        181
    roasted butternut squash with olive oil,
        181
buying and storing eggs, 105–6

Cabbage, Unstuffed, 158
café au lait, 47
café mocha, 47
cakes, 209–10
    Classic Cakes and Other Great
        Cuisinart Desserts (Sontheimer
        and Brownstone), 240
    Orange Processor Cake, 240
    preparing a pan for, 216–17
can openers, 18
canned tomatoes, 273
cantaloupes, 266

capons, 82
cappuccino, 47
Caprese Salad, 173
Carasso, Danone, 197
Carasso, Isaac, 196
carrots, 267
　Carrot Soup, 75
　Carrot Vichyssoise, 75
　Cider-glazed Carrots, 176
　storing, 63–64
　Sweet and Sour Carrots, 175
carving a chicken, 92–93
casseroles, 147
Cathy's Utah Apple Chili Sauce, 258–59
celery
　David's Pasta with Celery and Tomato
　　Sauce, 140–41
　storing, 63–64
chai, 48
cheese, 198–99. See Recipe List on p. 287
　Blue Cheese Spread, 206
　cheese biscuits, 253
　Cheese Strata, 122
　Fromage Fort, 204
　Goat Cheese Tarts, 138
　Mayonnaise and Sour Cream Salad
　　Dressing with Blue Cheese, 196
　parmigiano reggiano, 128–29
　yogurt cheese, 196–98
cheesecake, 209
　Dinah Shore's Cheesecake Cookies,
　　231
　Sweet Potato Cheesecake, 202–3
chef's knives, 8, 10
Chesterton, G. K., 190
chicken. See Recipe List, pp. 286–87
　about, 80–81
　breasts, 94–97
　broth, 66, 69, 86–87
　buying, 81–83
　carving, 92–93
　Chicken and Peppers, 99
　Chicken Breasts with Spiced Yogurt, 95
　Chicken in Peanut Butter Barbecue
　　Sauce, 98

Classic Bread Stuffing for Roast
　Chicken, 87
Classic Chopped Chicken Liver, 102
cutting up, 85–86
fat, 65
handling, 83–84
Honey Orange Chicken with Rosemary,
　100
Jil's Honey-Mustard Chicken Breasts, 97
livers, 83–84
pan gravy for, 92
poached, 41
rendering chicken fat, 103
roasting, 86–91
Sautéed Chicken Breast with Thai
　Sauce, 96
stuffing for, 87–88
chickpeas, 28
Child, Julia, 8, 80
　Mastering the Art of French Cooking, 34
Chili Sauce, Cathy's Utah Apple, 258–59
chives
　garlic, 23
　onion, 22–23
chocolate
　Berries with Chocolate Whipped
　　Cream, 225
　Chocolate Truffles, 260–61
　chocolate-strawberry ice cream soda, 59
　Chocolate Wafer Roll, 227
　quick chocolate icing, 217
　sandwich, 62
Chopped Chicken Liver, Classic, 102
chowder, 65
　Corn Chowder, 76
chutneys, 246–47
Cider-glazed Carrots, 176
Cider-glazed Vegetables, 176
Cinnamon Ice Cream, 229
Classic Cakes and Other Great Cuisinart
　Desserts (Sontheimer and
　Brownstone), 240
Classic Chopped Chicken Liver, 102
cleaning, 4
cocoa, 57

coffee
    about, 44–45
    decaffeinating, 47
    making, 45–47
    National Coffee Association, 45
    Russian Coffee, Hot, Cold, or Frozen,
        56
colanders, 15–16
cold black bean soup, 153
Comice pears, 270
conserves, 244
convection ovens, 211
cookie crust, for pie, 219
cookies, 218–19
    Dinah Shore's Cheesecake Cookies, 231
cooking
    as an art, 1
    The Art of Cooking Sicilian Macaroni
        and Vermicelli (Martino Corno), 125
    Austrian Cooking for You, 156
    management of, 4
    Mastering the Art of French Cooking
        (Child), 34
    planning, 2–3, 242–44
    Simple Cooking (Thorne), 6
    with water, 40–43
corn, 267
    on the cob, roast, 267
    Corn Chowder, 76
coulis, 200–201
cracking eggs, 108–9
cream, 192–95
Cream Cheese Frosting, 239
Cream Sauce, 250
creaming butter and sugar, 212–13
crème fraîche
    Berries with Faux Crème Fraîche, 223
    homemade, 195–96
    with strawberries, 196
croutons, 78–79, 274
Crumpacker, Bunny
    The Old-Time Brand-Name Cookbook,
        257
    The Sex Life of Food, 200, 263
Crustless Quiche, 118–19

cucumbers
    Cucumber Salad, 184
    raita, 248, 256
curry sauce, 251
Custard, Joan's Comforting, 234–35
cutting boards, 9–10, 25

Daniels, Josephus, 45
David's Pasta with Celery and Tomato
    Sauce, 140–41
de Gaulle, Charles, 199
decaffeinating coffee, 47
deglazing, 146
desserts, 207–22. See also Recipe List
    on p. 289
Dickinson, Emily, 163
Dinah Shore's Cheesecake Cookies,
    231
dinner, planning, 2–3, 242–44
double boilers, 15
Drop Biscuits, 252
dry beans, 171
durum wheat flour, 124
Dutch ovens, 147
Duxelles, 269
dying eggs, with onion peels, 28–29

Eau-de-Vie, 262–63
eggplant, 267–68
eggs. See Recipe List on p. 287
    about, 104–5, 213
    buying and storing, 105–6
    cracking, 108–9
    Crustless Quiche, 118–19
    dying, with onion peels, 28–29
    fried, 110
    Hard-Cooked Eggs, 106–8
    June's Shakshouka, 116
    poaching, 110–11
    scrambled, 109
    separating whites and yolks, 111–12
    shells of, 113–14
    Soft-Cooked Eggs, 106
    stuffed, 108
    Swiss Baked Eggs, 115

symbolism of, 21, 113–14
   whipping egg whites, 112–13
Émile (Rousseau), 191
equipment, for kitchen, 7–20
   baking pans, 14–15
   cutting boards, 9–10, 25
   double boilers, 15
   knives, 8–10
   measurers, 13
   mixing bowls, 13
   pots and pans, 11–12
   spatulas, 13–14
   tongs, 13
espresso, 47
Eton Mess, 226

Fadiman, Clifton, *Information Please*,
   190
Fast Food My Way (Pépin), 153
fennel, 268
fish. *See Recipe List on p. 287*
   Fishmonger's Salmon, 162
   Glazed Honey Mustard Salmon, 162
   leftover, 275
Fishmonger's Salmon, 162
flour, 213
folding, 213–14
food mills, 17
food processors, 17–18
Forster, E. M., 116
Francis I (king of France), 196
Franklin, Benjamin, 81
fried eggs, 110
fried rice, 274
Fromage Fort, 204
Frosting, Cream Cheese, 239
fruits, 264–74

garlic, 23–24
   chives, 23
   Garlic Bread, 36
   Garlic Butter, 36
   Garlic Soup, 69
   Oil and Garlic Sauce for Pasta, 132
   storing, 27–28

Gazpacho, 273
Glazed Honey Mustard Salmon, 162
glucosinolates, 135
Goat Cheese Tarts, 138
The Gondolier's Cook Book, 180
Goulash, Austrian, 156–57
grape leaves
   stuffed, 183
   Unstuffed Grape Leaves, 182
grapes, with sugar and cream, 196
graters, 15–16
gravy, for chicken, 92
greens, beet, 187
Guacamole, 265

Ham Salad, 274
Hamburgers, 151
Hard-Cooked Eggs, 106–8
hazelnuts, 261
heat, 4
Henry II (king of France), 125
Henry IV (king of France), 80
Hepburn, Katharine, 232
herb biscuits, 253
Herbal Iced Tea, 51
high tea, 50
homemade butter, 193
homemade crème fraîche, 195–96
homemade yogurt, 197
Honey Orange Chicken with Rosemary,
   100
honeydew melons, 268
Hoover, Herbert, 81
Hyde, Joseph, *Love, Time & Butter*, 90

ice cream, 220, 228–30. *See also* ice
   cream sodas
   Berry Yogurt Ice Cream, 230
   Cinnamon Ice Cream, 229
   Mint Ice Cream, 228
   from snow, 221–22
ice cream sodas
   Black and White Ice Cream Soda,
   59
   variations on, 59

iced tea, 51
icing, quick chocolate, 217
immersion stick blenders, 17–18, 79
In Defense of Food (Pollan), 164
Information Please (Fadiman), 190
iron pans, seasoning, 12
Italian Bread with garlic, oil, and tomato, 36–37

jams, 244–46
    Quick Blueberry Jam, 249
Jefferson, Thomas, 126, 135
jelly, 244
Jil's Honey-Mustard Chicken Breasts, 97
Joan's Apple Bread Pudding with Sauce, 236–37
Joan's Blueberry Buttermilk Muffins, 254
Joan's Comforting Custard, 234–35
juices, 43–44
    Rhubarb Juice, 53
    Tomato Juice, 54
julienning, 27
June's Shakshouka, 116

kitchen equipment, 7–20
    baking pans, 14–15
    cutting boards, 9–10, 25
    double boilers, 15
    knives, 8–10
    measurers, 13
    mixing bowls, 13
    pots and pans, 11–12
    spatulas, 13–14
    tongs, 13
knives, 8–10
    chef's knives, 8, 10
    sharpening, 9
kosher kitchens, 143

Lamb and Beans Provençal, 153–54
Lamburgers, 151
lassi
    Mango Lassi, 58
    strawberry, 58

latte, 47
Le Creuset cookware, 12
leeks
    Leeks, Turkish, 37–38
    Potato and Leek Soup, 74
    preparing, 23
leftovers, 274–75
Lemmon, Jack, 127
lemons, 268
    lemon zest, 16
    Limoncello, 262–63
    Preserved Sweet Lemons, 257
lettuce, 269
Lévi-Strauss Claude, 149
Limoncello, 263
Liver, Classic Chopped Chicken, 102
livers
    chicken, 83–84
    Liver, Classic Chopped Chicken, 102
Local food, 2–3
Loren, Sophia, 124
Louis XIV (king of France), 209
Louis XV (king of France), 191
Louis XVI (king of France), 191
Love, Time & Butter (Hyde), 90

Macaroni Club, 126
Macintosh apples, 264
main courses. *See Recipe List on p. 286*
management, of cooking, 4
mandolines, 20
Mango Lassi, 58
maple syrup, 222
Marco Polo, 125, 221
Marie Antoinette (queen of France), 191
Marinara Sauce, 132–34
marmalade, 244–45
Martino Corno, *The Art of Cooking Sicilian Macaroni and Vermicelli*, 125
mashed potato with sour cream and fried onions, 272
mashers, potato, 17
Mastering the Art of French Cooking (Child), 34

Mayonnaise and Sour Cream Salad
   Dressing with Blue Cheese, 196
measurers, 13
measuring, 210–11
meat. *See Recipe List on p. 286*
   about, 142–43
   Austrian Goulash, 156–57
   Breaded Pork Chops, 155–56
   browning, 144–45
   Hamburgers, 151
   Lamb and Beans Provençal, 153–54
   Lamburgers, 151
   roasting, 149
   salt pork, 64–65
   Sausage, Vegetable, and Bean Stew,
      160
   searing, 144–45
   Unstuffed Cabbage, 158
Medici, Catherine de, 125
Mediterranean Onion Relish, 34
melons, honeydew, 268
menu planning, 2–3, 242–44
mesclun, 172
microwave ovens, 19
milk products, 190–99, 213
"The Minimalist" (Bittman), 19
Mint Ice Cream, 228
mirepox, 42
miso, 65
mixing bowls, 13
mocha, 56
   café mocha, 47
   mocha ice cream soda, 59
   mocha macchiato, 45
molasses, 208
Morley, Robert, 123
Mornay Sauce, 251
Mouth Wide Open (Thorne), 6
Muffins, Joan's Blueberry Buttermilk, 254
mushrooms, 269
   Duxelles, 269
mustard
   Glazed Honey Mustard Salmon, 162
   Jil's Honey-Mustard Chicken Breasts,
      97

   mustard sauce, 251
   Shallot and Mustard Vinaigrette Salad
      Dressing, 173

National Coffee Association, 45
Nero (Roman emperor), 221
Nix v. Hedden (1893), 163–64
nonstick pans, 4, 8, 11
Norman conquest, 150
North American Blueberry Council, 254
nuts, toasted, 261

Oil and Garlic Sauce for Pasta, 132
The Old-Time Brand-Name Cookbook
      (Crumpacker), 257
olive oil, 64, 129–30
olives, 270
onions
   antibacterial quality of, 28
   Baked Onions, 31
   chives, 22–23
   legacy of, 21–38
   mashed potatoes with sour cream and
      fried onions, 272
   Mediterranean Onion Relish, 34
   Onion Soup, 70, 78
   peeling, 24–25
   peels, for egg dying, 28–29
   peels, for soup, 30
   Red Onions, Baked, 31–32
   Roast Onions with Thyme and Honey,
      32
   sautéed, 33
   scallions, 22
   slicing, 25–27
   Spanish, 22, 25
   spread, for bruschetta, 33
   storing, 27–28
   Venerable Vegetables, 179
Orange Processor Cake, 240
ovens
   convection, 211
   Dutch, 147
   microwave, 19
   temperature of, 211, 216–17

Paddleford, Clementine, 60
pan gravy, for chicken, 92
pans
    for baking, 14–15
    iron, seasoning, 12
    nonstick, 4, 8, 11
    pots and, 11–12
    preparing, for cakes, 216–17
parmigiano reggiano, 128–29
parsley, storing, 63–64
pasta. *See also Recipe List on p. 288-289*
    about, 123–26
    al dente, 127
    how to cook, 126–28
Pea Soup, Yellow, 78
peaches, 270
Peanut Butter Barbecue Sauce,
    Chicken in, 98
pear sauce, 270
pears, 270
peas
    Black-eyed Pea Salad, 188
    chickpeas, 28
    roast potatoes with, 271
    snow or sugar snap, 271
pecans, 261
pectin, 245
peelers, 15–16
peeling onions, 24–25
Penne and Broccoli, 135–36
Pépin, Jacques, 8, 204
    Fast Food My Way, 153
pepper grinders, 20
peppers, red, roasted, 271
pesto, 137, 248
    with pasta, potatoes, and string beans,
        138
    Pesto Tarts, 138
    Tomato Salad with Pesto, 138
pies, cookie crust for, 219
Pink Vichyssoise, 75
planning, 2–3, 242–44
poaching
    basic technique of, 41
    chicken, 41

eggs, 110–11
salmon, 41
Pollan, Michael
    The Botany of Desire, 265
    In Defense of Food, 164
pork
    Pork Chops, Breaded, 155–56
    salt pork, 64–65
potatoes, 168–71, 272
    baked, 169
    mashed potatoes with sour cream and
        fried onions, 272
    mashers, 17
    pesto with pasta, potatoes, and string
        beans, 138
    Potato and Leek Soup, 74
    roast, with peas, 271
    Russian Potato Salad, 185
    Venerable Vegetables, 179
pots and pans, 11–12
poultry shears, 86
prep work, 147–48
Preserved Sweet Lemons, 257
preserves, 244–46
processors, 17–18
pudding, 220–21
puréeing, 67–68

Quiche, Crustless, 118–19
Quick Blueberry Jam, 249
quick chocolate icing, 217
quick soup, 68

raita, 248, 256
Recipe List, 285–91
red onions, baked, 31–32
red peppers, roasted, 271
reducing a sauce, 43
relishes, 246–48. *See Recipe List on
    pp. 290–91*
    Mediterranean Onion Relish, 34
rendering chicken fat, 103
Rhubarb Juice, 53
rice, 19, 170–71
    basic recipe for, 170–71

cookers, 19
fried, 274
pudding, 220
Rice and Butternut Squash, 180
Unstuffed Grape Leaves, 182
roast corn on the cob, 267
Roast Onions with Thyme and Honey, 32
Roasted Beet Salad, 186
roasted butternut squash
with cream, 181
with olive oil, 181
roasted red peppers, 271
roasting
meat, 149
vegetables, 167
Roughing It (Twain), 104
Rousseau, Jean-Jacques, *Émile*, 191
Russian Coffee, 56
Russian Cream, 200
Russian Potato Salad, 185

salad, 171–74. *See also Recipe List on
p. 285*
salad dressings
Blue Buttermilk Salad Dressing, 189
Mayonnaise and Sour Cream Salad
Dressing with Blue Cheese, 196
Shallot and Mustard Vinaigrette Salad
Dressing, 173
Vinaigrette Salad Dressing, 172
salad spinners, 19
Salade Olivier, 185
salmon
Fishmonger's Salmon, 162
Glazed Honey Mustard Salmon, 162
poached, 41
salsa, 246–48
salt pork, 64–65
Salzburger Nockerl, 120–21
samovars, 49–50
Sandburg, Carl, 21
sandwiches
avocado, 266
chocolate, 62
tomato, 273

sauces. *See Recipe List on pp. 290–91*
about, 246–48
reducing, 43
sausage, 78, 160
Sausage, Vegetable, and Bean Stew, 160
Sautéed Chicken Breast with Thai Sauce,
96
sautéed onions, 33
sautéing, 4, 66, 145–46
scallions, 22
scrambled eggs, 109
searing meat, 144–45
seasonal food, 2–3
seasoning iron pans, 12
semolina, 124
separating egg whites and yolks,
111–12
The Sex Life of Food (Crumpacker), 200,
263
shallots, 23
Shallot and Mustard Vinaigrette Salad
Dressing, 173
Shallot Bread, 36
Shallot Butter, 36
sharpening, of knives, 9
Shen Nung, 48
Shore, Dinah, *Someone's in the Kitchen
with Dinah*, 231
shortcake, biscuits for, 253
simmering, 29
Simple Cooking (Thorne), 6
slicing onions, 25–27
slow cookers, 19, 147
Slow Roasted Tomatoes, 177
Smith, Maria Ann Sherwood, 265
Smith, Sydney, 39
smoothies, 44
Banana Anna, 55
variations on, 55
snow ice cream, 221–22
snow peas, 271
soffritto, 42
Soft-Cooked Eggs, 106
Someone's in the Kitchen with Dinah
(Shore), 231

Sontheimer, Carl, *Classic Cakes and Other Great Cuisinart Desserts*, 240
soup. *See also Recipe List on p. 286*
  about, 4–6
  basic ingredients of, 62–63
  making, 64–68
  quick, 68
  quick breads. *See Recipe List on p. 291*
  removing surface fat from, 67–68
  thickeners for, 66
sour cream, 194–95
  Mayonnaise and Sour Cream Salad Dressing with Blue Cheese, 196
spatulas, 13–14
spreads. *See Recipe List on pp. 290–91*
split pea soup, 78
squash, 3, 160–61
  butternut, roasted, with cream, 181
  butternut, roasted, with olive oil, 181
  Rice and Butternut Squash, 180
starters. *See Recipe List on p. 285*
steaming
  basic technique of, 41
  vegetables, 168
Stew, Sausage, Vegetable, and Bean, 160
Stewart, Martha, 106
stock, 62
storing
  eggs, 105–6
  garlic, 27–28
  onions, 27–28
  vegetables, 63–64, 166
strainers, 15
strawberries
  with crême fraîche, 196
  strawberry lassi, 58
  strawberry shortcake, 253
The Street Where My Heart Lies (Bemelmans), 60–61
string beans, with pasta, 138
stuffed eggs, 108
stuffed grape leaves, 183
stuffing, for chicken, 87–88
sugar, 207–8
  creaming butter and sugar, 212–13

sugar snap peas, 271
Suleiman (sultan of Ottoman Empire), 196
Sullivan, Thomas, 52
Summer Borscht, 72–73
Summer Sauce for Pasta, 139
  uncooked, 139–40
sweating vegetables, 146
sweet and sour dishes
  Sweet and Sour Carrots, 175
  vegetables, 176
Sweet Potato Cheesecake, 202–3
Sweet Roasted Tomatoes, 178
Swiss Baked Eggs, 115
symbolism, of eggs, 21, 113

Talleyrand, Charles Maurice de, 142
tarts, tomato, 138
tea, 47–52
  afternoon tea, 50
  bags, 48, 51–52
  herbal iced tea, 51
  high tea, 50
  iced tea, 51
temperature, of oven, 211, 216–17
Thai sauce, for chicken, 96
thermometers, 18–19, 91, 211
thickeners, for soup, 66
Thorne, John
  Mouth Wide Open, 6
  Simple Cooking, 6
Tolkien, J. R. R., 242
tomatoes, 163–64, 272–73
  canned, 273
  David's Pasta with Celery and Tomato Sauce, 140–41
  sandwich, 273
  Slow Roasted Tomatoes, 177
  Sweet Roasted Tomatoes, 178
  tarts, 138
  Tomato Juice, 54
  Tomato Salad with Pesto, 138
tongs, 13
Truffles, Chocolate, 260–61
Turkish Leeks, 37

Twain, Mark, *Roughing It*, 104
tzatziki, 205

umami, 128–29
uncooked summer sauce, for pasta,
    139–40
unsalted butter, 212
Unstuffed Cabbage, 158
Unstuffed Grape Leaves, 182

vanilla extract, lemonade, 214
vegetables, 163–66, 264–74. *See also*
    Recipe List, 287–88
    Cider-glazed Vegetables, 176
    roasting, 167
    Sausage, Vegetable, and Bean Stew, 160
    steaming, 168
    storing, 63–64, 166
    sweating, 146
    sweet and sour, 176
    Venerable Vegetables, 179
Venerable Vegetables, 179
Vichyssoise, 74
    Carrot Vichyssoise, 75
    Pink Vichyssoise, 75

vinaigrettes
    Shallot and Mustard Vinaigrette Salad
        Dressing, 173
    Vinaigrette Salad Dressing, 172
vinegar, 172–73

walnuts, 261
water
    about, 39–40
    boiling, 40
    cooking with, 40–43
watermelon, 273–74
whipped cream, 193, 223–25
whipping egg whites, 112–13
White Sauce, 247–48, 250
Wilde, Oscar, 174
The Williamsburg Art of Cookery, 240

Yellow Pea Soup, 78
yogurt
    Berry Yogurt Ice Cream, 230
    cheese, 196–98
    Chicken Breasts with Spiced Yogurt,
        95
    homemade, 197